Extreme Taboo Sex Short Stories:

How to Have Rough Forbidden Anal Sex, Role Play, Cuckold, BDSM, Domination. Discover Submission Fantasies and Domination

Sex Positions for Couples

Make Your Couple's Sex Life Amazing with The Leading Top Sex Positions and With Techniques and Tips for Awesome Fantasy Time.

© **Copyright 2019 by CHASECHECK LTD - All rights reserved.**

The content contained within this book may not be reproduced, duplicated or transmitted without direct written permission from the author or the publisher.

Under no circumstances will any blame or legal responsibility be held against the publisher, or author, for any damages, reparation, or monetary loss due to the information contained within this book. Either directly or indirectly.

Legal Notice:

This book is copyright protected. This book is only for personal use. You cannot amend, distribute, sell, use, quote or paraphrase any part, or the content within this book, without the consent of the author or publisher.

Disclaimer Notice:

Please note the information contained within this document is for educational and entertainment purposes only. All effort has been executed to present accurate, up to date, and reliable, complete information. No warranties of any kind are declared or implied. Readers acknowledge that the author is not engaging in the rendering of legal, financial,

medical or professional advice. The content within this book has been derived from various sources. Please consult a licensed professional before attempting any techniques outlined in this book.

By reading this document, the reader agrees that under no circumstances is the author responsible for any losses, direct or indirect, which are incurred as a result of the use of information contained within this document, including, but not limited to, — errors, omissions, or inaccuracies.

Table of Contents
Table of Contents
Introduction
Chapter 1: The Art of Kama Sutra
Chapter 2: Benefits of Kama Sutra
Chapter 3: Trying Tantric Sex
Chapter 4: Getting Ready for Sex
Chapter 5: Beginner Sex Tips
Chapter 6: A Massage to Get Ready
Chapter 7: Getting Things Started
Chapter 8: The Secrets to a Great Massage
Chapter 9: Trying Dirty Talk
Chapter 10: Orgasm
Chapter 11: Female Ejaculation
Chapter 12: Best Sex Positions for Him
Chapter 13: Best Sex Positions for Her
Chapter 14: Best Sex Positions To Bring Couples Closer
Chapter 15: Increasing Male Orgasmic Control
Chapter 16: Pregnancy Sex Positions
Chapter 17: Oral Sex Positions
Chapter 18: How to Have Better Sex
Conclusion

Introduction

First off, I would like to thank you for choosing this book, and I hope that you find it informative and helpful no matter what your needs may be. Congratulations on taking these first steps in improving your sex life. This can be a hard topic for some people, but we are here to strip away all of those awkward feelings about sex. Here, we will celebrate sex as something natural. The goal of the book is to help people improve their sex lives because sex should be something that helps bring couples closer and to improve their overall wellbeing. Sex should not be done only for procreation.

This book will walk you through all of the various aspects of sex and foreplay. The first thing we are going to go over is kama sutra and tantric sex and the benefits of practicing them. These are two common topics that get discussed in the world of sex, but so many people don't actually know what they are or what they even mean. They are not both the same, as you will soon find out, and they will bring something a bit different into your sex life.

Besides that, we are also going to go over how to get your body and mind ready for sex. One of the most common issues people have when it comes to unsatisfactory sex is that they aren't able to get out of their own head enough to really enjoy what is happening. With the right preparation, this doesn't have to be a problem.

Then we will look at some tips that can help out those who may not have all that much experience in sex. Everybody has to begin somewhere, and there is no need to feel ashamed.

After that, the next couple of chapters are going to go over the various ways that can get you and your partner ready for sex. We will go over some tantric massage techniques, preliminary games, dirty talk, and other secrets of a good couples massage. These tend to be things that people like to avoid because they are afraid of messing them up, which makes sense, but you won't have to worry about that anymore after you have read this book.

Next, we will go over the orgasm. This is the main goal that everybody is aiming for when having sex, right? So why shouldn't we discuss it and what it means and how to improve your chances of having multiple orgasms? This will naturally bring us into our next subject, female ejaculation. This has been seen as the lost unicorn in the sex world, but we are going to dispel the myths that you may have heard and explain to you exactly what it is.

Then we will move into specific sex positions for you to try. First, we will go over the best sex positions for him, then the best positions for her, and then the best positions to bring both of your closer.

After that, we will look at some exercises that men can use in order to increase their orgasmic control. This is a common issue that men can run into, and it does not mean that they have anything wrong with them. With these exercises, men can learn how to control their orgasms so that they are able to last long enough to please their partner.

Then we will go over the best sex positions to use when your partner is pregnant. Sex during pregnancy is often seen as impossible or tricky, but there are positions out there that can make sex during pregnancy easy. After that, we will go over the best sex positions for oral. Oral sex is often forgotten about, but it can make things more interesting.

Lastly, we will wrap everything up with talking about things that you can do to improve your sex life. While the goal of the entire book is to improve your sex life, these exercises can be used in addition to everything else that we will talk about.

Making a choice to not be stuck in the same monotonous sex every night is a big decision. Having amazing sex should not be a mystery, and with this book, it no longer will be.

Before we begin, I would like to ask that if you find any part of this book helpful and informative, please rate and leave it a review.

Chapter 1: The Art of Kama Sutra

For many people, when they hear the words "Kama Sutra," they automatically see some contortionist sex positions. They think it requires positions that use acrobatics, yoga, and maybe even some primeval pornography. This is only partly true.

The *Kama Sutra* actually covers much more than what people in the Western world see. To simply say that it is just a book full of spicy sex positions is providing this ancient, sacred Hindu text a disservice.

Kama Sutra isn't something that magically turns everyday sex into sacred lovemaking. That part is only like 20 percent of what it is about. Real, sacred lovemaking is mainly about a deep connection and spirit, which is the reason why the sex positions of the *Kama Sutra* only take up about 20 percent of the text. The rest of it helps to guide you through the art of love. Kama Sutra also helps you with things like:

- Etiquette
- Family life
- Balancing your masculine and feminine energies in yourself and in the partnership
- The philosophy and nature of love
- Proper grooming
- What triggers and sustains desire
- Self-care
- The practice of different arts like poetry, cooking, and mixing
- Many other non-sexual, pleasure-oriented facets of life

It helps you to live a good life and not simply how to have amazing contortionist sex.

Kama Sutra, which is also written as Kamasutra, is a Sanskrit word made of two words, "kama" and "sutra." Both words have different meanings, but when they are combined, the meaning makes up the premise of what Kamasutra is all about.

"Kama" in Sanskrit translates to "desire," and includes both the aesthetic and sensual desires. However, when it comes to Kamasutra, it places emphasis on sensual desire. In the majority of world religions, a person's sexual desire is viewed as taboo.

However, within Hinduism, "kama" is one of the "four goals of Hindu life." Their four goals of life include, "kama," "artha," meaning success and abundance, "dharma," meaning truth and virtue, and "moksha," meaning release.

In Sanskrit, "sutra" means thread or line, but in the sense of Kama Sutra, it is talking about a thread of verses that create a manual.

Where Does it Come From?

Kama Sutra comes from the ancient Hindu book called the *Kama Sutra* that was written by the Indian philosopher Vatsyayana Mallanaga between 400 to 200 BCE. What is interesting is that Vatsyayana said that he was a celibate monk. He also said that bringing together all of this sexual wisdom was the contemplation of deity and a form of meditation.

Vatsyayana wasn't the teacher of this wisdom but simply composed the Kama Sutra from a book that was written much earlier, in the seventh century, called Kamashastra, or *Rules of Love*. This other book is a lot larger, but it also looked at the love-customs and partner compatibility of Northern India.

The *Kama Sutra* was written in a difficult and complex form of Sanskrit. Even when it was translated to English, the ideas still come off as a bit abstract to the modern reader. Thanks to Bhagwan Lal Indraji and Sir Richard Francis Burton, we can look at the complex translation from the Kama Sutra. This excerpt is about the different varieties of moaning that take place during lovemaking:

"The whimper, the groan, the babble, the wail, the sigh, the shriek, the sob, and words with meaning, such as 'mother, 'stop,' 'let go,' or 'enough.' Cries like those of doves, cuckoos, green pigeons, parrots, bees, moorhens, geese, ducks, and quails are important options for use in moaning."

Not exactly what you would think of when it comes to moaning, is it? Luckily, people have studied it more and more translations have been written that make it easier to understand.

Sex and Beyond

As stated above, Kama Sutra isn't just about sex. For example, a large part of Kama Sutra is about flirting and courtship. It states that if a man wants to attract a woman, he should hold a party and ask his guests to recite poetry. When the poetry is read, people should leave out certain parts, and then the guests compete to complete the poem. It also suggests that the man and woman should play together, meaning they should do things together like swimming.

Kama Sutra also focuses a lot on dating with the aim of getting married. Finding your ideal partner involves making sure that you possess the same qualities that you would like your partner to have.

When it does come to sex and intimacy, Kama Sutra also includes the nonsexual aspects. There are eight categories of embrace. The first four are expressive of mutual love, and the other four are to increase pleasure during intimacy and foreplay.

1. Touching Embrace

This helps a man and woman get acquainted, develop the hots for one another, and the man feels passion fire up so that he starts looking for an excuse to get closer with the purpose of brushing his body against her.

2. Piercing Embrace

The piercing embrace happens when a part of the man touches the woman's private parts, such as her breasts, without a known intention, but as an accident. But because of the touch, the man feels an instant sexual urge to grab her breasts when secluded or in the dark.

3. Rubbing Embrace

When a couple passes each other in the dark or down a lonely alley, or even in public, they realize their sexual attraction towards one another, so they make a point or rubbing their bodies against one another because of their desire to feel each other up.

4. Pressing Embrace

The rubbing can move to something else that is guided by intense arousal. This happens when one person pushes the other against a wall and presses their body tightly against the other to bring them closer so that they can feel their partner's intimate parts.

5. Twining of a Creeper (Jataveshtikaka)

This embrace occurs when a woman clings to her man in the way that a creeper twines around a strong plant that stands tall and steady. She then pulls the man's head towards her so that she can kiss him, while intently staring deep into his eyes.

6. Climbing a Tree (Vrikshadhirudhaka)

This embrace occurs when a woman places a hand around his shoulder, reaching to touch the back of his other shoulder. One of her feet is placed on his thighs, and the other foot is on his feet, just like she was getting ready to climb a tree. These moves show that she wants a kiss from him.

7. Mixture of Sesame Seed with Rice (Tila Tandulaka)

You know what it is like to be laying down and to be spooned or to spoon your partner? This is what this embrace is like. Whether you choose to lay face to face or front to back, you both need to be laying next to one another and have your legs and arms entwined.

8. Milk and Water Embrace (Kshiraniraka)

The act of sex is imminent; you become vulnerable to your partner. This is the type of embrace that happens with a sexual union when two bodies are pressed against one another as tightly as you can like you are entering into one another. The woman should be sitting on his lap, facing him, so that they can feel each other up in the best way possible, enjoying whatever sensations happen.

Besides embracing one another, Kama Sutra also covers kissing. The Kama Sutra actually has 26 forms of kisses that range from kisses to showing affection and respect, to those that are used during sex and foreplay. The best kiss for sexual partners is one that based on being aware of the emotional state of your partner when you two are not having sex.

Other aspects of intimacy and foreplay include mutual massages, rubbing, biting, pinching, and using the hands and fingers to stimulate each other, as well as many different forms of cunnilingus and fellatio.

Kama Sutra is also inclusive of same-sex relationships, as well as sex "games" like group sex and BDSM.

Chapter 2: Benefits of Kama Sutra

Everybody understands that changing up sex positions and trying new things is good for their sex life. Even still, people choose to stick with what they are used to for one reason or the other. Let's take a moment to look at the benefits of trying new things in bed, specifically Kama Sutra.

- Different Perspective

When you change up your sex positions, you are also changing your perspective in bed. You get to see new areas of your partner's body and experience different types of stimulation.

This is a very important thing for men because their eyes are the second most important zone to his penis. Women love with their ears, but men love with their eyes. Men have visual sex, which is why they are more likely to watch porn. When they get to see something new that is also exciting, it only makes the sex that much better.

For example, in missionary, you only see each other's faces, but if you move to doggy style, he gets a perfect view of her rear end. The same is true if the woman gets on top. They get a nice view of each other's chest.

- Tone The Organism

In Eastern medicine, there is a notion that all parts of the organs and body are connected, and each part can be influenced by another part. Genitals of men and women have many representative areas of every vital organ within the body. During sex, and in various sexual positions, these parts are stimulated. This means that you can be helping other areas of your body when you are having sex.

- Different Sensations

In all the sexual positions that we will talk about in later chapters, the penis will touch a different area of the vagina and enters at varying depths. This changes how sex feels for him and her. For women, they are all different. They feel different things even if they are stimulated in the exact same spot. For men, they feel pretty much the same thing all the time.

- Help Women Reach an Orgasm

The worst thing for a woman is not reaching orgasm during sex. Every woman is unique in what she needs in order to climax, so trying out new things in bed can help her to get exactly what she wants.

Why would you risk your relationship when all you need to do is change up your positions so that she actually has an orgasm? It is important for men to understand exactly how their partner's body works so that they know what she needs.

- Boost In Confidence

Simply following Kama Sutra can help boost a person's self-confidence. The actual *Kamasutra* book provides tips on how to boost a person's confidence and guides you to help make your personality magnetic.

Chapter 3: Trying Tantric Sex

Tantric sex is probably one of the best things to try out if you want to achieve the biggest orgasm of your life. If you don't believe me, then continue reading, If you do believe me and want to learn how, then continue reading.

Tantric sex is a Hindu practice that dates back more than 5,000 years ago. The word tantra is Sanskrit means "woven together." Buddhist and Hindu meditation practitioners often use the union of tantra as a way to help weave together the spiritual and physical, which also weaves women to men, and the Divine to humanity. The main purpose of the practice is to become one with God. The way that the Western achieves this is by teaching people to have slow intercourse without reaching orgasm.

Couples who have chosen to try tantric sex say that they reached more pleasure and have experienced a sense of "becoming one with each other" that is very loving and profound. The main goal of this sexual practice is to be enlightened and not trying to win a gold medal for gymnastics of the carnal type. If this comes off as a bit confusing, this of it this way. If having a quickie is the sexual equivalent of take out, tantric sex is the Michelin-starred meal, lovingly and slowly prepared and more delicious thanks to the wait.

Practice Makes Perfect

You will start things out by facing each other and looking deep within your partner's eyes. Your clothes should remain on while doing this. Remain focused only on the other person's eyes. This is going to help keep the two of you intimate. Some people have said that to keep the tension down during this act is to switch up which eye you are looking at, but some consider this to be cheating the practice. Your eyes are the windows to your soul. The point of this act is that the two of you are gazing into each other's souls.

Check in with your breathing. Yes, you could be breathing wrong during this practice. You should try to get your breathing synchronized with your partners. You both should be breathing in at the same time and then breathing out at the same time. Then you will transition into what is known as breath exchange. You will breathe in as your partner breathes out, and then you will breathe out when they breathe in. This is meant to mimic you breathing into each other. This should be practiced for about ten minutes before moving on.

For Starters

To transition this into tantric sex, you will do the same thing described above but without any clothes on. You are going to sit in your partner's lap, facing them. Next, you will wrap your legs around their waist and start to practice your breath exchange. Now you will start to caress and kiss each other. After some time, penetration can take place, and the two of you can start very slow intercourse. Make sure that you continue to caress and kiss one another. Your eye contact should be maintained through all of this.

Now things get to get a bit more interesting. Once the two of you get more proficient, you could actually build the ability to have longer orgasms. For men and women alike, this is a different way of having multiple orgasms. This will make you remain at the top of your pleasure without actually having an orgasm. You will get to enjoy all of the same feelings as having an orgasm, but it can help you last for several minutes, or even hours, without ever having a regular orgasm. This is able to create an emotional merging, as well as profound sex. There are some women who have been able to have an orgasm while doing specific exercises.

Other Ways to Tantra

What we have gone over is only one way to perform tantric sex. The good news is, tantric sex isn't really goal oriented, so there isn't a right or wrong way to do it. The trick of tantra is to take your mind off of the orgasm and focusing on making foreplay more enjoyable and rewarding until you are both ready to reach its natural end. This is often easier said than done, so in order to delay orgasm, tantric experts offer different methods such as massage, breath control, and meditative techniques.

The first thing you can do is to start by turning down the lights and shutting out the world around you. Loosen up your body. Tantra focuses on moving the energy through your body, so you should shake your limbs vigorously to help energize and unblock your body before you get started.

You may also want to stay off of the bed. Sometimes getting onto the bed will trigger your sleep button, which means that you two will choose to have a quick romp instead of a deep connection and loving sex, which is the goal of tantra.

You can try to lay down with your partner on the floor, with some blankets and pillows to make it more comfortable, and slowly start to touch one another. Take your time to leisurely make your way across their body.

Start experimenting with different types of touches, such as gentle strokes, light feathery touches, and firm massages. The aim of this is to heighten each other's senses in a slow and intense way so that you can build each other to a peak but not taking each other all the way. When done the right way, this is able to prolong the sex and your pleasure for hours.

If you start to find that your mind is wandering, refocus yourself on your breaths. Practice the breath exchange that was discussed earlier. This will help to keep your both focused and bring you closer together.

Above all else, don't give up. The first time you try this, don't be surprised if you don't last more than ten minutes or so. Try again. Tantric sex is going to take some time to get the grip of because we have all become used to our western way of sex. This means that we all expect sex to have an obvious beginning, middle, and end.

Tips and Tricks

Tantra isn't a one-size-fits-all practice. There are different things you can do to improve your practice and to make it more satisfying and unique.

- You don't have to get naked. You can begin things while clothed, and you can remain clothed, or you can choose to remove all of your clothing. The important thing is to do whatever feels comfortable for both of you. This will look very different for everybody.

- Focus on your breathing. Deep breathing is a very important part of tantric sex. When you focus on your breath, it gives you the chance to be present in the moment and to fully immerse yourself in the experience.

- Use all of your senses. Light a few scented candles. Play some sensual, soft music. Slowly touch your partner. Start into one another's eyes. Savor the taste of the kiss. Engage every sense during your tantric practice, and this will help you to feel every ounce of pleasure more fully.

- Go at things slowly. An important part of tantra is to learn how to feel and experience things on a deeper level. The best way to achieve this is to go slowly. You shouldn't rush tantra. Instead, you need to relax your mind and enjoy every second.

- Explore everything area of your partner's body. Stroke you hands slowly over their body. Use your tongue to explore their mouth as you kiss. You can also gently glide your lips up and down their chest. Let them do the same thing to you.

- You can experiment with things as well. For example, kink and BDSM often incorporate tantric ideas. When you are practicing tantra, there is no rule that says you have to stick to traditional practices. You can think outside of the box.

- There is no need to go full tantra. You can add in elements of tantric practices into your bedroom game. This could mean meditation as part of foreplay or focusing more on your deep breathing to help slow things down.

The Importance of Reconnecting

With our lives constantly being over-scheduled, we don't make sure that we take the time to stop and stay focused on our partners. Couples have come to realize that a normal monogamous relationship isn't working for them anymore. There are some couples who decide to have an open relationship for this reason alone. Performing tantric sex is a way to enhance your sexual pleasures and the relationship in several different ways. First, when you emphasize the breath, it helps to connect both of you on a more intimate and deeper level. This alone is able to help open your heart up to being more forgiving, loving, and closer to your sexual partner.

Second, since tantric sex is performed at such a slow pace, this will give you the chance to see how sensual your mind and body can be. Being able to enjoy sex for an hour or more is equivalent to turning a single taco from a fast-food restaurant into a Mexican feast. Either one is going to take care of your hunger, but that feast is going to provide you with more pleasure, satisfaction, and delight.

Last but certainly not least, you may not enjoy the thoughts of not having an orgasm, but his can help both of you create connectedness and ecstasy beyond the normal orgasm.

Chapter 4: Getting Ready for Sex

The secret to an invigorating sex life lies within the mind. Do you remember when sex seemed like a seven-course feast? You didn't know what was coming next, every mouthful made you tingle from head to toe, and once you reached the end of it, you felt content and satisfied. Nowadays, it seems like a bowl of cereal; convenient, quick, and fills a gap, but it's not something you would want to have every single day.

In order to get great sex back, you need to put it on the brain. When you make sure that you turn your brain on before you have sex, it will trigger your libido. Let's take a moment to look at some ways to get your mind ready for sex.

Take It Slow

How come a man can go from watching a slasher film to hopping into bed and instantly feeling horny, but a woman hops into bed and starts to think about everything they have to do the next day? The female brain and the male brain work differently. A woman's brain works by multitasking, but a man's brain typically focuses on one thing at a time.

Studies have found that a woman needs a transition time of 10 to 30 minutes between activities. That means that if you want to have sex before going to sleep at night, turn off the television and take some time before jumping into bed. During this time, you could have a warm aromatherapy bath or a massage to help put one another in the mood. The best scents for arousal are sandalwood, bergamot, chamomile, or lemon.

Just Say Yes

For some, having sex can be like having to go to the gym. Their body and mind start to rebel against is, but once they do it, they feel great. Standard wisdom has said, for a woman, the sexual cycle goes from desire to arousal, to orgasm. There has been new research that has found that women who are in long-term relationships will experience desire after they become aroused. That means, sometimes, you simply have to be receptive to your partner's touch instead of giving in to the voice that's telling you to go to sleep.

When you give into that touch, your brain will start to focus on pleasures that follow and will then increase the blood flow to the right areas. Even if all you have is a quickie and you don't orgasm, the biochemicals released during sex are still released, which will help you to want to have more sex, more often.

There are ways for women to help get themselves aroused instead of waiting on their partners to initiate. You can start by tensing your pelvic floor muscles. All of these muscles support your pelvic floor, as well as your genitals, and helps to stimulate the arousal process.

Morning Person

While most people think about having sex right before bed, mornings are actually the best time for sex. This is the time of day when your body has produced more sex hormones, such as testosterone. If setting aside time in the morning to have sex is out of the question, you should still use those early-morning hormones to help get your mind ready for a night of passion. Simply thinking about sex during the day can often be enough to make you want it.

That means, instead of just giving your partner a peck goodbye, take some time to look deep into their eyes and then give them a long lingering kiss. Wrap things up by whispering, "Our room, 10 pm." This will not just leave your partner anticipating the night to come, but it will also turn you on.

Getting the mind ready is only part of getting ready for sex. You also want to make sure that your body is ready as well.

Fantasy

You can also use your mind to help trigger your desire for your partner. There is a simple exercise you can do for this. You and your partner sit across from one another, hold hands, and then stare into one another's eyes. Don't say a word, but both of you should start to think about the last time that you had sex and really enjoyed it. This helps to create a connection between the mind and body. It works a lot like how you shiver when you recall a scary experience. When focusing on all the little sexy details, it will ignite your body and turn you on. You will also get to see the arousal on your partner's face.

Get Some Sleep

There is nothing worse than falling asleep before sex. One of the main reasons why new parents lose their sex lives is that they are too tired. Sex just doesn't sound good when you haven't had enough sleep. If you have noticed that you are too tired to get intimate, you need to make sure that you make sleep a priority. Make sure that you are getting the recommended seven to nine hours each night. To improve your sleep, you should make sure all devices are turned off.

Ask Questions

One of the most common reasons why you may be turning your partner down is out of boredom. This boredom doesn't have to do with just positions. You also have to rediscover what you both want. You should always ask questions, like: "Do you like it when I do this?" This will help you to feel more comfortable and confident when it comes to asking for what you want. You should also feel comfortable looking outside of your own bedroom for new inspiration.

Talk To Your Doctor

This tends to apply more for women, but men, feel free to talk to your doctor if you haven't been experiencing any sexual desire. For women, you should speak with your gynecologist if you have noticed that you have been having a hard time getting turned on for your partner. There are medical reasons that could cause this. Depression, menopause, hormonal imbalance, and some medications can impact your libido. Fortunately, topical and oral medications, lubricants, and hormone therapy can help get your mojo back. You should never feel embarrassed to talk to your doctor about this, that have heard everything.

Understand Her Cycle

Women are influenced by their cycle. They will find sex more enjoyable at different times of their cycle. From day one to 14, women produce more testosterone, which means it is easier to get turned on and reach climax. Women also experience a surge in libido during days 24 to 28 because of the nerve endings that are stimulated by the thickening of the uterine lining.

Food

We know a healthy diet is important for a long and healthy life, but the foods you eat can also affect your libido. Foods like honey, peanut butter, and bananas contain vitamin B, which naturally boosts your libido. Celery contains androsterone, which can help aid in female attraction. There are a lot of other foods out there that act as natural aphrodisiacs as well.

Kick Those Bad Habits

There are already plenty of reasons to stop smoking, but I've got one more for you. Smoking can actually hurt your sex life. Cigarettes narrow the blood vessels, and this makes it harder for the blood to flow to the genital region, which is very important for both men and women when it comes to sexual stimulation. You should also make sure that you don't drink too much. Too much alcohol will act as a depressant and decrease your libido.

If you make sure that you follow at least some of these tips before you have sex, your mind and body will be ready, and one won't let the other down.

Role Playing

Have you ever felt like you would want to be somebody different behind closed doors? Have you ever felt the need to change up the power dynamics in your relationship? Have you found yourself fantasizing about being a robber, schoolteacher, or police officer? Does it make you feel like you're gross or weird to feel that way?

It shouldn't. Roleplay within a relationship is actually very healthy. In spite of what you might have been told growing up or what might have been said on early morning bad cable shows, sex isn't something that is dirty, and role-play isn't a sinister act that only deviants and sinners indulge in.

Role-play is a healthy practice for couples, married, or otherwise, that can help you to improve and strengthen your connection with your partner. The desire to pretend to be somebody else doesn't have anything to do with dissatisfaction with your partner or sex life. It has to do with safety and trust.

Role-playing is simply the act of acting out your or your partner's fantasies, and this act of playing out fantasies often happens when you feel secure and safe in your relationship. Role-playing is a great indicator of feeling physically and emotionally safe with your partner.

Role-play has the ability to be a healing experience and can help to strengthen the relationship of the individual. It is a great way to express your desires or yourself. While movies and porn may make you think that women and men already have their fantasy roles laid out, that isn't necessarily the case in reality.

For example, if you are the woman in a heterosexual couple and your boyfriend is a high-powered financial analyst, and he wants you to spank him and treat him as a "bad boy," he could be hinting that he doesn't always need to be in control. The two different roles, the submissive and the dominant character in this type of sexual exploration, can change the bonds between people. It can enliven, deepen, and strengthen the relationships, whether you switch between a submissive and dominant role or remain static.

The fantasies you have are a lot more common than you believe. There are three common fantasies:

1. Public or spontaneous sex

2. Bisexual fantasies
3. Dominant and submissive

Chances are, you have had one of these fantasies before.

For the dom and sub fantasies, it gives you the chance to have an unequal power distribution in a controlled and safe situation. It gives you the chance to release your inhibitions and to be taken over by pleasure, and either have a gain or loss of control.

Humans have a subcortical circuit for submission and dominance. The majority of us will display these two sides several times throughout the day. A partner who would like to be dominant might have, or currently, feels weak and helpless during certain points of their life and benefits from getting to feel as if they are in control in a certain area.

With a bisexual fantasy, simply wanting to role play in a bisexual role, doesn't mean that you actually have homosexual tendencies. This, in no way, means that everybody is bisexual, but a lot of people have experienced sexual interest towards a person of the same gender.

With a spontaneous fantasy, it is one of the "just can't wait to have you" type of things. This is something that we have all heard about and thought about, if not, we've given it a try. The thought of having sex in a public setting can be quite invigorating because of the danger behind it.

There is no need to be afraid of the idea of foreplay. It does not mean that you feel unhappy in your relationship, and it doesn't mean that you think your current sex life is boring. Simply wanting to be another person during sex doesn't mean you are going to hurt your relationship and the life that you both have outside of the bedroom.

The key to having a healthy and successful role-play is trust. Without trust, boundaries may end up being crossed, and your lines can be destroyed. It is all about having mutual respect and a good understanding that this is simply an exploration of fantasies, and the most important element of it all is consent.

Through this act of self-expression, there is an opportunity for validation and acceptance from your partner, which can lead to an intimate and emotional connection. The lowered inhibitions and sexual confidence that is needed when you role play can only be reached through safety and trust in your relationship.

If you are able to engage in role-playing with confidence, you aren't being some sexual pariah. Instead, you are proving that you have faith in your lover and partnership with them. If you can comfortably open yourself up to that level of vulnerability, you are reaffirming your connection.

Roleplay equals communication. When you are in tune with your sexual self, you are traveling an enlightened path. You want to feel relaxed enough in your relationship to feel like you can ask your partner for whatever it is that you want without feeling shameful.

In order to have good communication, you have to be in tune with yourself. Having a good understanding of what you desire and being aware of the level of openness and comfort you have to act out that desire is going to help you talk to your partner. If you have a solid relationship, then this communication should be fluid. So what should you do if you think role playing is for you? Here is where you need to start.

1. Think About What Your Fantasies Are

First, you each need to figure out what you want. In your head, what turns you on? Is it a teacher you had in college? Maybe you have always wanted a massage therapist to take things a step further. You may have even fantasized about being your favorite book character. Your only limit is your imagination. Think about any type of scenario that turns you on, even if it is something as simple as a first date with a person you have lusted over. Your dirty thoughts are the best inspiration for role-playing games.

2. Talk About It

There are some fantasies that can happen spur of the moment, like pretending to meet them for the first time. Others are going to need some prep work. If it is something really kinky that involves whips, leather, or some type of costume, you are going to have to give your other half a heads-up.

You can start things off by saying, "I can't stop fantasizing about..." Then you can gauge their interest in it. If you notice they perk up a little or get into it, then you can take things to the next level.

3. Be Kinky or Not

There are some fantasies that are all about power, such as officer and criminal, or student and teacher. One of you is going to have to have power over the other in some way. This is a great way to explore a power exchange dynamic in a playful way. But not every scenario is going to have the power play. Pretending to pick them up in a bar, or acting as if you are on a blind date gives you the chance to be somebody that you don't think you are, such as overtly sexual, aggressive, or bold.

4. Start Slow

For some, role playing is going to feel silly. You may feel uncomfortable or awkward "playing pretend," even if it is something that turns you on. This is why it is best to begin slowly and with something small. You may try sexting about your fantasy at first. This gives you the chance to be imaginative without having to look at the other person or speaking. For some, this is all they want or need. For others, after they get comfortable with typing things, it is going to be easy to say their "lines" as the scene plays out.

5. Dress Up or Not

Imagination is extremely powerful, so costumes aren't always needed. If you aren't interested in buying costumes and the like, then skip it. But if the act of dressing up helps you get into your role, then go for it. If you aren't sure if you need the costume or not, try it with the costume and without to see which way you prefer.

There are a lot of places to buy costumes online. There are adult stores that you can buy things from, and you can also try Halloween stores, especially when they have their sales after Halloween has passed. You may even find some things in your closet that will work.

6. What Do I Say?

The first few things that you say as your character may seem silly or awkward, and that is okay. This is something new, and nobody expects you to be perfect when you first start out. It is okay to fumble and laugh. If the fantasy has a strong connection for you and your partner, then the words will come and you can follow each other's lead.

You might know how you would like things to end. If you do, you need to tell your partner. But you might also want to be surprised; in which case you should imagine what your character would say and go with it. There isn't a critic in your house that is going to tell you what you should and should not do. If the role play ends with both of you naked, sweaty, and satisfied, then you have done well.

Chapter 5: Beginner Sex Tips

If you took the time to compare your sex life to today's dating scene, you might think your sex life is blander than mashed potatoes. That said, you should never get "wild" just because that is what everybody on TV is doing. Research has found that spontaneity and openness are able to lead to a longer-lasting relationship. Don't let other people mess with your mind.

After you have gotten used to talking candidly about sex with your significant other about what you want to try out and what you don't, it will become a lot easier to do in the future. A lot of people prefer to have a partner who feels empowered. This is going to help you to build respect and improve communication between the two of you. So, for those of you who are still new to improving your sex life, or haven't really gotten started with your sex life, let's go over some tips on how you can make some changes.

- Casually Mention It

Every sex expert out there will tell you that if you are having problems talking with your significant other about your sex life, you can let a song, erotic book, or movie provide you with inspiration. The conversation can easily be started with, "I saw this movie," or "I read an article about…" After that, you can let the conversation naturally continue.

- Don't Be Afraid to Be The Initiator

If your partner is normally the one that initiates sex, change things up a bit by showing them how much they excite you and flip the switch so that you can get things started. Everybody loves to feel as if their partner can't resist them.

- Practice Some Non-Sexual Touch

While this may have more to do with putting in some work when you aren't having sex, it can end up leading to an overall better sex life. You shouldn't reserve touching for solely when you are naked. Find a way to add in some hand holding, back rubs, hair stroking, and any other non-sexual touching that will encourage you and your partner to show affection for each other. You will learn more about each others' bodies in a way that is a lot deeper than simply have sex.

- Toys

If you would like to experiment with some toys, begin with simple ones. The easiest one to try is a vibrating ring. They fit over the penis and can be used with a condom. Most guys like these because, well, they vibrate of course. They also provide stimulation for the clitoris, so it really won't matter which position you are in, everybody wins. It isn't just pleasurable for one or the other.

Even if there isn't a penis around, vibrating rings can be used as a massager. You don't have to use them on the genitals.

- No Toys, No Problem

Even though it is exciting when you introduce new things into the relationship, you don't have to have toys to increase the heat.

It isn't always about bringing things into the bedroom. It could be about changing up the location. It might be an erotic book or porn. It might be creating a playlist of songs that turn you on. After two songs, anything might happen.

The most important thing is you don't need to make it complicated. Try to find just a few phrases that you think you can pull off and try them out first. If talking seems too hard, just begin by getting more verbal when you are having sex. Moans and groans can help you get used to being more vocal during sex. This will also help your partner know they are going things that you like.

- Lubes

The easiest thing to add to your sex life is lubricants. Water-based lubes are easier to clean up since the main component is water. These are normally cheaper. There is one drawback to this type of lube. They normally dry up faster than the silicone-based ones. The silicone-based ones last longer and are thicker. If you are having sex underwater, you are going to need a lube that won't wash off. If you are trying anal sex, where lube is very important, silicone-based lubes are your best option.

- Remember to Communicate

This one should be a no brainer, but anytime you begin pushing the boundaries in the bedroom, you have to make sure your partner is consenting to the new things.

If you are into any type of verbalizing or fantasy play that is going to involve your partner saying stop, they need to be able to do that. Everyone needs a safe word. Although you aren't into discipline or bondage, you might need some way to tell your partner it's time to stop.

If your significant other wants to do something you aren't into, say something like: "I appreciate you telling me about your fantasy, and I would like to explore it by talking about it. Right now, it isn't anything that I would be willing to actually try." When you let your partner know that you aren't comfortable with it, you are letting them know that there isn't anything wrong with their fantasy. They don't need to feel ashamed or guilty about asking about it.

Basically, sex is all about what is and isn't pleasurable and comfortable for your partner and yourself. There isn't any way to be an advanced sexual partner. When you have sex with your partner, if it is fulfilling and fun, then it is perfectly fine. Never do anything new just to keep away from a breakup.

Anything you explore needs to be done to enhance your relationship. You need to build on everything you have already created.

Chapter 6: A Massage to Get Ready

Massages are a great way to get rid of any tension you may have, spread healing energies, improve your blood circulation, and when we are talking about tantra, they can help to sexually arouse your partner. Massages are the best way to help sexual partners show one another extra intimacy.

By nature, humans crave touch, and massages are a natural and an easy way to get that much-needed human touch. So how can you achieve this? First, there is no need to head out and get some special certification or training to help you perform your tantric massages. The only thing you really need is to have a yearning and intention to genuinely satisfy your partner through the intricate capacities of your hands.

What Does Tantric Massage Mean?

Before we head into the actual massage techniques, we should go over what a tantric massage is, how it differs from other types of massages and the biggest benefits of it. The tantric massage that we will go over was first created from many different sources, which are mainly a mixture of tantric philosophy and influences from the most important Western thinkers.

The main parts of tantric massage include:

- Experiencing a spiritual awakening is the true and ultimate goal of the practice of tantra and tantric massage.
- You should never wear clothes during the massage, so private parts will, the majority of the time, be exposed.
- It helps to heighten or boost orgasmic or sexual experiences.
- It helps to get rid of blockages in various areas of your spirit, mind, body, and consciousness.
- Tantric massage is focused on using and the potential of your sexual energy so that it will benefit you and won't limit you.

Benefits of Tantric Massage

Just like with any type of massage, a tantric massage comes with many different benefits, as well as some added benefits that make the tantric massage all the more special. The main benefits of having a massage are:

- Increased wellbeing
- Relieves stress, anxiety, and pain
- Improves the mood
- Improves immunity and health

When it comes to tantric massages, you all get these benefits:

- Higher spiritual awareness
- More intense sexual experiences
- Improves sex drive and libido

With all of that out of the way, let's take a look at some techniques and tips to help you get started with your tantric massages.

Getting Things Setup

For those who have never gotten to have a tantric massage, the thought of a tantric massage is often intriguing, if not intimidating. There are some people who think it is taboo, which is an unfortunate byproduct of our society.

Then you have those who have received a tantric massage, and they see it as a unique, irreplaceable, and exciting practice that can do a lot for a person and their significant other's wellbeing. Since most people don't understand what it is and how it works, they don't even view it as an option for them.

In order to have a good tantric massage session, you are going to want you and your partner to take turns massaging each other. This type of massage is going to require the receiver to be completely open and receptive and to be fully willing to surrender themselves to the experience completely.

To help get things underway, the following are some ways to get things prepared before you get started with the massage.

- Get The Space Ready

You are going to want to get the room where the massage will take place ready. This can be any private space you have in your home, like the bedroom or living room. Make sure that you have plenty of comfortable bedding and soft pillows at your disposal. You can also set the mood by adding some candles, and you can use scented candles to help increase the mood. Make sure that you place your candles in safe areas, away from anything flammable, because the last thing you will want to do is set something on fire in the middle of a massage. Turn the lights off or dim them slightly.

You should also make sure you have something drink nearby, like water or wine. You can also have some light snacks close by to help keep your energy up. You can even feed each other. An oil diffuser can be used to give your room a fresh and soothing scent.

- Get Yourself Fully Prepared

Before you get the massage started, make sure that your mind and heart are open. If you have something that is causing you any sort of discomfort, it is a good idea to try to avoid bringing that up right now, but it might be a good idea to take some time to work through your problems in order to relax further. The main discomfort that people will experience is due to self-consciousness and insecurity about different areas of their body. While you massage one another, it is extremely important to keep your attitude playful and show them you are interested in discovering new interactions.

You may also want to take a shower or a bath before you start the massage. It is a good idea to do this together, but make sure that you stay away from any sexual interactions during your shower.

Once that is done, stand face to face and stretch to get rid of tension.

You need to also be wearing comfortable clothing. Make sure that whatever you have on is loose enough that you can take it off easily. However, doing all of this fully nude is a very good idea. Since tantra is about the slow accumulation of sexual energy, it is okay to begin things with your clothes on.

- Start by Slowly Building Sexual Energy

After you have taken your shower and you have stretched, sit down so that you are face to face and in a comfortable position. This could mean that you are cross-legged, or you could have your legs draped over one another in order to help the energy from your erogenous zones to be closer.

Simply sit like this and start into each other's eyes for at least five minutes. As we talked about in the tantric sex chapter, the eyes are the most important part. This will likely feel uncomfortable when you first do this but carry on and stare at each other as long as you can. As you begin to feel all of your tension fall away, you have created a real connection. This is what the goal is of this exercise. This is the connection that you have to have so that you can revel in the tantric massage and sex. Do your best to make sure that you don't lose eye contact during this.

Begin the Massage

After you are fully ready, whoever wants to receive the massage first can lay down on the surface that you prepared. There are a couple of simple massage methods that you can use, and all of them are beginner-friendly so that you can use them right away. You will want to have some massage oils to make these massages more enjoyable.

- Start on The Back

Add about two tablespoons of massage oils in your hands. Smear the oil across your hands and then rub them together so that you can get the oil and your palms warmed. This will feel better for your partner. Once you have warmed your hands, place them on their low back and let your hands move up their back, over the neck and shoulders, and then back down the back over the butt.

- The Hand Slide

Now that there is a good layer of oil over your partner's back, you can begin to slide your fingers down the spine and then massage all the way down their low back and over their buttocks. Then make your way back up to their neck, over the should, and down their arms and across their fingertips. Do this around five times. As you are massaging them, communicate with them and ask for some feedback on how all of this feels or what they like about it. If your partner doesn't like to talk a lot, you don't have to push them to talk. You need to remember that this is supposed to give them a sense of relaxation and wellbeing.

- Pull-Ups

To change up the motions, try moving one hand after the other as you move up the sides of your lover's body. Start by placing your hands at their hips with your fingertips pointed towards their spine and then pull your hand up to their spine. Once you do both sides, move your hands to their waist, and make the same motion to bring your hand to their spine. Then move your hands up to the side of their breast and pull your hands up to their spine. Lastly, start at their armpits and pull your hands up to their spine. You want to do both sides with each of these.

- Kneading

This is a crazy easy motion, especially for those who have every baked bread. Even if you haven't made bread, it is still a straight forward movement. All you need to do is squeeze their back and buttocks between your fingers and thumbs in a sinuous motion. Then you will allow your hands to glide to another area of their back and then repeat this action over and over until your kneaded all the way up their back. Then you can move your way back down. When you are working in fleshier areas, such as the butt, you can add a little more pressure, so you shouldn't about squeezing it a bit more and spreading their cheeks as your knead.

- Feather Stroke

Before you move down to their thighs, lightly stroke their shoulders, arms, neck, back, and butt with only your fingertips using an extremely light stroke. You should do this for around five minutes. If you have long fingernails, feel free to lightly scratch their skin. You should do this in circular motions and from side to side. The goal is to have this light and prickly touch to create sensual eagerness for your lover because they don't know what area you are going to touch next.

- Foot Caress

You might need to use a bit more oil for this. Rub your oily hands together and then rub the oil down and across their thighs and calves slowly. Knead the back of their legs as well. Do one leg at a time. The feet, whether you realize it or not, is an erogenous zone, so make sure you give them some considerable attention. Add some extra oil to each foot, rubbing it over the ankles, heels, and between the toes. Using the palms of your hands, slide them along the bottom of your partner's foot a few times. Gently rotate their toes clockwise and counter-clockwise. Then move your forefinger between each toe. Gently pull the toes away from the body.

- Flip Them Over

Your partner is probably feeling pleasured after everything you just did to their back, so now you can bring the attention to their front. Have them flip over as you apply more oil to your hands. Smear the oil over their belly and slowly start to slide up their stomach, over their nipples, and then back down to their belly. Continue to do this a few more times. As you do this, it spreads energy into their bodies. If your partner is a female, make sure that you a gentle with her breasts. Men can handle firmer strokes across their chest. You can also knead a man's chest if you want.

Once you have finished massaging your partner, it's your turn to get massaged. Allow the massages to progress naturally and let what happens next, happens. People who are more experienced in tantra and tantric massages will also use yoga poses during their massages. You don't have to use yoga poses in order to have a successful tantric massage.

Chapter 7: Getting Things Started

The most wonderful thing about playing sex games is that they are all foreplay. Does anybody actually have to justify making sex more intimate, longer-lasting, creative, and playful?

What is foreplay? Foreplay is any type of sexual activity before you have intercourse. With that said, intercourse doesn't even have to be on the menu or the grand finale. Foreplay is hot enough when it is done right. Most women call it "the whole point of having sex." It doesn't matter if it involves a quick text, back rubs, dirty talk, dry humping, spanking, fingering, oral sex, neck kisses, touching each other while spooning, or making out, foreplay is all the sensual things you do before the "huge event," whatever this might mean for you.

Why is foreplay important? There are many reasons why foreplay is so important. It is important for women to feel turned on and excited enough to enjoy sex. Jumping into sex without leading up to it can feel painful, uncomfortable, and boring. Even if you only have time for a quickie, it needs to have some type of lead in so it can be fun for everyone.

You don't go jogging without warming up first, do you? That is all well and good, but it won't get you heated up for sex. All the talking, kissing, touching, and rubbing before sex is just as important as the sex itself. It can help get the blood going to all the right places, boosts the libido, gets you in the mood, and relaxes you. If it is done right, you are going to get your partner primed for an exquisite orgasm.

This definition makes it seem like penetrative intercourse is the only definition of sex. It is best to call it "arousal activities." There are LGBTQ couples who don't actually penetrate each other, and they consider things such as oral sex to be the main event. So, when you call oral sex foreplay, it can be a noninclusive way to look at sex. When you look at foreplay as an appetizer and not the main meal can make it sound like it isn't as important as the man's orgasm.

You should think about foreplay as any activity that can build up arousal, whatever it might be. Sex doesn't need to be a linear experience that begins with a kiss and ends with sex.

As long as all parties involved consent, there isn't a right or wrong way to do foreplay. If oral sex is the main event, then the rubbing and touching that leads to it will give you the arousal you need. Any activity that can get a person "aroused enough to have fun with the other stuff" is considered foreplay.

Here are some classic foreplay activities:

- Spank your partner
- Tell her you enjoy reading her poetry
- Play with your partner's testicles
- Tell him that you love when he plays his guitar (or whatever instrument he might play)
- Nibbling your partner's earlobes
- Fingering your partner's anus
- Biting and kissing your partner's neck
- Fingering her vagina
- Sucking and licking nipples
- Caressing your partner's body all over
- French kissing
- Kissing and licking your partner's anus
- Squeezing and caressing your partner's breasts
- Stroking her penis
- Stroking his penis

You can focus on certain body parts like the back of your partner's neck or their pubic bone. The main part is taking the pressure off of yourself and making your partner have an orgasm. If it feels good for everyone involved, then you are on the right track.

Foreplay can trigger physical and physiological responses that make sex possible and enjoyable.

Physical Responses

Foreplay can actually get the juices flowing because it increases your sexual arousal. Don't confuse this with sexual desire, but it can do that, too.

Sexual arousal can cause many responses from your body; these include:

- Increases blood pressure, pulse, and heart rate
- Lubricates the vagina. This makes intercourse enjoyable and prevents pain.
- Dilates the blood vessels in the genitals.
- Makes the nipples hard and causes the breasts to swell.
- Blood will flow to the genitals, which in turn cause the penis, clitoris, and labia to swell.

Physiological Responses

Foreplay does feel good, but it goes a lot deeper than that. When you engage in foreplay, it can help build emotional intimacy that makes you and your significant other feel connected both in and outside the bedroom.

If you aren't in a relationship, no need to worry; foreplay can lower your inhibitions, and this makes sex even hotter between virtual strangers and couples.

If stress halts your libido, foreplay just might take care of this problem. When you kiss, it releases serotonin, dopamine, and oxytocin. This cocktail can lower your cortisol levels while increasing your feelings of euphoria, bonding, and affection.

Foreplay Means Something Different for Everyone

When talking about sex, foreplay has been defined as an erotic stimulation that precedes sex. If you take sex completely out of the equation, then foreplay becomes defined as a behavior or action that precedes these events

Whatever this event is might not look the same to someone else as it does to you, and this is fine.

You don't even have to put intercourse on the menu if you don't want to. Foreplay is its own thing, and it could be all you need to have an orgasm. If fact, research shows that women can't reach an orgasm just by having sex.

As long as all parties are consenting, foreplay could be anything that you want it to be. You can begin before things get heated up. You need to begin somewhere, but why does it have to be during sex. You don't even have to be in the same room to start.

You can use foreplay to prolong your playtime. If you know that you will be getting together in a couple of days or later today, you can use foreplay to start the party and keep going. Below you will find some foreplay tips. You can find one that you really like and try it out on your partner or get adventurous and try them all. The time you spend on your partner's body before penetration increases their pleasure along with yours when the main course happens.

You don't even have to be in a relationship to play sex games that are intended to be used as couples. Anybody who doesn't mind getting closer would be a great candidate for sex games.

When you find yourself needing to break the ice or get closer, take a look at these ideas for sex games.

- Who's More Powerful

This could be a thumb war, wrestling match, pillow fight, or tickle war. The main thing is you have to do it completely naked. The point of this game is competing, getting each other all worked up, and struggling against your significant other. Whatever the case, the person who surrenders first, has to do a sex act on the other. You need to make sure you agree to the act before you begin. Your partner might not like losing, and you might pick something that they don't like doing.

- Leave notes

You don't have to be creative to get your partner going. You can just leave them a note. Put it on their pillow or hide it in their bag. This shows that you can't wait to be with them later.

- Hide and Seek

This is definitely an R-rated version of the children's game. When you know that your significant other is coming home for the day, take your clothes off and leave a trail for them to follow. Make sure the clothes lead to where you are. Once they open the door and see the clothes, give them time to find you. The best part is they get to decide what happens next. You can then switch roles if you would like to.

- Sexting

Foreplay doesn't have to begin in the bedroom. It can begin when you wake up. This is so easy, and you can do it anytime and anywhere. A text telling them what you want to do to them or how hot you get just thinking about them. You can also tell them certain things they can do to get you all hot and bothered. This shows then that you are thinking about them and everyone loves that. Send them a text that says: "Can't wait to get naked with your later" can get your significant other excited before you ever get into the bedroom. If you are careful, you can even send them a nude picture of you to show them what they can expect later.

- Pick Your Tool

Let your partner try to bring you to orgasm by using a toy or object of your choice. This makes for some great foreplay whether you orgasm or not.

- Meeting For Drinks or Dinner

When you meet your partner for drinks or dinner, make out quickly in the parking lot before you go inside. Once you are inside, play footsies under the table, meet in the restroom for another make-out session. You could "accidentally" drop your fork to take a peek at what they might be wearing under their clothes. These are just a few ways to turn drinks and dinner into foreplay.

- Santa's Bag

If you have any sex toys, put them in a bag. Just make sure they are clean. Ask your significant other to reach into the bag without looking and get one. Whatever toy they pick out is the one that gets used for the night. This keeps either partner from feeling self-conscious about adding a toy to sex.

- Kiss Them Like You Mean It

Don't greet them with a chaste kiss on the cheek. Lock eyes with them, press your body against theirs, and kiss them deep and long.

Use your hands and tongue, and be sure to moan enough to make them excited about what is about to happen. Don't forget to end the night with another fabulous kiss.

- Buy an Adult Board Game

There are more of these on the market than you might think. Some will use cards. Others take a pair of dice. Some games are more traditional. There are some games out there that incorporate all three.

You could get a Jenga set if you don't have on already. Take each block and write down a command like "kiss my neck" and keep going from there. When you play with your partner, whoever extracts a block successfully from the tower, their partner has to perform the command. You can also come up with a punishment from when the tower gets knocked down. You can get naughty and creative on the punishment.

- Tell Them It Is Game Time

You don't have to be coy when all you want to do is get them naked and make wild passionate love to them. Tell them as graphically as you can that all you want to do is get them hot and wet or hard and keep them there all night long.

- Red Light, Green Light

This is not the game you remember from your childhood. You are going to lay down on your bed either naked or in something that makes you feel like a goddess. Have your partner stand at the door to the bedroom. You get to see how well they know you by asking them questions about you. The questions can be anything from personal to sexy. You could ask things like: "Where is my dream vacation?" or "What is my favorite sex position?"

When they get the answer right, they can take a step toward you. If they get the answer wrong, they have to take a step backward. Your significant other is going to learn more about you while going crazy with your teasing. When your partner finally gets to you, let the fun begin.

- Light Candles

There isn't anything like candles to set the mood for all the sexy things you want to do. Tea lights don't cost a lot of money, so stock up and light them when you want to get busy. Plus, candlelight makes your skin look great.

- Timed Penetration

Find some sort of timer. You could use your cell phone, hourglass, or stopwatch. Now choose a time. It could be 30 minutes, ten minutes, or an hour. Now get busy with your partner any way you want. The kicker is there can't be any type of penetration before the time runs out. Once the timer goes off, have all the fun you can handle.

- Turn Music On

Everyone has a song or two that touches them in their special place. You need to find out what your significant other's is and add your to it to create a playlist that will get them all hot and bothered.

Here are a few of my personal favorites:

- The Weekend – Earned It
- Nine Inch Nails – Animal
- Barry White – Let's Get It On
- Donna Summer – Love to Love You

- Play Truth or Dare

This one is old, but it's still good. You might need to focus on the dares more than the truth. It all depends on your mood. If you think that they might be hiding something, by all means, stick to the truth but be careful, it might blow up in your face and not in a good way. You could dare your partner to try to kiss you without using their hands. Try to pleasure you by only using the tip of your tongue; this is the best time to uncover all your fantasies.

- Dance

There isn't anything hotter than two bodies being pressed against each other. Feeling your partner's hot breath on your cheek while you sway to the rhythm of your sexy playlist can up the heat factor in the room.

- Mirror

You and your partner need to sit down while facing each other. Start by touching, licking, kissing, or lightly touching your partner. Now they have to repeat what you did to them to you as close as possible to what you did to them. This can get very hot. It's a great way to communicate with them about what you like without actually having to talk to them. Then you get to switch roles. This also helps you pay attention to each other better.

- Sexy Underwear

These aren't just for women. If you can find the right one that fits perfectly, you can really turn your partner on. Low rise briefs are always a good choice.

- Make Out Time

You can go old school and make out. Press your partner up against a wall, get them in the back seat of the car, or just fool around on the couch.

- Striptease

I'm not talking about swinging around a pole. You don't even need to have moves. Just dim the lights, put on your playlist, and slowly take your clothes off. Make sure your expression doesn't show any signs of fear or uneasiness. You can totally fake confidence.

- Make An Erotic Picnic

Place a picnic on your bed that is full of sexy goodies that are meant to be shared. Juicy cherries and strawberries along with some chocolate sauce and whipped cream to dip them into can make for a fun night. You can feed each other and then lick each other clean. Chocolate is a natural aphrodisiac, too.

- Slowly Remove Their Clothes

Since foreplay isn't a sprint, it is a marathon. You aren't in a hurry to get finished. Rather than stripping all your clothes off and getting down and dirty, begin by taking off your partner's shirt. Wait a few minutes and then take their pants off, then remove her bra, etc.

until they are completely naked. As you remove an article of clothing, focus on the skin that was revealed. After you take their pants off, you can massage their legs. When the shirt is gone, lick and kiss their chest.

- Massage

Human touch is powerful, and a massage can work wonders on the mind and body. Light those candles and get out your massage oils. There are some massage candles that can be used as both.

Begin at their feet and move up their body. Make sure to hit all their sensual points and linger in those special places when you feel like it.

You can begin by massaging your partner's legs from their upper thighs to their ankles. Now, focus on their feet, kneading their heels and all the parts of their feet. Now, work on their toes. Pull on each of them separately. You get bonus points if you suck them.

A bit of warning here, my partner hates having their feet touched, so you might want to ask their permission before you touch their feet.

- Quality not Quantity

If you can improve the quality of foreplay, she won't ever bug you again about quantity. If you just act like you are going through the motions to have sex with your partner, they will notice, and it is going to take longer to get them excited.

Basically, do what you would like to do and enjoy it; if you like her calves, stroke them. If you love how her butt looks in those jeans, kiss it, or give it a smack. When a man loves what he is doing, it will show, and this will turn her on even more.

- Erogenous Zones

A body is full of hot spots that beg to be touched. Nibble, lick, and kiss your way through all their zones.

- Find Out What Turns Them On

If you have any doubts, just ask them what they want. Most women really appreciate it when their partner makes sure that they are satisfied. If they see that you are trying very hard to please them, they will return the favor.

- Skin to Skin

You might remember dry humping from your teen years. Well, it isn't just for teens. The anticipation of two bodies rubbing together in different states of undress is the hottest thing ever.

- Toys

There is a lot more to sex toys than just a dildo shaped like a penis. Vibrators of various sizes and shapes can be used outside the body on any of the erogenous zones.

You can also find nipple and finger vibrators that can take foreplay to a whole new level.

- Sensory Play

All that dry humping and kissing is probably going to get the job done, but you can take it even farther with some props. Put a blindfold on your partner and then tease them with various temperatures and textures by using your tongue, ice cubes, feathers, etc.

- Tell Them What You Want

Talking about what you want during sex isn't just for foreplay. This makes sure you get what you need and want. Tell them what you want them to do to you and what turns you on.

- Soapy Shower

How wet hands and skin sliding across one another's bodies while you are lathering each other up with soap can take showering to a new level. You might not even want to get out of the shower, ever.

It's amazing at all the things you can find at home, or you could buy a seduction kit online.

That's it. Have fun. You might even think of some games on your own. The important thing to remember is that both parties have fun and enjoy each other.

Chapter 8: The Secrets to a Great Massage

We have gone over the art of the tantric massage, but if you don't want to take things to that extreme yet, you can still give your partner a simple massage. These techniques will help to make the simple massage more pleasurable.

In our life, it is very easy to let our emotional distance and stress get in the way of having a healthy relationship with our significant other. An erotic massage can help to create physical closeness and intimacy while helping to relieve stress and letting them get into the mood for sex.

When you add in erotic massage to your relationships, it can help to bring you both closer together emotionally and physically. It does not matter if your partner is always stressed or they aren't feeling inspired; an erotic massage can be exactly what you need to explore brand new levels of sexual bliss.

Three Important Areas of Erotic Massage

For you to get all the benefits of an erotic massage, let's look at the essential elements and how to use them.

- Environment

Setting the scene is very important because the environment could easily break or make the experience. This doesn't have to be time-consuming or expensive. If you incorporate the three things below, you will be doing fine.

First thing, you need to create an environment that doesn't have any distractions. Get any laptops, tablets, or phones out of the room you are going to be in. Unplug the television and cover up any devices that have harsh displays. You will also want something comfortable for them to lay on, and you can use some aromatherapy.

- Mindset

Before the massage, you need to ask yourself:

- How could I make their experience as enjoyable and relaxing as possible?
- How can I stay focused through the whole massage?
- How could I communicate with them to give them the most pleasure?
- What should I look for in their responses or reactions?

How you answer these questions could help you keep the right mindset throughout the entire session. It might take you some time to figure this out; it is going to be worth it to give your partner an erotic and relaxing experience they deserve.

- Technique

Even though the mindset and environment are needed for an erotic massage, it wouldn't be a massage without a technique.

There are some techniques that you can use during the massage:

- Effleurage

At the start of any massage, you should begin with gentle and light touches. These are called effleurage. The reasoning behind this is to get their blood circulating and get them prepared for the massage.

Use the palm of your hand and start with a gentle touch. You can do this in any pattern you want. Circular motions are the most common. They will cover the most area. Make sure you keep the pressure constant and make sure you pay the same attention to all areas of their body.

- Kneading

This is the most common technique that is used during the massage. It is easy to learn how to do.

Use your fingertips and thumb, take the muscle tissue between them, and squeeze at different intervals. This is great for large muscles of the buttocks, upper arms, and thighs.

- o   Friction

This is normally associated with deep tissue massages. This technique could be used when you need to work out tight kinks. Using your fingertips and thumb, put some gentle pressure on the knot and work it slowly in a circle.

When the knot starts giving away to the pressure, add more pressure while making sure your partner doesn't feel any discomfort.

To lighten the hurts but feels good feelings that are associated with this technique, you can change up the pressure during the session to give your significant other some time to recuperate every once in a while.

- o   Stretching

If your significant other has some stubborn areas of stress with knots, stretching could give them the best relief. This technique uses manual manipulation on your significant other's joints. You could rotate their ankles and wrists gently, bend and stretch their elbows and knees, and keep working on getting their limbs as loose and free as you possibly can without using force.

- o   Percussion

The chopping motions that are used with this technique might not seem erotic at all, but this could be a fun way to experiment and see how each other likes it.

There are different ways to do this technique. You could use the side of your hands to make a fast chopping motion to the upper back and things. You could use your fingertips to tap out any knots or kinks your find in their lower back, face, and neck. Percussion is useful to have in your massage arsenal.

The Science of An Erotic Massage

If you have never really entered the world massage, then you may be asking yourself how a simple massage can provide you with the benefits that we went over in the tantric massage chapter. This is a fair question. Humans are sensory-seeking creatures. From a very young age, humans are taught that touch is something we want and is good. We touch people in order to give and receive comfort, show signs of solidarity, and provide warmth.

We touch our partners to show them that we care about them and to provide them with satisfaction and joy. This means that massage can be an easy way to show your significant other that you care about them and their wellbeing. Also, think about the fact that there are certain levels of openness and trust that comes along with a sensual massage.

Very few women are going to be open to receiving an erotic massage from a man if there isn't some level of trust between them, as this contributes to the positive feelings and benefits of an erotic massage.

There are many different processes that the body undergoes when it receives a massage. Some of these processes, like the relaxation of muscles, are local. Others, like the release of endorphins, affects the entire body. But what the exact mechanisms behind the things that are happening?

There are various theories among experts. Some researchers and scientists believe that physical touch through massage session is able to improve circulation. This will, in turn, increase how much oxygen gets delivered to the muscle and will help to improve the healing process. Others believe that massages engage the lymphatic system.

This will help to remove waste from the knotted area and will improve muscle movement and healing. Still, there are those that believe all of the benefits of massage are based in the nervous system. Touch causes an electric sensation that travels from the original point of touch all the way to the brain, which will release endorphins and other happy chemicals. So which one of these theories is right?

Right now, there aren't any right or wrong answers. It is possible that none of the above are correct, or they all could be. But whatever the exact reason is for those "good" feelings, there is no arguing with the scientific research that backs the benefits that come with a massage.

From lowering depression and anxiety levels to control inflammation following physical activities, massage has certainly shown that it provides many benefits to those who undergo treatment.

Eroticism and Massage

After you have a good understanding of how massage works and all of the benefits it provides, it is easy to see how erotic massage came to be. After all, when you mix two things that help to make you feel, which in this case is sex and massage, it makes sense that those good feelings are going to be amplified.

Erotic massage, though, is not all about sexual pleasure. Instead, there are two ways to pleasure your partner during an erotic massage session. Of course, sexual pleasure is one of these two sources. But, the other pleasure source is from the actual massage.

The orgasm should be seen as a by-product of your massage session, but it should not be the ultimate goal. As you move your hands over their body, your partner is going to feel more relaxed. The tension is going to leave their body, ever so slowly, until all of their muscles are loose and relaxed. This is the reason why climax becomes more likely. As they relax, so will their inhibitions.

With an erotic massage, your partner is going to slowly lose their signs of self-consciousness, anxiety, and fear. This is the magic of an erotic massage.

Targeted Massage Combinations

Knowing the massage techniques outlined above is a great start, but to make sure that your partner receives the satisfaction they deserve, it is important that you know the areas of the body that you should target and in which manner. The techniques can defiantly be used from head to toe, but sometimes a routine that includes targeted combinations of different body parts can provide more satisfaction.

The orgasm is the greatest possible release that a person can experience. While orgasms can vary in intensity and length, with the right massage routine, you can help to increase the strength of the orgasm. That's what this targeted massage routine is going to help you do.

Begin by having your partner lay flat on their back on a comfortable surface, be it bed, table, or floor. You will start with an entire body once over. This is basically a quick rundown of the more thorough routine you will be doing, but it will help to get the blood pumping. With only your fingertips, start at their forehead. Grave the side of the face with both hands and then slowly move your way down to their neck and chest.

Do not touch their nipples, but do lightly touch around the chest or breasts and then down the sides of their torso. Once you get to their hips, you are going to start to branch out with one hand on one leg and the other hand on the other leg.

Simultaneously move your way down their legs. Remember that you should keep your touches light and feathery, and then trace your way back up a little ways and then back down again. Make sure you notice your partner's cues during this once over so that you can be a good idea of where their most sensitive areas are.

Once you have finished the once over, move back up to their neck. You will work your way down their body once more, but this time you will be spending time kneading the tight kinks and knots out of their body, but you should also add in some light touches to excite and arouse them. You can also use some of the other techniques that we discussed early in the chapter, like stretching. Pay attention to how your partner responds to the different methods.

Since this massage is meant to increase the orgasm, you will want to maximize the touches to the pubic region you make to help excite them. If you are massaging a woman, this does not mean you have to spend a bunch of time on her clitoris. Instead, use light pressure just above the pubic bone. Run your fingers over their stomach and stop at the very top of the public bone right above the hips but just below their belly button.

With the palm of your non-dominant hand, press down slightly. Make sure that your partner isn't uncomfortable. With the dominant hand, slowly work across their genitals, gently grazing across the sensitive areas.

When massaging a woman, feel free to insert your middle and ring fingers into her vagina at this point and press the palm of that hand up against the clitoris. As you move your entire hand up and down, the middle and ring fingers will be hitting the g-spot, and the palm will be rubbing the clitoris. When massaging a man, you can start stroking him.

As you notice them getting closer to climax, you can press down onto the pubic bone a bit more firmly and increase the intensity of your strokes.

These are only a few of the most common techniques that are used during an erotic massage session. You can experiment with various touches. Just remember to watch your partner and their reactions.

The next time you notice that your partner is feeling stressed out, offer to give them a massage and try out these techniques.

Chapter 9: Trying Dirty Talk

Dirty talk doesn't have to be complicated, weird, awkward, or creepy. Dan Savage, a popular sex columnist, summed up sex talk with this very simple statement, "Tell 'em what you're going to do, tell 'em what you're doing, tell 'em what you did." Simply put, dirty talk should be straightforward and simple.

While it can be and should be simple, most of us end up freezing up in the moment, and we end up saying something we heard once in a porn, and it will come out sound weird, awkward, unnatural, or very unsexy.

Given how easy dirty talk can go wrong, why do we even want to bother with trying it at all? The simplest answer is that when it is done right and is said by a person that you are attracted to, nothing is sexier than vocal sex. The biggest sex organ is the brain, so it only makes sense that we get turned on by what a person says during a moment of passion. This will also work in reverse. When you say your fantasies and desires that normally get kept to yourself to a rapt audience, it can be a big turn-on.

When you will get to the heart of dirty talk, having good dirty talk can take us out of our regular lives and really put us into the act of sex. While you might be physically feeling what is going on, if your mind is not there, the pleasure reward can fall short. This is the reason why people often fantasize when masturbating. Dirty talk helps us get out of our own heads into the body. The simple sounds and tones can help all of our daily worries melt away and remember how amazing our partner feels.

Now that you know why you should try dirty talk, let's look at how you can make it work.

Don't Make It Complicated

You shouldn't try to be a porn start right off the bat. Say the things that feel natural, and definitely don't think you need to have some sort of elaborate narrative before you get things going. This isn't some strange Shakespearean monologue that you have to recite, and there is no need to talk every single time. Dirty talk doesn't have to just happen during sex. Picking the right moment to say something like, "I can't wait to feel you inside me," can do the trick.

Think about your senses, if vulgar or profane language isn't something that you typically use, then don't feel like you have to. Chances are, your partner would be turned off if you all of a sudden started using words you have never used before. Your aim should be to be playful, and you should start early. While your partner is at work or picking up some things from the store, drop a few hints about how you want to play.

This helps to build the anticipation of sex. You can easily send a text that says, "I can't stop thinking about tonight..."

Give Instructions

You have two forms of dirty talk. One form helps to build anticipation for sex, and the other is simply instructional and happens, most of the time, during sex. Giving some direction or instructions can be pretty sexy. You could tell your partner something like, "When you get home, I want you to put on your best lingerie, and then I want you to lay, face down, on the bed, and wait for me to come home and play with you." This combines both forms of dirty talk and can be used to add in some role-playing.

You Don't Have to Go X-Rated

It is very important that you know how to read your partner when it comes to dirty talk. You should not say things that are really vulgar unless all of the signs point to that. You can easily say things that are way too X-rated and then end up turning your partner off. If this happens, it will likely be embarrassing, but you should be able to recover from it.

If Things Don't Work Out, Talk About What Went Wrong

If something you say causes nervous laughter, that is fine, but there could be times when what you say can trigger them. They may not know the best way to verbalize why those words hurt them in the moment, but if you feel as if you took things too far, you should make a point of talking to them about it later on.

It will help to make sure that both of you understand that dirty talk carves out an erotic space and that you don't actually feel the way the person is talking. It is all about play. Think about how some people like to be called "daddy," but they aren't interested in incest. Instead, they like the dominance and authority the word gives them.

If you do take it too far, then do your best to correct it. Honor what your partner is into and what they are comfortable with, and talk with them about the things that they don't like. But, you should never make them feel like that owe you an explanation for the things they don't like. If they want to tell you, they will. This is true for you as well.

Try These Out

So, to make things easier for you, if you really don't know what you should say to your partner, I will provide you with a list of lines that you try using. You will have to fill in the blank on some things, but I think you will get the gist pretty quickly.

1. "Fuck me hard."
2. "I love it when you moan my name."
3. "I want you to use me like a toy."
4. "You taste so good."
5. "I'm going to come for you."
6. "It makes me crazy when you _____."
7. "When I get home, I want you in my favorite skirt with no underwear…"
8. "Yes, please. More."

9. "Right there. Touch my _____."

10. "I've been thinking about what I want to do with you…"

Give some of these a try the next time you want to get your partner in the mood and see how it feels.

Chapter 10: Orgasm

The orgasm has long been viewed as the peak of sexual excitement. It's a very powerful feeling of pleasure, which involves releasing accumulated erotic tension. While everybody's goal with sex is an orgasm, there isn't a lot now about it. During the last few centuries, theories about the orgasm have changed. For example, experts have only recently started talking about the female orgasm. Many doctors in the 1970s claimed it was perfectly normal for a woman not to experience an orgasm.

Orgasms are able to be defined in several ways with different criteria. Medical professionals talk about physiological changes that happen within the body. Mental health professionals and psychologists talk about cognitive and emotional changes. There isn't a single, overarching definition of the orgasm.

Sex researchers have tried to define orgasms in models of sexual response. While the process for orgasm can differ between people, there are several basic physiological changes that often occur in most incidences. Master and Johnson's Four-Phase Model includes:

- Excitement
- Plateau
- Orgasm
- Resolution

Kaplan came up with his own model, but his is different from most sexual response models because it includes desire. The majority of models don't include non-genital changes. It is important to understand, though, that not every sexual act is preceded by desire. Kaplan's three-stage model is:

- Desire
- Excitement

- Orgasm

Benefits of Orgasm

A 1997 cohort suggested that men's mortality risk was lowered when they experienced a high number of orgasms than in men who had fewer orgasms. There is also some research that suggests ejaculation can help to reduce the risk of prostate cancer. Researchers found that a man's prostate cancer risk was 20 percent lower in those who ejaculated at least 21 times a month than those who ejaculated only four to seven times a month.

There are a lot of hormones that are released during orgasm, which includes DHEA and oxytocin. There are some studies that suggest these hormones may help protect against heart disease and certain cancers. Oxytocin, along with other endorphins that get released during the female and male orgasm are also relaxants.

Types of Orgasm

Not surprisingly, since experts haven't come to a consensus in regards to a definition of an orgasm, there are many different types of orgasms. Sigmund Freud stated that immature and young females can only have an orgasm through clitoral stimulation while mature women are able to have an orgasm through vaginal stimulation. We will go over a few of those types.

- Pressure orgasms – this orgasm comes from indirect stimulation of applied pressure. This is a type of self-simulation that is common in young people.

- Tension orgasms – this is a common type of orgasm. It is created through direct stimulation, often when the muscles and body are tense.

- Blended or combination orgasm – these are a variety of orgasmic experiences that blend together.

- Relaxation orgasms – this orgasm comes from deep relaxation through sexual stimulation.

- Multiple orgasms – these are a series of orgasms that happen over a short period of time.

There are actually a few orgasms that both Dodson and Freud discounted, but there are others who believe they are real. For example:

- G-spot orgasms – this is an orgasm that is caused by the stimulation of an erotic zone inside the vagina through penetrative intercourse, which feels very different from orgasms caused by other forms of stimulation.
- Fantasy orgasm – these are orgasms that result from mental stimulation.

The Female Orgasm

Men and women go through similar yet different physiological processes when experiencing an orgasm. Here we will talk about the process of the female orgasm following the Masters and Johnson Four-Phase Model.

1. Excitement

When a woman is psychologically or physically stimulated, the blood vessels in her genitals will dilate. This increased blood flow will make the vulva swell, and fluid will pass through the vaginal walls. This makes the vulva wet and swollen. Internally, the vagina expands at the top. Breathing and heart rate will quicken, and her blood pressure will rise. The blood vessel dilations can cause a woman to look flushed, especially on her chest and neck.

2. Plateau

As the blood flows to the lower vaginal area, it will reach a limit and turn firm. Breasts can also increase in size by 25 percent and increase the blood to the areola, which makes the nipples look less erect. The clitoris will then pull back against the pubic bone, which makes it look like it has disappeared.

3. Orgasm

The genital muscles will experience rhythmic contractions that are about 0.8 seconds apart. For women, their orgasms last longer at about 13 to 51 seconds. Since women don't have a recovery period, they can continue to experience orgasms if they are stimulated again.

4. Resolution

The body will slowly return back to its previous state, with a reduction in breathing, pulse rate, and swelling.

The Male Orgasm

1. Excitement

When a man experiences psychological or physical stimulation, he gets an erection. Blood flow has increased in the corpora, which is the tissue that runs through the penis, which causes the penis to grow and become hard. The testicles will draw up as the scrotum tightens.

2. Plateau

With the increased blood flow, the testicles and glans will increase in size. The buttock and thigh muscles will tense, the pulse quickens, blood pressure rises, and breathing increases.

3. Orgasm

Semen, which is a mixture of 95 percent fluid and 5 percent sperm, is forced through the urethra by contractions in the pelvic floor, vas deferens, seminal vesicles, and prostate gland. These contractions also cause the semen to be forced out of the penis, causing ejaculation. Orgasm for a man tends to last for ten to 30 seconds.

4. Resolution

The man is now in the recovery phase, where he can't have any more orgasms. This is what is called a refractory period, and how long it lasts varies between men. It could be a few minutes to a few days and tends to become longer the older the man becomes. At this point, the testicles and penis return o their original size. Their pulse and breathing will be fast.

Multiple Orgasms

People find the idea of multiple orgasms intriguing and fro good reason. It is perfectly normal to want to experience one right after the other, as well as simply tapping out after the first. Here, we will go over why the female body is designed to experience multiple orgasms, and strategies to make them more likely to happen.

Having multiple orgasms doesn't necessarily mean that you have another orgasm right after your first one without a moment's rest, but you can do that. Multiple orgasms simply mean that you have several orgasms during a single sexual encounter.

In order to experience multiple orgasms, it will require some experimentation on your part. After you have your first, you will need to figure out what can make it happen again. If you find that your clitoris is so sensitive that you can't touch it, use the rest of your body. Try out different forms of stimulation. This could be playing with your breasts or getting your partner to kiss everything except the clitoris. The main point is to continue the arousal in whatever way works for you. Continue this for however long you want, and you can always check back in with the clitoris to see if some of the sensitivity has gone away.

That being said, sometimes stimulating the sensitive clitoris could be the ticket. There are some women who say continuing to run the clitoris gives them the chance to embrace what seems like unbearable overstimulation, which can result in more orgasms. It all depends on what you are able to handle. If you like oversensitivity, then do it. If it hurts or doesn't seem to be creating a pleasurable feeling, stop touching the clitoris to try to have more orgasms.

You can also use Kegal exercises to help extend your orgasms. As you reach your first orgasm, push your hand over your vulva and pulse it between orgasm contractions as you squeeze your thighs.

Doing this can intensify and increase the orgasmic contraction and bring you into another orgasm.

You also need to make sure that you breathe during the entire experience. There are some people who will unconsciously hold their breath as the orgasm builds, but concentrating can help. When you reach an orgasm, breathe purposefully, slowly, and deeply while contracting your pelvic floor muscles. This breath work can lead to multiples for some people.

These tips are a great place to start, but don't get upset if they don't work the first time. It takes practice and learning your body.

Chapter 11: Female Ejaculation

Ejaculation has been described as a powerful experience that is only associated with male sexuality and penises. What most people don't realize is that it is possible for a female to ejaculate from the vagina or vulva. This could happen after, during, or even before sex and with or without an orgasm. Since there is a lot more knowledge about women and people, who were assigned the female persona at birth do possess sexuality. We aren't just passive sex objects. We are more aware and open about our sexual appetites, desires, and biology. Squirting is only one small part of it.

What Is It?

While having sex, some people who have vulvas will experience an involuntary release of fluids. This is what is known as female ejaculation or, as some people call it, squirting. Even though everyone who has a vulva identifies themselves as a female, and everybody who identifies as a female won't have a vulva.

"Squirting" has gotten more attention recently because more people are talking about it. There is more accurate information about the sexual reality of people who were assigned the gender of female. Their bodies are still thought of as being a mystery or myth. Squirting is often thought of as something to try to reach or just a part of being completely liberated sexually. This puts a lot of unnecessary pressure on women.

Some people think that squirting is just a party trick that specific people have to perform. But that doesn't make anyone feel empowered. What about people who identify outside the gender norms? How can we talk about female ejaculation?

Squirting History

It seems as if ejaculation has been around for a long time. During 2010, Joanna Korda and her associates looked through numerous ancient literary texts and found many references about sexual fluids being ejaculated.

In the ancient India text the *Kama Sutra*, they talk about "female semen that falls constantly." In a Taoist text written during the 300x called *Secret Instructions Concerning the Jade Chamber*, they talk about the difference between "the genitals transmitting fluid" and a slippery vagina. Joanna Korda and her conspirators concluded that this could easily be considered to be female ejaculation.

Most people wouldn't even consider it to be literature. They see it as pornography. Pornography is a normal way for anyone to learn about sex now. We checked out one popular porn side called Pornhub and found that some of the most popular videos were about squirting. The popularity of squirting increased a lot between the years 2013 and 2015. It still remains as some of their top 20 videos.

According to their data, women search for squirting videos 44 percent more than men do. As people age, the popularity of squirting will decrease.

People from Slovakia, Venezuela, Columbia, Vietnam, and South Africa will search for squirting videos when compared to other countries. In America, people from Wyoming, Montana, Utah, and Nebraska are more interested in squirting videos as compared to people from New Jersey, Maryland, California, and New York.

Most people who are assigned the female gender only experience something like a trickle rather than the large gushes that you see in videos. In fact, most people don't even realize it happened. Just like not squirting or squirting is "better," there isn't a right or wrong way when ejaculating.

What Is the Fluid That Gets Ejaculated?

Just because squirting videos are popular doesn't mean that it is accepted everywhere. During 2014, any pornography depicting female ejaculation was banned in Europe. This ban has been met with a lot of protests because it implies that ejaculating from the vulva or vagina is perverted while ejaculating from a penis is totally normal.

Censors couldn't see the difference between urination and female ejaculation. They consider urination to be and "obscene" act.

Scientists haven't agreed on what exactly is in the fluid of the female ejaculation. Even though it still isn't clear, female ejaculation fluid has shown to contain some urine, and it contains other fluids, too.

Dr. Amy Gilliland, a sex researcher, did a study in 2009 along with Doula and found that studies that have been done on female ejaculation noticed those studies didn't include how the people felt about the account.

Most of the participants reported that large amounts of fluid were released during their orgasm. Some stated there was enough that it sprayed walls, soaked the bed, and scared their partners.

Gilliland saw that some women who felt shameful about their ejaculation learned to feel more positive about their ejaculation later on in life once they heard other people's positive feedback, other's experiences, and learned more about female ejaculation.

Chapter 12: Best Sex Positions for Him

The tantric and kama sutra sex positions that we will talk about in this chapter are great for everyone involved, but it focuses on what will feel the best for him. While this chapter and the next will use the pronouns of he and she, this doesn't mean same-sex couples can't try these positions. They are adaptable to any couple who would like to try them.

Rock-a-Bye Booty

This one can be a bit tricky for people who aren't exactly flexible.

- Begin with the man on his back, and the lady slowly straddles him.

- Once he has penetrated her, he will lift his torso up, and she will position herself so that they are facing each other.

- Both will wrap their legs tightly around each other's buttocks. Both will link their elbows under the other's knees and bring them up so that they are at chest level.

This position will require a rocking motion since thrusting isn't possible in this position. The woman can squeeze her pelvic floor muscles to provide him with a stronger sensation.

Passion Pretzel (Blooming Orchid)

In the scheme of things, this position is fairly simple. If you or your partner have bad knees, then you may want to make sure you have cushions for your knees to rest on.

- To get into this position, start by kneeling face-to-face.

- Then you will both place the opposite foot flat on the floor and inch closer until your genitals reach each other.

- You both place your weight on your planted foot, and you both lunge back and forth.

This position places you in equal positions, and you share the reins. Everybody's arms are free to do as they will, as well. This will be a slow grind and not a lot of in-and-out action.

The G-Force

This is a fairly simple move that almost anybody can do. The man will have reins in this one.

- She lays down and pulls her knees as far into her chest as she can.
- He will kneel in front of her and grab hold of her feet and then thrusts into her.
- He can then bring her feet up to his chest. The woman will only have her upper back on the bed or floor.

Baby Got Back

For this one:

- The man will kneel and then sit back on his heels.
- The woman keeps her back to him and lowers herself onto his penis, either in a squat or plie. Her feet should be planted on either side of him.
- She places her hands on her thighs to help her keep her balance. He can also hold her rear to help with support.
- She slowly moves up and down, and she can nest all the way into his lap. She controls the movement with this position.

Tub Tangle

This one will take bath time to a whole new level.

- He will sit reclined in the tub, and she will straddle his lap while facing him.

- Once he is inside of her, he will move his torso up so that they are more face-to-face.
- They will both wrap their legs around one another's backs and link their elbows under the other's knees to pull them up to chest level.

This will require slight rocking instead of thrusting.

Lap Dance

For this one, you are going to need a tall-backed chair that you have padded with some pillows to make things more comfortable.

- He will sit down in the chair.
- She will face him and straddle him, sliding him inside of her, and then lean back a bit. She should rest her hands on his knees.
- One at a time, she will bring her legs up so that her ankles are resting on his shoulders.
- She will then move her buttocks back and forth, and at whatever speed she likes.

This will take some balance power on the woman's part.

The Milk and Water Embrace

This is great for all types of people.

- He sits down on the bed, a short stool, or chair.
- She then sits down on him, with her back to him.
- She then controls the thrusting.

This leaves all hands free to do as they will.

Torrid Tidal Wave

This is great for an intense make-out session.

- He will lay on his back, keeping his legs together.
- She will straddle his penis and then move to lay stretched out on top of him, pelvises aligned.
- She will lift up her torso so that she is resting on her hands.
- The slightest movements will provide pleasing friction.

The Tug of Love

For this position:

- He will lay down first with his legs wide open.
- She will down on top of him and allow him to enter her. Her legs should be on either side of him stretched out in front of her.
- Then she will lean back onto the bed.
- Once both are laying down, he will grab her hands and gently pull them to move her.

This is great for couples who have a foot fetish.

Life Raft

This is designed for sex in the water. You will need a pool and an inflatable pool bed.

- She will position herself on the pool bed on her stomach. Her vagina should be in the middle of the bed.
- He stands behind her with her legs wrapped around his hips. He should not push downwards. He enters and starts thrusting.

The important thing is to make sure the vagina stays out of the water because the water, especially if it is chlorinated, can dry things out.

Brute

This is a very male dominant position.

- She will lay down and pull her knees to her chest.
- He will stand with his back to her, straddling her hips.
- He then squats down and slowly enters her and continues to move slightly up and down.

The man needs to be very careful not to hurt himself.

Piston

This can be quite a tiring position.

- Both are standing and facing each other.
- He will lift her off the ground, placing his arms under her butt and thighs.
- Having a bed or sofa behind him will allow her to let her legs rest on it to help take some weight off of him.
- He will then "piston" himself up and down.

This might be easier to get into if he starts out sitting on a bed or sofa.

Missionary

This is a common one and one you have already performed, but it is a very intimate position.

- She will be on her back with her legs open.
- He will rest on his elbows as he thrusts in and out.

Helicopter

For this, the penis will need to be slightly flexible. Not every man will be able to do this. Basically, if you are standing, you should be able to push your erect penis down towards the ground comfortably before trying this.

- She will begin by laying on her stomach, with her legs straight and wide.

- He will then lay down on his stomach, facing the opposite direction, legs straight and wide.

- He will back into her until his thighs are over hers, and he can push his penis into her. He can then slowly and carefully thrust in and out of her.

Face to Face

This is great when you want to be intimate. Plus, it doesn't take a lot of effort.

- She will need to be sitting on the edge of a sofa, bed, or any other surface that is about 12 to 20 inches off the ground.

- He will kneel in front of her.

- She can drop herself slightly over the edge to help line things up.

- He can grab hold of her legs or waist when he starts to thrust.

Book Ends

Some couples struggle with this one, so you will need to experiment.

- Both will begin on their knees facing each other.

- He will spread his knees so that he can be closer to the bed while she will remain tall.
- Once he has lowered himself so that he is in line with her, he can slip his penis inside.
- If comfortable, he can move his knees back together.

Jellyfish

This can be a difficult position. It requires some strength and balance for both people.

- He starts by kneeling in the bed, his butt resting on his ankles.
- She will straddle him, squatting so he can enter.
- Both will wrap their arms around one another.

You will be doing more of a grinding motion rather than thrusting.

Hang Loose

This is a variation of missionary.

You will do the same thing you did for missionary, except this time, you will be on the edge of the bed so that her head can hang over the edge.

Big Dipper

This is a tiring sex position, so don't plan on being here too long. You will need a sturdy chair that faces your sofa or bed.

- He will position himself so that he isn't quite sitting in the chair, with his hands resting on the chair and his feet on the bed or sofa. He will be completely elevated off the ground. He will look like he is going to do a tricep dip.

- She will then straddle his as she is facing him, but she should not place any weight on him.

- He will then lower himself and push himself back up, moving in and out of her.

Reverse Missionary

This is another one that will require some penis flexibility.

- She will start by laying down with her legs spread apart.

- He will lay down on top of her but facing her feet. His legs should rest on either side of her.

- He will slowly push his penis into her.

Any position that requires him to move his penis backward needs to be done carefully and the partner should never pull on the penis. It is very easy to hurt the suspensory ligaments.

Ballerina Sex Position

This one will require the woman to be flexible to do this comfortably.

- Both will start by standing and facing each other.

- She will raise one leg up until it rests on his shoulder as she balances on the other.

- The raised leg will be pretty much straight so that he can get as close as possible.

- He can wrap his arms around her as he starts thrusting.

Screw

This is a simple position that anybody can do.

- She will start by lying down on her side.

- He will position himself behind her legs and place his hands on either side of her torso.
- She will turn her upper body to face him as he starts penetrating her.

Stand and Carry

This is a standing position that does not use a couch, bed, or wall.

- She starts off lying down, and he will lean over her. She wraps her arms around his neck and her legs around his waist once he enters you.
- He then wraps his arms around her and brings her to a standing position. He can grab her butt to help move her up and down.

Bent Spoon

This isn't one of the most popular sex positions, but it is great if you want to shake things up.

- The man will lay on his back, and she will lay on top of him, back to his chest.
- He will then enter her.
- She will then spread arms out to help keep her steady, and he will spread his legs to keep his balance.
- Once ready, she will bring her knees up to her chest and rest her feet on his knees for support.

X Marks the Spot

This is another variation of the missionary positions.

- She will start by laying in her back with the man on top.
- Hence the name, their bodies will make an X.

This might be a bit tricky at first, and possibly awkward, but once you get into it, it should get easier.

Italian Chandelier

This position is very submissive for the woman and gives the man a lot of power. It is super easy to move from missionary to the Italian Chandelier.

- Begin by getting into a regular missionary sex position.
- He will then come up on his knees, bringing them closer to the woman, which should force her legs apart.
- He then wraps his hands under her hips and butt and then lifts them up.
- She will help out by planting her feet on the bed. The goal is to have her hips and waist pushed into the air.

Down Stroke

There is a lot of stimulation for both people with this move.

- She will lay on her back close to the edge of the sofa or bed and raise her legs into the air so that they are pointed towards the ceiling.
- He will stand in front of her and grab her legs, pulling her toward him so he can enter her.
- Once he has her lifted towards him, he will lift her waist off the bed so that only her shoulders and upper back are touching the bed.

Exposed Eagle

This is one of the hardest Kama sutra positions we will discuss in the book. It requires a lot of strength and flexibility.

- The easiest way to start is to begin in cowgirl position. She will straddle and face him with her knees on either side.

- She will then lay backward until her back in on his knees and thighs. He has the option of raising his knees if she can't bend all the way backward.

- He will then raise his upper body so that he is in a more seated position.

- He can support himself by placing his arms behind him, or he can wrap them around her back.

Bended Knee

This is an easier version of the ballerina.

- Both will start out on their knees facing each other—they need to be close.

- He stays on one knee and lifts the other up and out to plant his foot.

- She will then lift the leg in front of his raised nee and rest her leg over his.

- He can then enter and begin thrusting.

Acrobat

This is a variation of the reverse cowgirl.

- He will begin by lying on his back, and then she will straddle him, facing away from him.

- She will stay on her knees and will then lay back onto him.

Viennese Oyster

This is a more complicated position that will require some flexibility.

- She will start on her back and grab her legs, pulling them apart and back.
- She will want to get her legs so far back that they are touching or almost touching the bed on either side of her. She can then wrap her arms around her legs.
- He can then enter. He could also hold her legs back.

Crab

This is another one that should only be done if he has a great deal of penile flexibility because she will be bending the penis back quite a bit when she sits on him.

- Begin by getting into a cowgirl position.
- She will then move her feet so that they are planted on either side of his shoulders.
- She then bends back, slightly, supporting herself on her hands.

This position should not be used during rough sex because it could damage the penis.

Bouncing Spoons

This is a super simple position that any couple can do.

- He will sit upright in bed with his back supported against the wall or headboard. His legs should be relatively straight out in front of him.
- She will stand over him, back to him, her feet positioned on either side of his legs.
- She will then move down onto her knees and sit back onto him, guiding his penis inside of her.
- She can then lean back so that she is rested against his chest.

Side Ride

This is another variation of the cowgirl position and is super easy to do.

- He will begin by lying down with his knees bent slightly so that his feet are flat on the bed to give him thrusting leverage.
- She will then sit on his lap, letting him enter her. Instead of having her back to him or facing him, she will sit sideways. This means she will face left or right.

Deep Impact

Hence the name, this position will allow for deep penetration. This is great for rough, passionate sex.

- She will lay down and point her legs towards the ceiling.
- He will be position on his knees, facing her.
- She will rest her legs against her shoulders.
- He then grabs her thighs and holds her tight as he thrusts.

Twister

This is definitely an "exotic" sex position.

- She will start by lying down her side. For this example, we will use the right side.
- He will then lay down on his right side. His head will be at her feet and her head at his feet.
- They will both bend their left knees and raise them up to the ceiling.

- She will lean forward and push her body through the newly created gap so that his leg is now over her waist. She should not be lying on his right leg.

- He will be sandwiched between her legs with her left legs over his waist.

- He should now be able to start thrusting.

See Saw

This is fun but can be quickly tiring. This is also a very unique position.

- He will sit down on the bed.

- She will sit in his lap, facing him.

- She should spread her legs wide so that she can get comfortable.

- She can then start to lean back, and either rest her hands on his shoulders or place them behind her.

You can either move up and down or grind on each other.

Intersection

This position will require you to form a cross with your bodies.

- Both will start out lying on their sides. She will have her head at one end and her feet at the other. He will lay across the bed.

- She will open her legs so that he can lay down on top of the lower one and penetrate her.

Doggy Style

This is a position that everybody knows and can do.

- She starts on her hands and knees with her legs spread apart.
- He is positioned behind her on his knees and enters from behind.

Sockets

This is a variation of scissoring.

- She starts by lying on her back with her legs spread wide.
- She will then bend her knees and plant her feet so that she can lift her lower back and waist off of the bed.
- He will then lay on his side at the other end of the bed.
- He should move down towards her in order to enter her. As he does so, he will slide his leg on hers. If he is on his right side, his right leg will move under her left leg and will move his left leg over her left leg. If he is on his left, he will do the opposite.

This is another position where his penis will need to be flexible.

Turtle

This is a variation of doggy and will require a bit more flexibility.

- She will begin by getting into the doggy position by resting on her knees.
- She will lower herself down so that she is resting on her ankles.
- Then she will lean as far forward as she can. She can reach behind and grab hold of her legs to help her lean further forward.
- He will then be on his knees behind her, penetrating her.

Lazy Wheelbarrow

While this may have lazy in the name, it still takes a lot of effort.

- He will start by sitting on a sofa with his legs together.
- She then sits down on him, facing away, with her legs together.
- She will start to lean forward as far as she can so that she can place her hands on the floor. Her stomach will be resting on her thighs.

Fire Hydrant

This is another doggy style variation.

- Both will get into a regular doggy style position.
- His knees should be positioned inside of hers.
- He will then start to lift one of his legs up and forwards so that his foot is planted at her side.
- The leg he moved will be under her leg so that her thigh will be resting on his thigh. The goal is to look like a dog peeing on a fire hydrant.

Chapter 13: Best Sex Positions for Her

The goal for these positions isn't to have an earth-shattering orgasm. The journey of lovemaking is about becoming one, being orgasmic, moving, connecting, feeling, and breathing with your partner. When you learn to explore your sexuality while being conscious of everything around you and you learn how to harness its power to experience a profound connection with other humans, you will transcend the need for specific techniques and just get into the flow. This flow will move into every area of your life.

Yab Yum

For this position:

- The guy is going to sit either on a bed or any other flat surface. He will fold his legs in the position of the half lotus. If this is too uncomfortable for him, have him sit on the edge of the bed or a chair and allow his legs to dangle.

- The woman is going to sit on his lap. Her legs will straddle his. She needs to wrap her legs around his waist. If this isn't comfortable for her, she can place a pillow under her bottom. If you are sitting in a chair, her legs could just dangle over his.

- She is going to raise herself up so she can put his penis inside her vagina. It doesn't matter whether it is hard or soft; either one is fine.

- Place your upper bodies against each other to create more skin on skin sensation. You can wrap your arms around one another.

- When you feel the time is right, you can begin to rock back and forth and let your bodies do the rest.

"Fitting On Of the Sock" or "The Rolling Tickle"

These are actually two different positions, but they blend together great and are great if you aren't very flexible.

- The woman will lay down on her back with her head resting on a pillow.
- The man is going to kneel down between her legs. He will sit back on his heels. If he needs to support his knees, he can put a pillow between his heels and butt.
- The woman is going to place her legs across the man's legs.
- The man is going to place his penis along the length of the woman's vulva. He will rock back and forth to stimulate the vulva. He uses his hands to stimulate her other erogenous zones.
- Once the woman is extremely excited and well lubricated, the man can place his penis inside her vagina.
- The woman is going to raise her pelvis up to meet him. Make sure you find your rhythm.
- If the woman is fairly flexible, she can bring her knees up to her chest.
- The man will be able to penetrate her very deeply while she is rolling her things down and up. If she needs help or support, he can place his hands under her bottom.

Congress of a Cow

For this position:

- The woman is going to bend forward at the waist while keeping her feet and hands on the floor
- The man will come up behind her and penetrate her.
- All the woman has to do is keep her balance while he thrusts away.

Yawning

- The woman is going to lay down on her back.
- The man is going to kneel in between her legs.
- The woman will spread her legs as wide as possible on either side of the man's waist. She will lift her legs as high as she possibly can. To alternate the sensations, she can try moving her legs up and down.
- Since you are both supported on the floor or bed, this is a great position to let your hand wander all over each other's bodies.

Tripod

- Both the man and woman will stand facing each other.
- The man is going to put one hand under one of her knees and bring it off the floor. You have now become a tripod.
- The man will now penetrate the woman.
- This works best if both parties are about the same height.

Launch Pad

- The woman is going to lay down on her back.
- The man will penetrate her while staying on his knees and facing her.
- The woman will lift her legs up and bring her knees into her chest. She can rest her feet on his chest if she would like.
- The man can lean over her while she raises her hips so he can penetrate her deeply.

Coital Alignment Technique

- The woman is going to lay down on her back with her legs spread open.

- The man is going to place himself in between her legs and penetrate her. This is just like performing a normal missionary position.

- Rather than him beginning to thrust in and out, he is going to move forward over her body. This changes the angle of his penis. His penis is now going to point down and will be more in contact with her vagina's back wall.

- While the man is in this position, his pubic bone and possibly penis will be in constant contact with the woman's clitoris.

- The woman doesn't need to just lay there. She can move to keep her clitoris in constant contact with his penis and pubic bone.

- The woman can also wrap her legs around his back and pull him farther into her vagina.

- The woman will get more out of this position if she can get a rhythm going with her man.

Swan Sport

- The man is going to lay down on the bed or floor on his back.

- The woman will sit on top of the man while facing his feet. She is going to place her feet on top of his thighs.

- She now has the opportunity to go as fast or slow as she would like.

- She needs to be able to keep her balance while sitting on her man.

- The man can help her keep her balance by holding onto her waist.

Upavitika

- The woman lays down on the floor or bed with her knees bent and feet on the bed.
- The man kneels between her legs and penetrates her.
- Once she has been penetrated, he can straighten his legs out.
- The woman will bring one foot up and place it over his heart.
- She gets to control the situation with her foot over his heart.

The Mastery

- The man is going to sit on the sofa or side of the bed with his feet flat on the floor. He needs to have his butt and thighs on the bed.
- The woman will either kneel down or squat on his lap.
- The woman can then wrap their arms around his neck.
- Help him penetrate you. Once he is firmly inside you, you can lift yourself up and down on top of him, and he can thrust into you.
- You might find it easier to just rock back and forth or grind against him.
- This position puts the woman in power since she is on top. She can find the rhythm she lays to bring both of you to orgasm.
- Since you are facing each other, you get to kiss and fondle each other.
- To change things up, you can place your hands on his knees and lean back a bit. Just be careful.

Pearly Gates

- The man is going to lay down on his back. He needs to bend his knees with his feet on the bed.

- The woman is going to lay down on top of the man. The woman's head will be to the side and above his.

- The man will now penetrate the woman while in this position.

- If you have problems keeping your balance, spread your legs, and keep them bent, so your feet are on the bed. You could also spread out your arms to help you balance, too.

- The man can wrap his arms around the woman's chest or waist to help keep them balance while playing with her breasts.

- When the woman has her balance, she will be able to thrust back and forth on his penis while he thrusts up into her.

- Since his mouth is right by her ear, he can talk dirty to her or nibble on her neck and ear.

Pretzel

- The woman is going to lay down on her side with the leg against the bed straight and the leg on top crooked out just slightly.

- The woman will need to raise her top leg slightly toward her chest and place the arm on top either in front of her or behind her. Just make sure the arms are very comfortable.

- The man is going to come in on his knees and straddle the woman's straight leg while remaining on his knees. Once he has penetrated her, he will keep his torso upright while thrusting into the woman.

- The woman won't be able to do much in this position, so she is at the mercy of her victor.

The Wheel Barrow

- The woman is going to bend forward at the waist with her hands and feet on the floor.

- The man will come up behind the woman and penetrate her from behind. Once he has penetrated her, he can lift one or both feet off the ground. Again this depends on how strong each of you are.

- The woman's hands and arms might become extremely tired while doing this position. If you have to, you can squeeze your legs together a bit to help you keep your balance.

- While the man is thrusting in and out, the woman just needs to keep her balance. That's pretty much it.

The Bodyguard

- You are both going to stand up straight.

- You are going to be facing in the same direction.

- The man is going to come up behind the woman and penetrate her.

- If he is taller, he is going to need to bend his knees a bit.

- Once he is inside, he will just thrust in and out, and you can push yourself back into him.

Asian Cowgirl

- The man is going to lay down on the floor or bed on his back.

- The woman is going to straddle him, but instead of being on her hands and knees like regular cowgirl, she will squat. This means that most of her weight is going to be supported by her feet.

- The woman can use her hands to take the weight off her feet by placing them on the man's chest or beside him on the bed.

Irish Garden

- To start this position, the man will sit on the bed with his back straight. He needs to keep his legs out in front of him and opened wide. He can bed his knees if it is more comfortable.

- The woman will get on her hands and knees, facing away from him and move backward toward him.

- She will lower herself onto the man by straightening her legs out behind the man make sure there is one leg on each side of his waist.

- Now she can lower her shoulders and head to the bed.

- The woman is responsible for all the movement here since she has the man pinned to the bed.

The Amazon

- The man will lay down on his back with his legs raised slightly with his knees bent.

- The woman will come in and squat down on him.

- He is going to need to bring his legs closer to his chest, so they don't get in your way.

- Now, sit on his penis and set your pace.

- The man will automatically push you up with his thighs.

Pump

- The woman is going to stand on a short table, sofa, or bed. Her legs stay bent just a little bit.

- The man will penetrate her from behind while he is standing.
- The woman can place her arms on a wall in front of her if there is one to help her push back against him.

Superwoman

- The woman is going to lay down on the bed on her stomach. Her arms will be stretched in front of her on the bed.
- The woman's legs need to be hanging off the side of the bed. Her waist should be even with the edge of the bed.
- The man will penetrate her from behind while he is standing and will begin thrusting.

Bull Dog

- The woman will get on her hands and knees. Then she is going to bring her legs together.
- This man will penetrate her from behind in a slightly squatting position.
- He will put his feet to the outside of her legs. He can keep himself steady by placing his hands on her shoulders or waist.

Legs on Shoulder

- The woman will lay down on her back and bring her legs up, so they are pointing at the ceiling.
- The man will be positioned on his knees but keeping his back straight. He will penetrate her.
- The woman will rest both her legs on one of his shoulders.
- The man will wrap one arm around her legs while placing the other hand on her stomach.

Prison Style

- Both the man and woman will be standing and facing in the same direction.
- The man will penetrate the woman from behind.
- The woman will bend at the waist until her chest is parallel to the ground, and she is looking at the floor.
- The woman can spread her legs while the man keeps his closed.
- Now the woman needs to put her arms parallel to her body.
- The man will reach forward and grab her wrists and bring her arms behind her back. He gets to control her by keeping her arms behind her back.

Burning Man

- The woman is going to face a table or countertop and will bend forward until her stomach is touching the surface. Her feet will stay on the ground.
- The man will come up behind her and penetrate her.
- The woman's legs are going to act as an anchor that will keep you in place. This allows the man to give some intense, hard penetration without falling.

Praying Mantis

- The woman will lay down on her back with her legs open.
- The man will kneel in front of her pelvis and penetrate her. He will take one of her legs and bring it up slowly so that it points the ceiling. He can then place it on his shoulder or wrap his arm around it.

Betty Rocker

- The man will lay down on his back with his legs slightly apart.

- The woman will straddle him while facing away. While she is sitting straight up, she will place his penis inside of her.

- Once he is firmly inside, she will begin leaning forward while supporting herself with her arms on his legs.

- Now the woman will begin to rock back and forth by using her arms and legs. She could also move up and down on his penis.

Thigh Tide

- The man is going to lay down on his back with his legs straight in front of him.

- He will raise one knee just a bit and put his foot on the bed.

- The woman is going to face away from the man. She is going to place one knee on either side of the man's bent leg while sitting on his penis.

- She will raise herself up and down on him. She can hold on to the man's leg to help keep her balance.

Fast Fuck

- The man will lay down on his back. His knees will be bent slightly and his feet on the bed.

- The woman will straddle him. She can either stay on her feet or knees. She will lean forward while resting on her elbows or hands. She will position herself, so she is raised above the man just slightly.

- She won't be resting on his crotch.

- The man will begin thrusting into her quickly. It isn't going to be a deep penetration, but it will feel wonderful.

Jughead

- The man is going to lay down either beside a couch or bed while keeping his back on the floor.

- The man will put his legs up on the bed or sofa.

- The woman will position herself above the man while being on all fours with an arm and a leg on each side of him.

- The man is going to lift his lower back and crotch off the floor so he can penetrate her.

- The woman will sit on his penis and thrust herself back into him. She can thrust as hard as she wants, or he can just push into her while she takes it easy.

Man Missionary

- The man will lay down on his back with his legs together. He can keep them straight or bend them at the knee.

- The woman will straddle him just like with the cowgirl position.

- The woman will lean forward over the man and rest her hands on his chest or stomach.

- She will then begin rocking back and forth. It is really like the normal Missionary position but reversed.

Chapter 14: Best Sex Positions To Bring Couples Closer

We've covers positions that are more pleasurable for him and for her, so let's look at some positions that will help to increase the intimacy in the relationship. While those sudden and desperate quickies, but nothing is better than sex that is soulful and rich. This can harness the bonding powers of neurochemistry and science.

Lotus Blossom

This is also known as the seated wrap-around and will require you and your partner to embrace one another, which is great for gazing romantically into each other's eyes.

This position can be used even if your goal isn't to have sex or orgasm. You can simply sit in their lap and look at each other or make out. To get into the position, one partner will straddle the other as you both sit in a cross-legged position. The person on top will wrap their legs around the bottom of their partner as you two face one another and embrace. The one on the bottom will enter the person on top with a penis or a toy.

Spooning 69

This position will allow the two of you to give and receive oral play while on your side. You get to have the closeness of spooning while also having the joy of the mouth-to-genital play.

You will both lay on your sides, facing one another but in opposite directions so that your mouth is aligned with your partner's genitals.

Breakfast Spoons

This is the spooning position but with morning sex. While it may not sound special, having sex in this cuddling position before you have both fully woken up brings something romantic to the relationship.

When your partner enters you from behind in the spooning position, they get the joy of being able to kiss your neck, hold your hands, or provide extra stimulation.

The Hound

This is an intimate spin on doggy style. This position allows for slow, deep thrusts, as well as quick, shallow thrusts. It is best to start things slowly and then speed it up. Alternate between deep and shallow. With this position, there is a lot more skin-to-skin contact, and all of her other erogenous zones are easily accessible. They can also nibble on the other's neck or ears, whisper dirty phrases.

How to get into this position. Both will start on their knees. The person doing the penetration will have their legs positioned on the outside of their partner and will curl their body around the other person and enter from behind. The one on the bottom will rest on their forearms and will be able to swivel their hips to get into a comfortable position.

Face-to-Face Standing

Face-to-face sex is great for kissing and intimacy. To get into this position, both partners will stand facing each other. It might be easier if one partner is braced against a wall. The penetrating partner will place themselves between the other's legs. They will penetrate their partner, and if possible, they can lift their partner's legs around their hips.

Drill

Missionary positions can be one of the most erotic positions because it places you in a face-to-face position. This position takes the standard missionary up a notch.

The woman will start by lying down, just like she would with regular missions. She will then raiser her legs up and wrap them around your partner's waist. She can cross her ankles to help keep her legs around him. This will allow you to grip their partner closer and pull them into her.

Teaspooning

This is one of the most intimate positions you can try.

He will start out on his knees, spreading them as wide as he comfortably can. She will then get on her knees in front of him, keeping her knees together. He will move closer to her, keeping his legs on either side of hers. He can then enter her, and his arms should be wrapped around her, holding her breasts, or holding her shoulders.

Sofa Spooning

You will want to make sure you have a comfortable, full-length sofa for this one.

He will lay down on the couch with his back pressed against the back of the couch. She will lay down in front so that they are laying back to chest. He will then enter her and start to slowly thrust with his arms wrapped around her.

This is great for a Netflix and chill moment.

The Mermaid

For this position, she will lay down face-up at the edge of a counter, desk, or bed. A pillow under her butt may be helpful. She will extend her legs into the air, keeping them together. He will stand in front of her, holding her ankles to keep him stable and allow him to thrust deeper.

The Sofa Spread-Eagle

This can be tricky if there is a large height difference.

She will start by standing on the edge of the bed, couch, or on two chairs, with her legs spread wide. He will stand on the floor in front of her. She will need to adjust her stance so that he can easily slide until their pelvises meet.

He'll do all the moving on this one, but she can do whatever she wants with her hands.

Chapter 15: Increasing Male Orgasmic Control

All men are looking to have an intense orgasm and an erection that will last long enough for them to reach orgasm. Reaching an orgasm is simple, but sustaining an erection and enjoying the orgasm will take a little more time and patience. Plus, your partner will thank you for lasting longer. Let's look at how you can control your orgasm and erection.

Muscle Strength

While having a six-pack might get you noticed, those aren't the muscles that help you during sex. To get the most out of your sexual experience, you need to work on your pubococcygeal muscle. These muscles sit on the floor of your pelvis and control your stream of urine and the muscle spasms that happen when you have an orgasm. This is why sex therapists and doctors recommend that you work on strengthening those muscles so that you don't have premature ejaculations and to improve the orgasm.

Kegel exercises aren't something that only women can do. They can also be used to strengthen the man's PC power. When you are urinating, you can squeeze this muscle to stop the flow of urine. Once you have figure out where the muscle is by doing this, you can squeeze that muscle at any time during the day. Hold the muscle for two seconds and then release. Do this 20 times, three times a day. You will start to hold the muscles for longer intervals. You should never stop with these exercises. Kegel exercises have to be performed on a regular basis in order to keep those muscles strong.

Edging

Nothing can help you to strengthen your control and erection better than edging, or holding back right before you orgasm. You stop as soon as you feel like you are about to orgasms, rest until you are in control again, and then continue with sex. This can be done until it becomes second nature. This can be practicing during masturbation, and once you are ready to orgasm, you can stop edging.

The best way to edge is, once you stop yourself, don't start again until your breathing is under control, and then wait 30 seconds before you continue on. If you find this does not work, you can also stop ejaculation by squeezing the top of your penis or gently pulling the testicles right when you are about to have an orgasm. Then you will do this all over again. After edging has been mastered, you will be able to have a dry or contractile orgasm. Basically, you will get the same pleasure sensations of an orgasm, but you won't lose the erection. This means that you can have multiple orgasms before you finally finish.

Stop Masturbating

I understand that I just told you to practice edging while masturbating but hear me out. Masturbating is probably not going to give you and eye-rolling and mind-blowing orgasm for a man at least. The male body releases 400% more prolactin after they have penetrated a vagina than it does after masturbation. Prolactin is the male hormone that makes them feel sexually satisfied. Our evolutionary forces have always rewarded behaviors that are connected with reproduction. Having vaginal-penile sex is something that is passed through our genes.

Deep Breathing

If you ask a sex therapist the best way to have a full-body orgasm, they are going to tell you that controlled breathing will do it for you. If you make sure that your breathing remains regular and deep, this is going to allow for a more intense arousal to build. The orgasm will remain more satisfying. Breathing to quickly is going to increase your excitement and will ultimately push you over the edge.

Breathing can intensify the male orgasm by taking more oxygen into the arousal process. Shallow breaths in through the nose and deep breaths out through the mouth will help to remove muscular and psychological tension that will help to intensify the orgasm.

Use the Brain

Orgasms get started in the brain. Our brains are in control of everything and are active in the genitals. Women have a lot of activity within the brain area that is connected to emotions, whereas men only experience brain activity in their secondary somatosensory cortex that deals with physical sensations. The good thing about this is that in order to have a better orgasm, you have to have your partner focus on the penis while you are focused on the sensation that you are getting from their touch.

Keep Your Feet Warm

This may sound crazy, but scientists have found that men who have cold feet will have a harder time reaching orgasm than those who are wearing socks or have warm feet. When the man is comfortable, he is going to be more relaxed. This relaxation is the key to have better orgasms. If you are afraid of being made fun of for wearing your socks, you can turn the heat up or place them into some warm water before she shows up.

Sex Positions to Sustain an Erection

Maybe you struggle with maintaining an erection, and that is what keeps you from enjoying your orgasm. There are some positions that can help with this.

One way to help things along is by having your partner straddle you. They will sit on your lap, facing you, and will lean back a bit and slide their pelvis up and down along the penis. You will also tease them with your fingers by rubbing their clit. Once you get hard, you can turn this into seated cowgirl, or you can simply stroke yourself while they continue to rub themselves up and down you.

You can also try the wake-up curl. Morning wood is something that shouldn't be taken for granted. This is the time when testosterone is the highest, so have morning sex. Both of you will be on your side, and you will slide up behind her. This means you won't have to worry about morning breath, and she will have a tighter feeling, which will help keep you hard.

Lastly, you can try the pointer dog. This is like doggy-style, but the woman will spread their legs further apart. This will allow you to pull out whenever you need to slow things down or to stroke yourself to keep the erection going. As you do this, you can continue thrusting your fingers into her.

Chapter 16: Pregnancy Sex Positions

Some couples think that they can't have sex once pregnant, especially later on in the pregnancy. The truth is, sex at any point during pregnancy can happen as long as everybody remains comfortable. There is no need to worry about your baby hearing things because they don't understand language, and the sounds are very well muffled.

If both parties are okay with it, then you can try some of the following sex positions. All of these positions help keep him off of the belly and will make things easier for the mom-to-be. That said, there are some women who don't feel like having sex. It is up to the hormones, so you will need to go with the flower.

Some of the best positions for you to try during pregnancy are those that will keep the pressure off of the belly and the woman off her back. When on her back, it can cause blood flow compression, which can cause her to end up becoming lightheaded, and can cause other problems. So the next time you want to have sex while pregnant, try these positions:

- Anal Sex

If this is something that the two of you have already been doing, you can continue to do so. Trying anal for the first time while pregnant would not be a good idea since most women experience heightened sensations, so it might not be enjoyable. For those who are used to it, you can try anal in any position that we are going to discuss.

- Seated

This is a lot like the lap dance kama sutra position, except you won't be facing him. He sits in the chair, or wherever, and you will sit on him. This puts her in control of everything.

- Standing

There are two options with this. You can face each other, or he can be behind her. Which one works best is going to depend on how far along she is. Facing each other isn't going to work late in the pregnancy. After the third trimester, he will probably need to be behind. This will limit his thrusting ability, so it helps for those who are experiencing with heightened sensitivity.

- Doggy Style

This will keep her off her back and doesn't add any pressure to the belly as long as she stays propped up. This places the man in control of the movements, so he needs to check in with her to make sure he isn't too rough.

- Spooning

Both of you will be laying on your said facing the same direction. The man has a little more control in this position, but the depth and speed won't be as much as with doggy style.

- Cowgirl or Reverse Cowgirl

This places the women in charge of the movement and will keep pressure off of her belly. This works well for women experiencing extra sensitivity.

You should also have pillows at the ready to help her get comfortable, and pregnancy pillows are great. You may also want to think about using toys and lube.

While you can do most sex positions while pregnant, there are things that you should never do.

- Missionary is not good with the woman on the bottom because it can compress blood flow, especially after the 20-week mark.

- Any prone position where the woman will have to lay on her stomach.

- And you should never blow air up the woman's vagina. This is something you should never do at any time, whether she is pregnant or not.

Having sex during pregnancy can require the two of you to get creative and figure out what is going to work for both of you. What may be comfortable at one time may not be later on. And you never know how the hormones will affect her.

Chapter 17: Oral Sex Positions

Oral sex can be a great way to get things ready for penetration, or it can be the main event of the night. If you are a woman who is not able to reach an orgasm through penetration alone, oral sex is what you are going to need to get things going. The following positions can give you new ways to perform oral sex so that it doesn't seem like the same old boring oral sex.

Spiderman

Most blow jobs won't allow you to have a good view, but this position will provide your partner with a full view of your body. You lay down on your back on a bed or table. Your head should dangle over the edge. They will come up behind you and lean over so that you are able to swallow their penis. You will be able to use your hands and mouth. They also have the ability to pinch and rub your nipples or clitoris while you are working on their penis.

Sidecar

Both of you will lay down your sides facing one another. Then you slide down until his penis is in your face. This could be called a lazy blow job if you want. Blow jobs don't have to kill your knees.

Leg Up

There are some women who have one side of their vulva that is more sensitive than the other. You will lift up that leg on the side that is more sensitive so that it is exposed. Then you will lick figure eights up and down the vulva to please them.

Deep V

You will start by laying down on your back at the edge of the bed. Grab your thighs and lift your legs up into a V shape. If you aren't this flexible, then you keep your knees bent and let your legs rest on your chest. He will kneel in front of you and start working on you. They can massage your thighs to help bring more blood into your vulva. This can help you to have an amazing orgasm.

Cliff Hanger

You sit on the edge of the bed and keep your legs dangling off the edge. He will kneel between your legs and go to work. They will use their hands to play with whatever they want to help heighten your pleasure.

Sofa So Good

You will start by laying upside down on your couch. Your head and back will be flat on the seat while your legs go over the back. Your partner is going to kneel over your face and facing the back of the couch. You can suck his penis while he licks you.

Doggy Does Oral

This is a very hot position that you will get to control the pressure and angle of. She will be on her hands and knees, just like in doggy, but he will kneel behind you and perform for her. This is also great for a rim job if you want.

Hail the Queen

The point of sitting on a person's face is not to actually sit on their face. You simply straddle their head and work your thighs. You hold yourself a few inches over their face while they work on you. They can still reach up and play with breasts, or anything else that they want to.

Corkscrew

The man will stand for this one as you kneel in front of him. Hold the base of his penis in both hands. Place the penis in your mouth and then tilt your head from side to side as your work up and down.

Fake Deep Throat

You can get the feel of a deep throat without having to gag by putting some lube on your hand and using it on the part of him that won't fit in your mouth. Move your hand as you would move your mouth. To make this more intense, look deep into their eyes.

Peace Out

You are going to be sitting in a chair while your partner kneels between your legs. The will place two fingers on each side of the clitoris and make the same motions you would if you were using scissors as they suck and lick the tip of the click. This will isolate the clit from the rest of the genitals and pinpoints the pleasure.

Swiper

Ask your partner to form some suction on the clit by placing their mouth over the labia and clitoris. Now have them shake their head in circles, side to side, and change the pace up. This is going to mimic how many of us masturbate. You can place some pillows under you to give them better access.

Supersize Me

Once you have your man right at the brink of an orgasm, stop and gently pull a bit on their testicles to stop them from having an orgasm. Give them a bit to recuperate and then go back to it. Once you have them begging, push a finger or vibrator against their penis and watch what happens.

Constellation

If oral sex is uncomfortable for you, you can try it on your side. This is great for people who have spasticity in their hips that makes it harder for them to spread the legs during oral sex. This will provide your partner with access to your genitals without having to be a position that causes pain.

Saddle Straddle

If your partner is more dominant, they will love straddling you as you suck and stroke their penis. You can use your hands and twist up and down their penis, and you lick the tip.

Live Show

If the two of you are into bondage, you can take charge by sitting them down in a chair and then blindfolding them. You can also take a bit further by tying their arms behind the chair. A safeword should be used. Then you will perform oral sex on them and take them to the edge by not allowing them to have an orgasm until you want them to.

Deep-Sea Diver

This is a great position for a rim job. This can be introduced in the shower. The receiver stays standing as the giver squats behind them and performing oral sex.

Butterball

This is another great position for rim jobs. The person receiving needs to be showered and fresh. They will lay down and pull their knees into their chest. This will give the doer the chance to reach the clitoris and breasts of the receive. If the man is the receiver, the woman can play with whatever she wants.

Shark Fin

Since oral sex doesn't work well underwater, the women will lay down with her hips at the edge of the tub. She will open up her legs but keep her feet in the water and enjoy everything her partner does to her.

Chapter 18: How to Have Better Sex

While you may not want to think about exercising when you want to have better sex, exercising has the ability to improve your sex life. Athletes train for years for their athletic endeavors, and sex is no exception. Practicing the following exercises can help to improve your strength and flexibility, which could be the answer that you and your partner have been searching for in order to make your sex life better. All of the exercises are things that can help both men and women.

- High Plank to Forearm Plank

Start by getting into a high plank position with your hands under shoulders. You want your body to create a straight line. From here, engage your core and carefully move your right hand and lower down onto your right forearm. Do the same on the left forearm. With control, move your right arm to bring you back up onto your hand, and repeat on the left side.

This helps to build upper body strength.

- Scissor Kicks

Start by laying flat on your back. Move your hands under your hips. Raise both legs straight in the air with your toes pointed. Try to keep your legs as straight as you can, and then engage your core and slowly lower your right leg to the ground. Don't touch the floor. Bring your leg back up and repeat with the other side. This is one rep.

This helps build up strength in the low back and abs and improves flexibility.

- Hydrants

Start on your hands and knees, keeping your wrists under your shoulders and knees under hips. Engage the butt and core and raise your right knee to bring it straight to the side. With control, bring the leg back down. You will do ten reps on one side and then do the other.

This helps to open up your hips and improves upper body strength.

- Wide Squat

Bring your legs into a wide stance and point your toes out. Keep your shoulders over your hips. As you squat down, make sure that your knees stay behind your toes. Press back up through your heels. This is one rep.

This helps build thigh strength and improves flexibility.

- The Bird

Begin by squatting down with your legs together, arms bent, hands together, and chest high. Keeping this low position, open up your left knee to the side and take a short step to the left. While you step, rotate your chest open to the left and open your arms so that the left arm goes behind you, and the right arm stays straight out in front.

Bring your left foot back to the starting position and bring both arms forward. Do this on the right side and return to the starting position. This is a single rep.

This will help tone up the upper back, calves, glutes, and quads, as well as improving flexibility. This is particularly helpful for women because it can help with woman-on-top positions.

- Squat with Knee Dip

Begin in a play squat position with your legs wider than shoulder-width and your toes turned out. Bring your arms out in from of you and then squat down. As you push back up, you will have all of your weight on your right foot. Allow your left leg to swivel on the ball of your foot so that the knee turns into the center. Bring the left arm back as you do this.

Turn the leg back out and squat back down. Repeat this movement on the right side. This should be one long fluid motion. One on each side counts as a single rep.

This helps to loosen up the hips, strengthen the obliques, abs, and legs, and helps your rhythm.

- Drop It Low

Begin by standing straight with your heels together, and toes pointed out. Clasp your hands together in front of you with your palms facing down. Making sure your shoulders stay over your hips, allow your heels to come, and your knees to point out to the sides slightly as you start to squat down.

As you move down, raise your hands over your head. Engage the core and then push yourself back up through your feet as you bring your hands back down to come to the starting position.

This will help to open up your hips, strengthen the core, butt, and thighs, and improve balance.

- Hip Swivel

To perform this exercise, begin by standing with your legs should width apart and keep your knees soft. Keep your elbows close to your side, bend your arms, and take your arms out to the side.

Rotate your hips to the right and come up on your toes on your right foot, and allow your butt to pop out to the left. From here, drop your right heel and swivel your hips to the left, bringing your left foot up on your toes. You will be drawing a half-circle behind you with your butt and engaging your core. One-half circle to each side is one rep.

This move helps to loosen up your butt and hips and tightens up the core. It also helps to improve your rhythm if you do this to the beat of some music.

Now that you have these exercises, you can turn on your favorite workout playlist and perform three sets of ten reps for each of these exercises.

Conclusion

Thank you for making it through to the end of the book, let's hope it was informative and able to provide you with all of the tools you need to achieve your goals whatever they may be.

The next step is to start trying some of these new positions and games to improve your sex life. One of the easiest places for most couples to start is with the massages. It is a very easy way to bring both of you together and to help get you both into the mood. You could even head out and purchase some massage oils to improve the experience. You can then start to work your way into trying some of the foreplay games and sex positions. If dirty talk is something that you have never done, that could be something that the two of you may want to try out. The possibilities are endless as to what you both can do. The main thing is to make sure that both of you are in agreement with what you want to try.

Finally, if you found this book useful in any way, a review on Amazon is always appreciated!

Kama Sutra for Beginners

The Sex Positions Bible to Drastically and Rousingly Increase Libido with Your Partner. Discover Secret Tips and Tricks from Ancient Times...

© **Copyright 2019 by CHASECHECK LTD - All rights reserved.**

The content contained within this book may not be reproduced, duplicated or transmitted without direct written permission from the author or the publisher.
Under no circumstances will any blame or legal responsibility be held against the publisher, or author, for any damages, reparation, or monetary loss due to the information contained within this book. Either directly or indirectly.

Legal Notice:
This book is copyright protected. This book is only for personal use. You cannot amend, distribute, sell, use, quote or paraphrase any part, or the content within this book, without the consent of the author or publisher.

Disclaimer Notice:
Please note the information contained within this document is for educational and entertainment purposes only. All effort has been executed to present accurate, up to date, and reliable, complete information. No warranties of any kind are declared or implied. Readers acknowledge that the author is not engaging in the rendering of legal, financial, medical or professional advice. The content within this book has been derived from various sources. Please consult a licensed professional before attempting any techniques outlined in this book.

By reading this document, the reader agrees that under no circumstances is the author responsible for any losses, direct or indirect, which are incurred as a result of the use of information contained within this document, including, but not limited to, — errors, omissions, or inaccuracies.

Table of Contents

Introduction

Disclaimer
Introduction to the Book
What You Will Learn
Why This Information Cannot Be Found on Google

Chapter 1: What Is Kama Sutra?

Common Misconceptions
A History of Kama Sutra
What the Kama Sutra Contains
The Benefits
The Criticisms

Chapter 2: Kama Sutra Tips and Tricks

What the Kama Sutra Can Do for Your Relationship and Sex Life
How to Begin Talking About the Kama Sutra With Your Partner
Beginner Tips for Incorporating Concepts From the Kama Sutra in Your Life

Open Your Mind

Rediscover Your Partner

Trust Yourself

Communicate

Express Yourself

Understand Your Body and Your Mind

Chapter 3: How to Begin Practicing Kama Sutra

Where to Begin
Understanding the Female Body
Understanding the Male Body
Understanding Orgasms
What to Do First

Lubrication

Silicone-Based Lubricant

Water-Based Lubricant

Oils

Gels

Kissing
Foreplay
The Importance of Foreplay
Kama Sutra Foreplay Techniques

Chapter 4: The Kama Sutra Massage Techniques

The Kama Sutra Classic Massage Technique
The Kama Sutra Erotic Massage Versus the Kama Sutra Classic Massage
The Benefits of Both
The Female Erotic Massage
The Male Erotic Massage

Chapter 5: Kama Sutra Sex Positions

Easy Kama Sutra Sex Positions

The Reverse Cowgirl

The Congress of a Dog

The Supported Congress

The Mare's Position

Afternoon Delight

The Lap Position

The Ascending Position

The Cross Position

Chapter 6: The Kama Sutra and Intimacy

What Is Intimacy?

The Importance of Intimacy
The Kama Sutra and Intimacy
How to Increase and Maintain Intimacy
Kama Sutra Sex Positions for Intimacy

> The Lotus
>
> The Position of Indra's Wife
>
> Half-Pressed Position
>
> The Hinge Position
>
> The Closed Door
>
> The Lock
>
> Variation of the Yawning Position
>
> The Standing Behind Position
>
> The Crab Position
>
> The Raised Feet Position
>
> The Waterfall
>
> The Sitting Duck

Chapter 7: Advanced Kama Sutra Sex Positions

Advanced Kama Sutra Sex Positions

> The Turning Position
>
> The Scissors Position
>
> The Plow
>
> The Peg Position
>
> The Posture of Splitting Bamboo
>
> The Suspended Congress
>
> Crossed Keys
>
> The Toad Position
>
> The Widely Opened Position

The Standing Position

The Fixing of a Nail

The Pressed Position

The Sphinx Position

X-Rated

Chapter 8: Other Kama Sutra Techniques

Techniques That Do Not Involve Penetration

Kissing

Scratching and Biting

Striking

A Note on Sexual Compatibility
Double Oral Sex Technique: The Roll
Oral Sex for Men
Oral Sex for Women

Chapter 9: The Kama Sutra Theories of Romance

Kama Sutra Cuddling and Embracing
Kama Sutra Theories of Relationships

The United Congress

The Congress of the Herd of Cows

The Gramaneri

Conclusion

What to Do Next?
How to Benefit From the Kama Sutra for Life

Introduction

Congratulations on choosing this book and thank you for doing so! There are plenty of books on this subject on the market, thanks again for choosing this one! Every effort was made to ensure it is full of as much useful information as possible; please enjoy it! If you find this book useful in any way, a review is always appreciated!

Disclaimer

Before we begin, there is one thing that I would like to mention. This book is not intended to replace medical advice. It is not responsible for the actions or the results of the reader. Please seek out the advice of a doctor before starting any health program. The author is not a medical doctor, and the information in this book is meant only to supplement your health decisions and actions, not dictate them. The wonders of autophagy are still being discovered as this book is being written. Please enjoy the information provided but also be wise in consuming it.

Introduction to the Book

The main focus of this book is to share strategies for maintaining a deep emotional connection with your long-term partner and how to accomplish this through the teachings of the Kama Sutra. Contained here are tips and suggestions on exactly how to continue to have an intimate and loving marriage for years and years from the perspective of the Kama Sutra.

What You Will Learn

In this book, we are going to delve into The Kama Sutra. This includes specific sex positions and techniques that you will learn about and can try with your partner in order to make your sex life more advanced than ever before.

I will begin by explaining what the Kama Sutra is, and I will share with you some ways that it can be incorporated into your own personal sex life. I will also share with you the other benefits of the Kama Sutra, such as how to increase intimacy, how to kiss and caress your partner, how to engage in rough sex and how a man can please a woman. After reading through this book, you will have a much deeper understanding of what the Kama Sutra can teach you about sex and love, and you will better understand the history of this guide.

Why This Information Cannot Be Found on Google

While there are many articles and blogs on Google that discuss the Kama Sutra, none of them are as accurate and as comprehensive as this book. Many online resources that focus on the Kama Sutra are only concerned with the sex positions, but there is so much more to learn and benefit from when studying this ancient text. In this book, you will find much more information than you would anywhere else. The Kama Sutra itself was not originally written in English, so this book is the best way to understand exactly what the teachings of the Kama Sutra entail.

As you will find out over the course of this book, the Kama Sutra is full of invaluable lessons that will change your sex life forever. Further, this book will not only improve your sex life but your relationship or marriage as a whole. The Kama Sutra is a book that contains deep and meaningful lessons about love, being in a relationship, sharing yourself with another person, different ways of demonstrating your love using physical touch, and much more. Through reading this book, you will find much more information than you would on the internet, as it breaks down the different sections of the Kama Sutra and presents them to you in a manner that is easy to digest, understand and implement in your own life. There is very little information on the internet regarding the Kama Sutra that goes as in-depth as this book does, and you will thank yourself for picking it up.

Chapter 1: What Is Kama Sutra?

We are going to begin this book by first learning a little bit about what exactly the Kama Sutra is. Then, we are going to learn a brief history of the Kama Sutra before we begin looking at how it can benefit you in the next chapter.

Firstly, what is Kama Sutra? When we say the term *Kama Sutra*, it is actually in reference to an ancient book. You may not have been aware of this fact, as most of the time we talk about Kama Sutra as a type of sex. While this book does guide you through sex by teaching you sex positions, it is actually a guide rather than a style of sex. Often, people will say "Kama Sutra Sex." As if it is a type of sex, when they are instead referring to a text. Throughout this book, you will see the term "The Kama Sutra," as I will be mentioning the book and its teachings.

You could say that the Kama Sutra is a guide to love and a guide to enjoying a pleasant life with your partner. This book can be seen as a guide to a long-lasting marriage that will help you to keep sex interesting. It will do this by showing you how to benefit from new forms of intimacy.

Common Misconceptions

Most often, the Kama Sutra is discussed in terms of wild and crazy experimental sex positions. There are numerous articles, blogs, and magazines that talk about the Kama Sutra in this way. The truth is, however, the Kama Sutra is a book that contains much more than just this.

You may have heard of Kama Sutra in conversations about sex or in articles that you read online. The truth is, however, this is a sacred book that was written long, long ago, which contains a guide for anyone who is looking to get more out of their relationship and their sex life.

A History of Kama Sutra

The book *The Kama Sutra* was written in Northern India. It was originally written in the language of *Sanskrit*. Sanskrit is an ancient Indian language. The original texts that gave rise to Buddhism were written in this language, which shows you just how much history is involved in the Kama Sutra. This book was written sometime around the second century AD, though nobody can be exactly certain of when.

The Kama Sutra is said to have been written by a man named *Vatsyayana*- who was an ancient Indian philosopher. It cannot be confirmed for sure if he wrote the entire book singlehandedly, but according to researchers, he made a significant contribution to the text.

The word *Kama* loosely translates to mean *affection, love,* and *desires*. This is quite telling, as the book is aimed at teaching the reader about all three of these factors. Affection, love, and desire are all very important when it comes to a long-term relationship or a marriage.

The Kama Sutra includes seven different sections or chapters. Each of these sections is focused on a different aspect of pleasure. These aspects of pleasure include both physical pleasure and emotional pleasure. Vatsyayana recognized that in a marriage, both forms of pleasure are equally important.

Only one of those seven sections contain sex positions, and the other six sections talk about a variety of other topics. These six sections each touch on a different category of sexual act or situation in which a couple can achieve a deeper level of intimacy. For example, kissing, touching, massaging, and so on.

Since the book was written in a time and place where it was surrounded by Hindu culture, it is considered disrespectful to the culture if the Kama Sutra is taken out of context. What this means is that it should not be read one single section at a time, rather it should be seen and consumed as a whole. This is because it was meant to be this way when it was written. The book is meant to be read all at once, from beginning to end. This allows a person to examine it in its entirety so that they can receive and benefit from the full scope of teachings that it contains.

What the Kama Sutra Contains

The Kama Sutra is a guidebook for love. Within the pages of this book are contained tips and tricks for everything involved in loving and caring for another person.

While the majority of times, the Kama Sutra is discussed in reference to the adventurousness of the sex positions it contains, this is only one small section of the book. The rest of the book contains a guide to many other forms of showing affection that does not include penetration. The Kama Sutra is said to be a guide to love, as it teaches its readers how to love and please their partner in a variety of ways.

The Kama Sutra was written with the intention that it would be read by men. This is likely because it was written so many years ago. The information that it contains pertains mostly to men who wish to attract and court a female partner. The book teaches men how to treat this woman whom he will eventually call his wife.

The Kama Sutra includes a guide to kissing, foreplay, loving touches, and other ways to achieve intimacy with your partner. These methods include bathing together and giving each other sensual massages- not necessarily the erotic kind.

The Kama Sutra also mentions same-sex relations in terms of one man having multiple women. It also touches on sexual encounters involving multiple men and one woman.

This book is full of information and tips for achieving a close emotional bond with your partner, which can be beneficial for any couple. As you can see, this book is much more than a book of wild sex positions.

When it comes to the section on sex positions, The Kama Sutra includes a variety of positions that range in difficulty level. It contains 64 sex positions in total. Later in this book, we will look at several of these sex positions in detail, including how to perform them and what benefits come of them. After reading about these sex positions and how to perform them, you can try to liven up your sex life by trying some of them out for yourself.

The Benefits

This book is full of information that can be useful in learning more about how to treat your partner lovingly in ways other than during sex. It can be useful whether or not you wish to learn more about sex positions in particular, as it can also help you to connect with your partner on a deeper level emotionally.

As your relationship progresses, it is important to keep sex and lust alive. When you become more and more comfortable with someone, the mystery and desire can begin to fade. This is completely normal. This happens because of the excitement of getting to know a person is no longer there. At the beginning of your relationship, everything you did together was brand new. At the beginning of a relationship, you are so eager to have sex with each other because the other person is new and hot and sort of like a novelty.
As you get used to being with your partner, it can be easy to lose those feelings of excitement and settle into the comfortability of your life together. This is by no means a bad thing. Getting to this point in your relationship is fun and comforting in its own way. This stage of a relationship is different from and in some ways, better than the early stages.

From a sexual perspective though, we don't want this stage of your relationship to bring with it the end of an exciting sex life. Introducing the concepts and lessons from the Kama Sutra can help you to maintain the lust and intimacy in your relationship. It can also provide you with new sexual adventures to take on together as an established couple.

The Kama Sutra contains a wealth of information about sex and different sex positions as well as including information about different positions from which to give massages, tips on kissing, and tips for men on courting women. There are a wide variety of sex positions included in this book, so there is no shortage of new positions to inspire you if you are feeling that your sex life is becoming stale. Information from this book can still be found to this day, even though it was written so long ago, not even in English!

The Criticisms

Though the Kama Sutra remains quite relevant to this day, several criticisms have been voiced regarding this ancient text and its contents, especially in recent years. In this section, we will examine three of the most popular criticisms that the Kama Sutra has received.

1. The Male Gaze

The Kama Sutra has received criticism for the way that it was written since it comes from the perspective of a man and discusses how to please a woman. Though this book mentions same-sex relations between two men, this is only in the context of men sharing one single woman. This can be seen as sexist to some.

2. Male Pleasure

Another criticism that has been voiced is concerning the way that this book discusses a man's ability to benefit from having many female sexual partners, and even mentions how he can have them all at one time. The Kama Sutra mentions that a man can have one wife and several mistresses, which is not a popular opinion in the year 2020.

3. Controversy

There has been debate about whether the Kama Sutra is a book that should be praised for the way that it teaches men how to prioritize intimacy and female pleasure, or whether it should be criticized for how it puts men in control in terms of sex. Even when it talks about relationships and love, it is written for a man who wishes to court his woman. Whichever way you view this book, it contains many valuable lessons. After reading this book, you are free to make your judgment about whether or not you think this book is still relevant.

4. Inclusion

Many people also think that the Kama Sutra should not be relevant anymore as it is not inclusive of different levels of ability and strength, as well as not including the potential for people with physical disabilities to try these positions.

5. Too Adventurous

For some, they may find that the Kama Sutra may seem like it is just a little too adventurous. Some people may think that this book full of positions that takes away from the deeper purposes of sex and simply wants to try to challenge the bodies of the couple during sex.

6. Realistic?

The Kama Sutra has been criticized for being a book that contains sex positions that are not realistic for the average human to try to recreate.

7. Sexism

This book has also been criticized for being sexist, as it is written for a man who wants to know how to please a woman physically and emotionally.

Chapter 2: Kama Sutra Tips and Tricks

Now that you have a solid understanding of what the Kama Sutra is and what it contains, we are going to go over some tips and tricks on how to get the most out of this book. After you read through this chapter, chapter three will focus on some of the specific techniques that the Kama Sutra contains and how you can begin to benefit from them.

What the Kama Sutra Can Do for Your Relationship and Sex Life

As I mentioned in the previous chapter, the Kama Sutra is not limited to the sex positions it contains. As you know by now, the Kama Sutra contains much more than this chapter alone. This is not to say that the chapter on sex positions is not of importance, as it can still provide you with a wealth of information about how to improve your sex life with your partner. For this reason, not only does the Kama Sutra give you tips and tricks for your relationship, but also some practical advice for trying new things in the bedroom.

How to Begin Talking About the Kama Sutra With Your Partner

It can be quite a difficult task, opening up to your partner about something that you wish to change about your sex life. This may be the first time you plan to have a serious conversation with them about sex. You may fear judgment or hurting their feelings, and you may fear that your partner will not be interested in what you are suggesting.

As we discussed in the previous chapter, your lust and desire for your partner may fade as time goes on. Using the information contained in the Kama Sutra can help you to keep your passion alive in the bedroom by providing you with new and exciting sexual adventures to embark on together.

You may feel unsure of how your partner will react to you telling them that you want to spice up your sex life. If you have been in this relationship for a while now and you feel that your sex life is becoming routine, chances are that your partner would agree with you. While this is true, your anxiety about bringing this up has likely increased the longer you have left this unsaid.

It is never a bad time to bring these topics up in conversation, regardless of how long you have been in the relationship or marriage. You deserve pleasure, passion, and lust, and sharing your thoughts with your partner should be a priority. Bringing up your desire for change can be seen as a conversation that will provide you both with benefits, rather than a critique. Letting your partner know that you are not criticizing them, but that you are simply looking for ways that you can both achieve more pleasure will show them that you mean no harm in bringing this up.

Begin by telling your partner that you have been reading about something called the Kama Sutra. They may have heard of this before, but it may help if you explain to them what the Kama Sutra is. As you know by now, many people have ideas about what the text is about, many of which are myths. Give your partner a background about the Kama Sutra, and tell them that you believe it can greatly benefit both of you in the bedroom.

Then, let your partner know that you have been interested in trying some of what you have learned in the bedroom with them. Explain to them what it is that you have wanted to try with them. Explain what it is and how it makes you feel. Whether or not you have tried it in the past with someone else, let them know that you would like to begin exploring it with them.

You can also ask them if there is anything that they have wanted to explore or talk about (that relates to sex) with you. This will open up a dialogue about sex and your sex life in general.

Finally, tell them that your goal is to improve your shared sex life and that you are open to any suggestions or conversations that they would like to share with you. Your sex dialogue should be a two-way street, so be prepared for a mutual exchange of thoughts and feelings.

Beginner Tips for Incorporating Concepts from the Kama Sutra in Your Life

The following subsection includes several tips for incorporating the Kama Sutra into your own sex life. This may be new for you, so follow the tips below to find out how you can get the most pleasure and benefit from this book.

Open Your Mind

Some of the concepts and sexual acts that you will learn about may be very new to you. While you do not have to do anything that you are uncomfortable with, try to read and understand with an open mind. These concepts may lead you to learn more about yourself and your partner.

Rediscover Your Partner

While you may know your partner like the back of your hand- especially if you have been together for some time now, it is important to remember that people grow and change. When it comes to incorporating new things in your sex life, your partner may surprise you with what they are open to and what they enjoy. As you begin to explore the Kama Sutra with your partner, try to view the experience as a rediscovering of each other. Rediscover their pleasure, their body, and their desires. Try to forget what you already know about them and view the experience as if you are learning about them for the first time all over again.

The beginning of any relationship comes with a lot of uncharted territories. You are exploring a new person's entire body- inside and out and letting them explore yours. This stage of discovery is something that we want to return to now and again during a long-term relationship or a marriage. This is because you should rediscover your partner's body as if it is the first time now and again.

People's desires change, and their bodies change. It is important to continue to learn and understand how best to please your partner as they grow and change. You should also expect the same from them in return. Revisiting your partner's body as if you know nothing about it can be a fun and flirty way to re-inject passion into your sex life. Try to remember the first time you had sex with your partner and channel that excitement and curiosity once again.

Trust Yourself

Trust yourself! At the most basic level, humans are animals. Just like any other animal, we are meant to have sex. This means that sex comes wired into our DNA and that we all have some knowledge of how to conduct ourselves during sexual intercourse. This is because our body can take over and follow its pleasure, its arousal, and its instincts. While you don't want to act like a complete animal in bed (unless you and your partner are into it), this is simply useful to keep in mind so that you can keep your nerves at bay. If you let your mind take control, it will get in the way of and inhibit this natural instinct that you came built with. Relaxation and being at ease will make the encounter much more enjoyable for both of you. If you are able to relax and enjoy the experience, your body will flow much smoother, and pleasure will come much easier to both you and your partner.

Communicate

It may seem like there is an expectation to pretend as you know exactly what you are doing and to seem like you have done it a thousand times before, but this is untrue. No matter who your partner is, they will be happy that you communicated and made sure that they were comfortable all along the way instead of pretending like you knew exactly what they wanted. Being able to communicate in bed is more impressive than not saying anything and guessing the entire time.

While some people may be embarrassed to be vocal and expressive in bed, many benefits can come of it, and many reasons why you may want to consider making a point to do this. By being vocal in the bedroom, you are able to communicate things to your partner without having to worry about ruining the mood or "killing the vibes." What this means is that you don't have to stop having sex or suddenly change your demeanor in order to talk to your partner during sex. By being vocal in the bedroom, you can communicate to them what you like, what you don't like, and what you want more of. This will make your enjoyment of sex better, and it will mean that you can experience more pleasure since your partner will know exactly what you want. You will also be able to please your partner better since you will know exactly what they want if they are vocal as well.

Express Yourself

Expressing yourself during sex allows you to express your pleasure. When you experience the physical bliss that is an orgasm, your body is always shocked at the level of pleasure it is feeling. If you have had an orgasm before, you know that the amount of pleasure you feel is so much that it begs to be let out in some way, usually by grasping something tightly or by screaming out in pleasure. By doing this, it actually enhances the feelings of your orgasm. Think of it this way- if you are experiencing an orgasm and you are holding your pleasure in so that you can remain quiet or because you are embarrassed about expressing yourself, your pleasure can only build to a certain level because there is no release for it. If instead, you let your pleasure out by exclaiming or grabbing onto the bed frame or a combination of the two, your pleasure can continue to build as it has an outlet. With no outlet, there must be a cap on it. Just like when you shake a bottle of soda, and it explodes out the top.

Expressing your pleasure during orgasm is very beneficial for your pleasure and for your sexual experience overall. At first, you may be unsure about how to do this, and you may be a little self-conscious about doing it with a partner. I can assure you, that your partner will most definitely be turned on by your exclamations of pleasure, as it will come as a sort of ego boost to them when they realize how much pleasure they caused you.

The first thing that you can do in order to become more comfortable with this idea is to try it on your own first. When it comes to anything sex-related, trying it first on your own is a great way to get comfortable with it before doing it with another person present. To try this on your own, do so when you are masturbating. This is a great time to try it as you are the person who best knows how to please yourself. Because of this, you can give yourself a strong enough orgasm- to the point where you will want to scream out in pleasure. When you come close to orgasm, open your mouth slightly. When you reach orgasm, allow whatever sounds escape your mouth to come out without holding them back and without judging yourself. You will likely find that you had an even better orgasm than usual because you weren't holding yourself back at all. You let your pleasure come about and let it out, which allows it to grow without putting a cap on it.

When you go to bed with your partner, try this same technique as you did when you were alone, and I guarantee that your partner will become extremely aroused by your orgasm sounds.

Understand Your Body *and* Your Mind

- The Body

The body is responsible for all of our physical sensations. The body houses all of our erogenous zones and our sexual centers. The body is our vehicle, and it is what allows us to feel pleasure at all. The body is responsible for our deep desires, our lust, our orgasms, our arousal, and our physical reactions to pleasure. There is something deep within that is not recognized by our conscious mind or our heart that moves us toward pleasure and away from pain. This is responsible for our deepest desires, and it wants desperately to seek them out.

The heart is the center of our body, and it provides us with our feelings of acceptance, warmth, comfort, happiness, and love. The heart is another important part of sex, and it is important for sexual comfort. If you are making love with someone whom you really care about, the heart will be where you feel those deep and intense feelings of inner warmth and connection.

- The Mind

The brain provides us with information about the situation we are in, allows us to use dirty talk, and makes our decisions, among other things. If the brain is distracted or tired or distressed, it will be very hard to know what we want, what we like, what we want to do, what to do next, etcetera. The brain is an important part of sex and sexual decision making.

Our emotions also play a large part when it comes to sex. While sometimes, we can perform the act of sex without emotions involved, this is not as sexually intelligent as we would like to be. Having sex with emotions does not mean that we are in love with every person we have sex with, but that we care for them, and we care for ourselves. It also means recognizing that we will have emotions surrounding desire, whether it is happiness, excitement, nervousness, joy. These emotions can all tell us something. Instead of blocking them out, we should be embracing them and listening to them. Being able to observe and read our own emotions, and the emotions of others is part of sexual intelligence. Emotions can also contribute to our enjoyment of sex as when we are feeling happy or in love. We tend to feel more intense pleasure when having sex with the person we feel strongly about.

The brain, the heart, and the body come together to form a sexual being, and this is responsible for all of our sexual preferences, desires, and comforts. It helps us seek out a partner and the activities that we get pleasure from. Being able to get in touch with your body means being able to look to all three of these parts of ourselves and listen to them as a whole and individually. This will ensure that you get the most out of your experiences with the Kama Sutra.

Chapter 3: How to Begin Practicing Kama Sutra

While you probably know how to please each other like it's second nature, rediscovering each other's bodies in a sexy way and learning new ways to please each other is great for couples who have been together for a long time. The Kama Sutra will help you to do this, and in this chapter, we are going to look at how you can benefit from this.

Where to Begin

Before beginning, we will first delve into the topic of the orgasm. We will look at the orgasm from both a male and a female perspective. We will look at the male body and the female body and how to please them, as well as how to give them a wonderful orgasm. This section will be helpful to you no matter how long you have been having sex, and no matter how long you have been with your partner.

Many people are out of touch with their sensuality, their desires, their fantasies, and even their bodies. By learning how to please the opposite sex, you will help your partner to discover their body and their body. This will also help you to become aware of this concerning your own body, and you will know how to get back in touch with all of these parts of your sexuality.

When it comes to sex, we all know that the cherry on top of a great session is the orgasm! There is no denying that an orgasm is the best part of being a creature that has sex for enjoyment and not solely to reproduce.

Understanding the Female Body

To give a woman an orgasm, you will need to understand the female body and all of the places that, when stimulated, will make a woman feel pleasure. Whether you are a female yourself or you are a male with a female partner, both sexes can benefit from learning more about the female body.

- The Clitoris

The clitoris is the place that many people know of as the spot to stimulate that is the easiest way to give a woman an orgasm. The clitoris is located very close to the vagina. It is a small bean-like structure that has many many nerve endings, which is why it can so easily lead to female pleasure. To find it, begin by placing a hand on the pelvic area, with the fingers towards the vagina. A woman can do this to herself, or a man can do this to find the woman's clitoris. Slowly move your hand downward, using your fingers to feel around. As you wrap your fingers underneath her, between her legs, feel around for a small lump-like structure. It is in a slightly different spot, covered by different amounts of layers and of different sizes on every woman, so explore around between the legs to find it. It will be towards the front of her body, right where her vaginal lips begin. On some women, you may even be able to see it with the eyes if there are not as many layers of vaginal lips covering it.

The clitoris is said to be the female penis. This is because it actually enlarges and becomes engorged when a woman is horny. It will be easier to find her clitoris if she is turned on. The clitoris is much larger than it seems, and this is because it extends up inside of the woman's body. Only a small part of it is located on the outside of the body, but the size of it is the reason why there are so many nerve endings located within and the reason why stimulating it will lead to such intense pleasure.

Once you have found the clitoris, you will then be able to stimulate it to give yourself or your woman an orgasm. Begin by gently placing two fingers on it and putting a bit of pressure. Rub it by moving your fingers in small circles- making sure to be gentle. Continue to do this, and she should begin to get more aroused the more you do this. By rubbing the clitoris, you will be able to stimulate the entire clitoris, even the part of it that you cannot see, and this will cause the woman to start to become wet in her vagina.

- The G-Spot

The G-Spot is a lesser-known spot than the clitoris, but a woman can have extreme amounts of pleasure if this spot is stimulated. To find this spot, you will need to insert a finger into her vagina. It is best to try to find this spot after you stimulated the clitoris for a bit because then her vagina will have begun to get wet- as it lubricates itself to prepare for penetration. You can use this to your advantage because it will make penetration more enjoyable for her and will reduce the friction of the entire vaginal area in general. When the vagina becomes very wet, it can lubricate the entire vaginal area, including the clitoris, which will then make it easier to stimulate the clitoris as well. No friction means smooth gliding, which results in pleasure and no pain. When she is wet enough, slide a finger inside of her vagina while she is lying on her back (a woman can do this for herself too) and make a "come here" motion with your finger, so that you are moving it towards her belly button. Feel around in this are, and when you feel a bumpy or rough surface, this is the G-Spot. Just like the clitoris, the G-Spot is slightly different for every woman, but they can all be in the same general area. The G-Spot will be a different size for different women, so be aware of this when trying to find it.

The reason that the G-Spot can give a woman intense pleasure is that it is actually connected to the clitoris. Inside the body, where the clitoris extends up into the woman, it meets the vagina, and this is the spot where the G-Spot is located. This thin wall between them allows for the pressure and stimulation to travel between them so that you are essentially also stimulating the clitoris when you are pleasuring her G-Spot.

To give a woman pleasure by stimulating her G-Spot, you will need to press on it over and over again until she reaches orgasm. This can be done using your fingers, your penis, or sex toys of a variety of sorts. We will talk about sex toys in a later chapter, but for now, we will look at the fingers and the penis. Stimulating this spot with your fingers is quite simple as you will have lots of control, and you will be able to feel around to see if you are in the right spot. When you have found the G-Spot with your fingers, gently press on it with the pads of your fingers and avoid curling your fingers around too much as you don't want your nails to scratch the inside of her vagina. Press with the pads of your fingers on her G-Spot with light pressure, but enough for her to feel what you are doing. Continue to do this, and you should feel her vagina getting increasingly wetter. As you do this, you can increase the speed of stimulation if she wishes. Communicate with her to see what she wants you to do (faster, slower, harder, lighter, deeper, shallower). A woman can do the same to herself in the bedroom. I just the same way, slide a finger inside of your vagina either with lube or after getting yourself a bit wet by watching porn or massaging your clitoris. Then, move your finger towards the front of your body and feel for the spot. Once you have found it, continue to stimulate it by putting pressure on it over and over again. It should feel good and get increasingly better the longer you do this. Eventually, the pleasure will build to a point where it feels as if you are about to orgasm. Continue to do whatever you were doing to get to this point, and orgasm will occur! This type of orgasm will be much more full body than a clitoral orgasm, as it includes the inside of the vagina and is also stimulating the clitoris from the inside.

The penis can also stimulate the G-Spot, but it is a little harder as there will not be as much control as there is when using fingers. Try to choose a position that will have the curve of the penis line up with the front of the vaginal wall, and this will give you the best chance of hitting the G-Spot. We will go into this further in chapter five, where we will look at specific positions. For now, though, knowing where the G-Spot is located as well as how to make a woman feel pleasure in that spot is a great start to being able to give her an amazing orgasm.

- The Anus

The anus is a very sensitive area for women, contrary to the beliefs of some people. While it is well-known that men have sensitive anuses and can receive pleasure here, it is a less well-known fact that so can women. Women have very sensitive anal openings because there are many nerve endings here and a lot of surface area. This means that when stimulated, a woman can feel a lot of pleasure here. Because this is an area that rarely receives stimulation. Therefore, when it does, it can be that much more enjoyable for a woman because she may not be used to the sensations.

The inside of the anus can give a woman lots of pleasure as well when stimulated. When a woman has her anus stimulated, it actually is only separated from the vagina by a thin layer, and similar to the clitoris and the G-Spot connection, she can actually orgasm from being anally stimulated because of the connection between her vagina and her anus. A woman can receive anal sex, and the penis making contact with her anal wall, especially the one toward the front of her body, can give her a very similar feeling to that of a vaginal orgasm.

The anus can also be stimulated with fingers, toys, or orally. Any of these ways can be enjoyable for the woman if she is open to receiving anal pleasure, as they will each give her a slightly different sensation. Think of how a warm tongue would feel vs. a smooth anal toy vs. the rough hands of the man she loves.

Understanding the Male Body

- The Penis

As we know, the male sex organ is the penis. A man can reach orgasm by having his penis rubbed, sucked on, kissed, or stimulated in a number of other ways. While you cannot easily tell when a woman is aroused, it is easy to tell when a man is aroused because his penis will become erect. This happens because then he can have sex with it- think of how hard it would be to have penetrative sex with a limp penis. When a man watches porn, sees a very attractive woman, or is touched in the right way, he will become erect. Then, by sliding his penis into a vagina repeatedly, into a sex toy like a fleshlight, or by having someone stroke it with their hand, he can eventually reach orgasm. Every man's penis is a different shape and a different size, and each man will like something slightly different in order to reach orgasm. There are so many things you can try and ways that a man could reach orgasm, there is lots of opportunity for exploration and trying new things.

We will revisit the topic of sex toys further in this book, so you will get more information on that very soon.

- The Testicles

A man's testicles may seem like they are there only to provide sperm for ejaculation, but they are also very sensitive erogenous zones for a man. If a man's testicles are stimulated, this can make him become very aroused and can make him erect if he wasn't already. A man's testicles can be stimulated during oral sex, during a handjob, or during sex in certain positions, and this will only add to the pleasure he is already feeling from having his penis stimulated in some way.

If you have ever had your testicles bumped in the wrong way, it definitely brought you a lot of pain for those few minutes afterward. Think of that level of pain but in terms of pleasure instead. This is what we want to unlock for you in your testicles. This level of sensation, but in the reverse- intense pleasure instead of intense pain.

Gently stroking the testicles with warm hands will get them used to touch so that they don't seize up and hug the body too closely. Gently rubbing the scrotum and massaging the testicles will add to whatever sexual activity is already happening. They can also be stimulated with the mouth during oral sex. The woman can move down to the testicles and gently suck or lick them to give a different sensation- that of warm moisture on sensitive skin.

A man can stimulate his own testicles while he is masturbating for added pleasure as well. If you are a man and you have never tried this, add it to your next masturbation session. Using one hand to stroke your penis and the other to massage your testicles will add a new dimension to your self-love sessions. Try this in the shower with a partner or without to enjoy the warmth or the water mixed with a massage and penis stimulation. You will never go back.

- The Anus

The anus is a well-known erogenous area of the male body. Males can get intense pleasure and even orgasm from being anally penetrated. This is due to the prostate gland being positioned right sat the spot where whatever is doing the stimulating would make contact with the anal wall. Right on the other side of this wall is the prostate, which happens to be extremely sensitive and leads to intense pleasure when stimulated in the right way.

A man's anus can be stimulated on the outside only, where-like a woman's, it is very sensitive due to a great number of very sensitive nerve endings being located there. This can be done using a tongue, fingers, a vibrating toy, or anything really. Beginning with this will lead the anus to relax and become receptive to being penetrated. Then, a sex toy or fingers can be inserted, and that's when the prostate will get its turn. When they prostate it pressed on over and over in a rhythmic pattern, it will cause a man to feel intense pleasure and eventually to reach orgasm. This is similar to the G-Spot in a woman where it needs to be continuously stimulated to eventually give her an orgasm.

Anal sex for a man is not just reserved for gay couples. Many heterosexual couples practice pegging, which is anal sex from a woman to a man using a sex toy. We will revisit this later, but this point is to say that the pleasure potential of a man's anus is not only reserved for gay couples and should be fully explored by any man or heterosexual couple wanting to unlock the full pleasure that a man's body is capable of.

Understanding Orgasms

We have discussed the female orgasm somewhat in this chapter so far, but in this section, we will look at it in a little more depth.

For a woman to reach orgasm, much of this is dependent on her mindset. She will need to feel comfortable being vulnerable in this space for her to reach her full arousal potential. She needs to reach this point in order for her to orgasm and in order for her to fully enjoy sex. For this reason, mindset and pleasure are very closely linked to a woman.

When the clitoris is rubbed in the right way, it will lead to orgasm, just like the penis of a man. Treating it like this can give both men and women insight into how it works and how to make the woman come. When stimulated physically with someone's fingers or a sex toy like a vibrator, this can lead to an orgasm for the woman. The clitoris is a structure that contains many nerve endings, which is what makes it so sensitive. When a woman is not aroused sexually, her clitoris is still there, but it will not be as enlarged as when she is horny.

A woman's vagina automatically swells when she is sexually aroused because of increased blood flow to her genitals, sort of like how your penis becomes erect when you get horny. What this means for you is that when your penis is inside of her, the walls of her vagina will tighten and swell as the blood flow increases, and you will feel this effect on your penis, resulting in added pleasure for you.

There are different types of multiple orgasms that a woman can achieve. Women are lucky in that they can have both back-to-back orgasms and blended orgasms. They are even able to have back-to-back blended orgasms in some cases! In this section, we will learn more about the different types of multiple orgasms.

We will now discuss blended orgasms. A blended orgasm is achieved when multiple different orgasms are achieved at the same time. This can be two different orgasms at the same time, or in some cases, even more than two! This type of orgasm leads to even more pleasure than a single orgasm and will lead the woman to feel more intense pleasure than ever before. During penetration, there is lots of opportunity for different types of female orgasms to occur. The two most common ways that a woman can reach orgasm are through her clitoris and through her G-spot. We will look at some ways that a woman can have both of these orgasms at the same time, as well as some other options for blended orgasms.

Any combination of these separate but simultaneous orgasms compounds to give the woman a mind-blowing, full-body, blended orgasm. This is especially so if the two locations of stimulation are a larger distance from each other- like the nipples and the clitoris for example. The best type of blended orgasm will vary from woman to woman, depending on her personal preferences and what her most sensitive erogenous zones are. Some of these zones include the clitoris, the anus, the G-Spot, and the nipples. Some women may have others as well, but this is largely dependent on the woman's body.

The first method is a clitoral orgasm during penetration. If the clitoris is stimulated while the man is penetrating the woman, she could have an orgasm through both her clitoris and her G-Spot at the same time. This type of multiple orgasms will make her feel pleasure like never before because these two places are extremely pleasurable even when achieved alone, so together it is a new level of orgasm! There are different ways that you can achieve this, but the most successful way is to penetrate her with your fingers while she rubs her clitoris at the same time. This way, you can feel your way around and stimulate her G-spot while she pleases herself. It may take some practice and will require a lot of communication, but eventually, you will both be able to time it so that she can have both of these orgasms at once. Another way that this can happen is while the man is thrusting his penis into her. While he is doing this, she can touch her clitoris using her fingers or a vibrator, or the man can stimulate her clitoris by using his fingers or a vibrator. Some specific positions will allow for the man's penis to reach the G-Spot when inside of her, and at the same time, the base of his penis or his pelvic region can rub her clitoris, causing both orgasms to happen at the same time. We will look at these specific positions later on in this book.

Another way that a woman can achieve a blended orgasm is through having both an anal and clitoral orgasm at the same time. This is similar to the blended orgasm in which the man is penetrating the woman with his penis while her clitoris is being stimulated, but in this case, it is done while you are having anal sex. The method will happen in a similar way to the vaginal penetration with clitoral stimulation, but the positions used will be slightly different as the positions used in this case would be ones that better allow for anal penetration while giving either the man or the woman free hands to stimulate the clitoris. Either the man or the woman can stimulate the woman's clitoris in a variety of anal sex positions using either their hands or a vibrating sex toy.

Another type of blended orgasm that is possible is a nipple orgasm and a clitoral orgasm. Not every woman is able to achieve a nipple orgasm, but if you are, then this could be a great option for a blended orgasm. If you are unsure whether you are able to reach orgasm through nipple stimulation alone, try this one in order to see if also your clitoris having stimulated leads to more sensitivity in your nipples as well.

One example of a position in which this type of blended orgasm can occur is the following. While you are sitting in a chair with your legs spread wide, your partner will get on his knees in front of you. He will then begin to give you oral sex on his knees. While licking and using his mouth to stimulate your clitoris, he will reach up to your breasts with his hands and massage your nipples with his fingers. Once he has done this for some time and began to please you, he will then switch and using his tongue. He will gently lick, suck and lick your nipples with his tongue, one at a time. While he does this, he will also move his hand down between your legs and stimulate your clitoris with his hand and fingers. Have him alternate back and forth using his mouth on your clitoris and then on your nipples. This will give you pleasure from both of these erogenous zones, and you will likely be able to experience a blended nipple and clitoral orgasm in this way, as long as he keeps stimulating both areas at the same time.

Not only can women have blended orgasms, but they can also have back-to-back orgasms. These orgasms occur one after the other and give the woman immense pleasure because she is able to keep coming again and again and again.

This type of repeated orgasm is only possible for women as the male body is unable to do this. This is because the male body has to wait for a refractory period after every orgasm. What this means is that there is an amount of time after an orgasm during which a man's body is unable to achieve an erection or have another orgasm. During this time, his body is recovering from the orgasm and needs this time to recuperate. The length of this period is different for every man, but it ranges between fifteen to thirty minutes in most males.

The great thing about the clitoris is that after orgasm, it may be very sensitive for a few minutes, but it maintains its "erection" and can be stimulated again a very short time after for a doubly pleasurable second orgasm. This can lead to a third and a fourth and beyond. This is why, as we discussed, it is beneficial to give a woman an orgasm during foreplay as it will increase her chances of orgasm during penetration because of how horny it will have made her. Sometimes, women's pleasure only builds after an initial orgasm instead of going back to zero before climbing again like a man's pleasure would have to. It is important for men to understand this difference because they can then take advantage of it and pleasure their woman to the fullest. While they await their refractory period, they can please their woman in a way that does not involve their penis, give her an orgasm, and then by the time this happens; he will be ready to get hard again and have a second round with her. All the while, she will become increasingly horny and pleased.

Another type of multiple orgasms that may be different from what you had in mind when hearing the words "multiple orgasms" is the simultaneous orgasm." This type of multiple orgasms is great for couples, especially long-term couples. This type of orgasm occurs when both the man and the woman are able to reach orgasm at the same time! The reason why this is great for long-term couples is that it takes practice and excellent communication during sex, but when mastered, it will unlock new levels of pleasure for both of you. When in a long-term relationship, one of the many positive things about having sex with each other is that you know just the right way to make each other orgasm. After having sex with each other so many times, you likely have this down to a science! This comes in handy here as you can use this knowledge to help you both orgasm at the same time. Since you know how to get your partner to orgasm in mere minutes, you can touch each other exactly as you each like at the exact same time in order to reach orgasm simultaneously.

Now, this is a little more difficult than it sounds, but it is entirely possible. To do this, begin with the intention of orgasming together. Both of you will stimulate the other person's genitals in the best way you know, so you will have to figure out a position that allows for both of these ways at the same time. For example, if your partner can make you come very quickly by giving you oral sex while also massaging your testicles and you can make her come very quickly by playing with her clitoris just the right way, then you will have to find a position where you can do both of these at the same time. This position could be one where you are lying on your back on the bed, and she is straddling your chest, facing your feet. She will bend forward so that her mouth reaches your penis, and she will hold herself up with one of her arms on the bed. She can then use her other free hand to massage your testicles. You will then slide a hand between her legs and begin playing with her clitoris, and you can even use your other hand to slide your fingers into her vagina if she wishes.

When you begin, start out slow. This will require a lot of communication between the two of you. Begin pleasing each other and communicating your pleasure with moans or simple phrases like "that feels good" the entire time. When one of you gets close to reaching orgasm, tell the other person. If your partner tells you that they are close to coming, ease up on the pressure or the speed on her clitoris, for example, so that she does not come yet. When, and if you are also close to orgasm, let her know, and you can both continue to stimulate each other's genitals until you both orgasm together at the same time!

One of the benefits of this type of orgasm in a long-term relationship is that when you care about a person deeply, you find pleasure in seeing them pleased. When you please your partner to the point of orgasm, it usually will make you also feel pleasure. Because of this, as each of you comes closer to reaching orgasm, it will make the other person more aroused. For this reason, a long-term couple will be able to do this act of simultaneous orgasms with ease.

Understanding The Female Orgasm Potential
Female ejaculation is a well-disputed concept in modern discussions about sexuality. There is evidence though, that it is possible and actually quite common. While the term *female*

ejaculation probably makes you think of something porn-related, it is something that can happen without theatrics and to a much lesser degree in your own sex life. Female ejaculation is often portrayed as a fountain of water spraying across the room; however, this is not the case in real life.

Female ejaculation does not have to occur, and, in many cases, it never does. It is sort of the icing on the cake or the cherry on top so to speak, but it is not necessary in order for the woman to be aroused or to achieve orgasm. Female ejaculation, commonly referred to as *squirting,* is different for every woman and does not have to involve a large amount of fluid like a male ejaculation. It also does not happen every time and does not only happen during orgasm. While it can happen at the time of orgasm, female ejaculation can also occur at any time during sex when the woman is extremely aroused. Thus, ejaculation can be a sign that the woman is feeling aroused regardless of whether she has reached orgasm yet or not. This is a good sign that indicates she is enjoying herself.

Ejaculation does not happen to every woman, but it can be something that can be practiced and learned if the woman would like to experience it. Some people become extremely turned on when they experience or witness female ejaculation, so if you or your partner feel that it would turn you both on, it is possible for the woman to begin trying to achieve this. For some people, it turns them on so much, even to the point of experiencing orgasm.

Female ejaculation has been linked to G-Spot stimulation, so the best way to achieve this is to have your partner stimulate your G-Spot with either his fingers, his penis, or a dildo.

What to Do First

The Kama Sutra text views sex as a spiritual act between two people that, with time, will increase a person's level of spirituality and sexual power. The book aims to help people to get in touch with their desires, which will aid them in reaching the full extent of their sexual power. It aims to liberate people in a sexual sense. These concepts were quite advanced for the time that the book was written, which is why this book is still so widely discussed to this day. Before you begin practicing the concepts of the Kama Sutra, it is important to understand this.

Lubrication

There are many different types of lubricants that you can use to make your sex glide easier and feel more pleasurable. The first type we will talk about is the synthetic lubricant. There are different types of these- water-based and silicone-based lubricants. The type of lubricant you choose will depend on what type of sex toy you are using and what your intended use is. I will go into more detail about the different types of lubrication below, but first, we will look at the benefits of using any lubrication during sex in general. Lubrication has been shown to have sex better in many ways, the first of which is that it makes all body parts glide better and slide easier, which means no painful dry skin on dry skin friction. Lubrication has also been shown to increase the intensity of both male and female orgasms. As I mentioned earlier, in order to have an orgasm vaginally for women or anally for either sex, constant rhythmic penetration is required.
Lubrication makes this possible because of the ease of movement it allows for will help with maintaining a rhythm of penetration.

Lubrication can also be used for masturbation with sex toys or with hands and fingers alone for both men and women because it will make toys or fingers move and glide easier, which will lead to more pleasure. Lubrication will make both clitoral stimulation and penile stroking more pleasant because it will eliminate any skin on skin friction that would occur because of a lack of a condom or, in the case of male masturbation the lack of a female's natural vaginal lubrication to act as a lubricant on the penis.

Silicone-Based Lubricant

Silicone-based lube is the type of lube you would want to use if you want to have sex in the bathtub, shower, or any environment involving water since it won't rinse off when it becomes wet. If you are not using it to have sex in a wet environment, the other benefit about it is that it will usually only need to be applied once and will stay thick and doing its job for the duration of your session. This makes silicone-based lube a great choice for activities involving anal sex because it is thicker and longer-lasting than other forms of lubrication. When having anal sex of any sort, ample lubrication is required, and choosing the longer-lasting sort of lube will be best.

The drawback though, is that this type of lubrication is not very easy to clean. This is because it cannot be rinsed off by only using water. This variety of lubrication requires you to use soap and scrub it off of whatever you are cleaning it off of, like a penis or your vaginal area. Silicone-based lubricants aren't ideal on a silicone-based sex toy because it can cause the toy to break down more quickly over time than it normally would.

Water-Based Lubricant

Water-based lubricant is very easy to clean as it can be rinsed off of your body or your sex toys with water alone. The drawback though is that if you enjoy shower sex, bathtub sex, pool-sex, or any sex involving the water, it will wash away immediately and will not provide any lubrication as soon as it gets wet. This is also why this type of lubrication may need to be reapplied a few times in a session. If you do not have much shower or bathtub sex and you use silicone sex toys, then water-based lube would be good for you.

Oils

As an alternative, you can use oil as a lubricant. Oil is beneficial because it is so versatile in its uses. Oil can be used as a massage aid for some sensual foreplay massaging. It can be used without being washed off before oral sex because of its natural roots and its flavor that would not be terrible in your mouth. If you prefer something natural as a lubricant, then oil will likely be your choice. Many people will use coconut oil for this purpose. It can be used as an edible lubricant as it is often seen in cooking and smoothies. The one drawback to oil-based lubricants is that they can't be used with condoms because they will deteriorate the condom and cause it to break.

Gels

There are some gels that are made for sexual encounters that also can be used with versatility. There are some aloe vera scented gels that can be used both as a massage gel for foreplay and as lube for penetrative sex. If you live in a hot place or take this gel with you on vacation, it can also be an after-sun gel for burnt skin. This way, soothing your partner's sunburn could turn into quite the sensual and even sexual experience.

Kissing

There are 16 different kissing techniques outlined in the Kama Sutra. This means that you will never run out of new and interesting ways to show your partner love through kissing them.

- The Normal Kiss
- The Straight Kiss
- The Turned Kiss
- The Throbbing Kiss
- The Touching Kiss
- The Bent Kiss
- The Pressed Kiss
- The Gently Pressed Kiss
- Kiss of the Upper Lip
- A Clasping Kiss
- The Kiss that Kindles Love
- The Turning Away Kiss
- The Awakening Kiss
- Kiss of Showing Intention

- The Transferred Kiss
- The Demonstrative Kiss

Foreplay

Foreplay is generally treated as the time before penetrative sex, where there is some kissing, some touching, and some sensual whispers. What happens during foreplay? In the media, foreplay is often given a bad reputation, as it is portrayed as something that must be done for the woman's body to get ready for sex, or for the woman to feel comfortable enough to begin having sex. While some of this is true, sex is much more than the act of a penis in a vagina. Sex can last much longer than the time between when the man inserts his penis and when he reaches orgasm. The Kama Sutra recognizes that there should be much more importance placed on foreplay, which is why there are several sections of the text which talk about what you can do to share intimate moments with your partner before penetration.

Sex between couples is much more than what happens when the man is inside of the woman. Treating sex as much more than just a physical activity means that we must include all aspects of sex in our discussions about how to have a better sex life. This includes foreplay. That being said, if foreplay is considered part of sex, then the positions in which you engage in foreplay are sex positions.

In this section, we will look at foreplay as a special part of sex, and I will introduce some different techniques for foreplay that focus on your emotional connection and intimacy with your partner.

The Importance of Foreplay

Foreplay is important to ensure that you will be able to have comfortable sex. This is because the man will have to be erect enough, and the woman will have to be wet enough for sex to happen smoothly and without pain. This is the most practical reason that foreplay exists.

Further, foreplay gives you a chance to connect with your partner on an emotional level before you begin connecting physically in such a deep way. This time to connect with one another can make the difference between lovemaking and the physical act of sex. Connecting emotionally while connecting physically will lead to longer-lasting love and more passionate sex.

As we discussed above, foreplay is an important aspect of sex. This is especially true for women. This is because a woman needs to feel comfortable and relaxed to feel sexual pleasure. Foreplay serves to make a woman feel comfortable, letting her hair down, and being vulnerable. This is true whether she is in a long-term relationship or having a one-night stand.

The woman will need to feel comfortable being vulnerable in this space for her to reach her full arousal potential. Further, she needs to reach this point for her body to reach orgasm. Taking some time to set the mood before you have sex will go a long way in terms of a woman's ability to become and stay aroused. This will benefit both the man and the woman because the man will have more fun if the woman is comfortable. Setting the mood also shows the woman that you are concerned with her level of comfort in her surroundings and are invested in her pleasure. Her ability to have an orgasm will depend greatly on her level of ease.

Many times, foreplay involves some kind of stimulation of the genitals, whether it is by oral sex or using your hands. This gets you ready for sex, as your body will respond by becoming more and more aroused. Once in a full state of arousal, you can achieve successful penetration.

There are some benefits to using only your hands to please your partner. When using your hands, you can feel your way around their body. This will mean that you will know exactly what you are doing and where you are touching them at all times. You can control the pressure with which you hold or stroke the penis or rub the clitoris when you are using your hands. For the man, he can feel his way around inside of the woman so that he knows exactly where he is. This way, he can aim for a specific location such as her G-Spot or the deeper areas of her vagina. If he were using his penis, he would not have as much control or as much perception of where he was in relation to her G-Spot.

The other reason why foreplay is so important for the woman is that it is quite difficult for a woman's body to reach orgasm during penetrative sex. If the woman can orgasm during foreplay, she will enjoy penetrative sex much more!

Another reason that foreplay will allow a woman to get more enjoyment out of penetrative sex is the following; The time spent getting each other in the mood for sex will cause the woman's clitoris to become engorged. This is similar to a male erection. The benefit of this is that when you are having penetrative sex, and her clitoris is engorged, it will more easily make contact with the shaft of the man's penis or with some part of his body as he is thrusting into her. What this means is that it will be easier for her to get clitoral stimulation during penetrative sex is her clitoris becomes engorged during foreplay.

Kama Sutra Foreplay Techniques

The first technique we will look at is setting the mood. This may not seem of importance, but it is a very important part of pre-sex behavior that is often overlooked.

As a couple, it is more important to set the mood and environment for your sex than it would be if you were having casual sex or a one-night stand. In a relationship, you have moved past the casual awkwardness of those types of encounters and onto real lovemaking.

When setting the mood, our focus is on creating an environment free of distractions where you can both focus on each other without becoming side-tracked. Another focus is to create an environment that is relaxing and calm. This will allow you to get in touch with your sensations and your deeper feelings to embrace your pleasure and move in ways that feel good to you without your thoughts running too much and getting in the way of your body and its own needs. So, what do I do to set the mood and make the environment relaxing? Read on.

If you are having sex in your bedroom or your home, it is a space that is very familiar to both of you. This may mean that all of your regular distractions are present all over the place, including your phone, your computer, and your textbooks or your work maybe. You don't want these things staring at you from across the room, reminding you that you have to study all night or send a quick email after your orgasm is over, so try to keep the room as free of these things as possible. Maybe leave your phone and laptop in the kitchen or the office, and make sure you put it on silent!

Secondly, we want the environment to be relaxing. Get rid of the harsh lighting of your overhead bulbs and turn on a few lamps with a soft orange glow or light some candles. The candles may seem cheesy, but there is a reason that they became so closely associated with romance. You don't necessarily have to go so far as having rose petals and chocolates, but some candles will be a nice touch for any day of the week.

Setting the mood in this way will allow you both to breathe and focus on each other and yourselves. We all deserve to have some time with our partner and our bodies, where we enjoy the feeling of pleasure. Use this time with your partner as a way to de-stress and let yourself unwind. Have some fun. Now that the mood is set, the next stages of foreplay can begin.

When you begin foreplay, begin by feeling around between your partner's legs slowly. Pay attention to their face to see what areas are most sensitive and responsive to your touch. Remember, this could vary by the day, so what they liked yesterday may not be what they want today.

When you find the spot that is most responsive (or spots, plural), continue to stimulate it, gradually increasing your speed and pressure as they become more excited and hornier. Listen to their audible cues to tell you when you are hitting the right spot, the right speed, and the right pressure and continue with this in order to keep exciting them. They may reach orgasm, or this may lead to some other type of sex. Being able to be sexually intelligent enough to know where to go, where to touch and how, and how to read the person and their cues takes time.

By stimulating a woman's clitoris, you can give her great pleasure if you know how to touch it the right way. During foreplay, try to give the woman an orgasm if possible. This will make her vagina extremely wet, which will lead to better penetrative sex.

How do you know when you have done enough foreplay? The answer to this is the woman's level of pleasure. It also depends on whether you are erect enough of course! If she has an orgasm during foreplay and you are both wanting to begin penetration, then that is an appropriate time to do so. If you want to extend foreplay even longer after she orgasms, by all means do so. If she does not orgasm during foreplay, you will know when you have spent enough time on this part of sex by how wet her vagina is and how ready she is to begin penetration. If she is getting very wet and is telling you she wants you to put your penis inside of her, it is safe to assume she is ready for you. If she is not too wet and she does not seem as passionate about the sex as she is when she is fully aroused, keep the foreplay going a little longer. You can use dirty talk to find out where she is at mentally as well. You can say something like, "do you want me to come into you?" "How wet are you?" or something of the sort. This will allow her to respond in a sexy way, telling you if she wants more in terms of foreplay, or if she is ready to take it to the next step.

Chapter 4: The Kama Sutra Massage Techniques

A great way to begin practicing Kama Sutra sex techniques is to start with a massage. Every couple can have a quick session of sexual intercourse, but this will not provide you with all of the potential benefits that the Kama Sutra contains. By starting with a sensual massage, you and your partner will share intimate moments together, which will have sex that much better once you get to that stage in this book.

The Kama Sutra Classic Massage Technique

The Kama Sutra talks about massages, including the best places to give massages and some techniques for doing so.

Sometimes, giving your partner a massage will lead to penetrative sex, and sometimes it will not. Aside from being part of foreplay, a massage can also be a relaxing gesture of love. Giving your partner a massage at the end of the day is a great way to get intimate with each other.

If you have massage oil, that is a great addition to any massage, but if not, you can use coconut oil. If you don't have either of those, you can use something like lotion to lubricate your hands and avoid skin to skin friction. Warm your hands before you start massaging them so that it feels nice and doesn't send a chill down their spine when you first make contact.

You can let your partner choose what type of massage they'd like- foot, head, back, shoulder, etc. Instruct them to lie in a comfortable position for their massage. Once you have lubricated your hands, put your hands on them lightly. Then you can begin to massage them gently.

The touch of a massage from a lover gives a person a sense of being cared for. It is a great way to deepen your bond. A massage is a great way to show your partner that you care about making them feel good.

After you have massaged their upper body or their feet, begin kissing their body where you just massaged it and then progress to kissing them on the lips. Let this encounter naturally progress, and let your bodies guide you. You can gradually move into touching each other in new areas, and maybe you will even begin touching each other's genitals, though that leads us to the next section of this chapter.

Eventually, all of this massaging could lead to sex, but it doesn't have to. We will discuss this in more detail below.

The Kama Sutra Erotic Massage Versus the Kama Sutra Classic Massage

Above, we saw an example of a classic Kama Sutra massage. This massage technique does not involve sex or massaging of the genitals. This style of massage involves the person's entire body or any specific location that they would like you to focus on. This kind of massage can be done anywhere and does not necessarily require either of you to remove your clothes.

Beginning with a relaxing massage such as the classic massage will help you and your partner to get into a relaxed and connected state of mind. Once you have finished with the classic massage, you may feel the urge to touch your partner and massage them in other places. This brings us to the erotic massage.

An erotic massage is a massage that involves the touching and massaging of a person's genitals. This leads to pleasurable sensations, but not necessarily to orgasm. An erotic massage can lead to orgasm, though that is not the sole intention.

Erotic massages can be given to both men and women, and they will lead to pleasure and relaxation. You can find a sample technique for a female and a male erotic massage outlined below.

The Benefits of Both

In this section, we are going to look at some of the many benefits that massages can provide you with.

- Relaxing

A massage, regardless of which type, is a relaxing way to unwind with your partner.

- Pleasurable

Massages are pleasurable, whether they are massages of the body or erotic massages. They bring a sense of pleasure in the form of human touch.

- Can be Done Man to Woman or Woman to Man

Massages are able to be done by anyone, to anyone. This makes them a great option for any kind of couple or relationship.

- Can be Done Anytime, Anyplace

Since you don't necessarily have to be naked, a massage can be done anytime, anywhere. This makes it a great option for any couple.

The Female Erotic Massage

This type of massage is an erotic massage, which is called the *yoni massage*. A yoni massage involves the woman's entire vaginal area, which is called the *vulva*. The vulva is a broad term for the vaginal area, which includes the clitoris, the large and small labia, the vagina, and the general areas around them. This area is full of nerve endings, so a woman can feel great pleasure from a massage in this location.

A Yoni Massage is done to open up the woman to her sexuality, her pleasure, and her sexual desires. As a partner, you can perform this type of massage for your female partner to unlock her hidden sexual energy and help her to get in touch with it. For this reason, this massage is a great addition to foreplay, though it can also be done independently of sex.

This massage can be done in a variety of ways, such as in a bathtub, in a jacuzzi, in bed or on the floor. The most important factor here is that the woman is feeling comfortable and relaxed, and the environment will play a big role in this.

To help the woman relax before her massage, begin by setting the ambiance. Ensure that you remove distractions so that she can focus on her pleasure.

You can prepare your hands in the same way that you lubricated and warmed your hands for the classic massage, but be sure that you are using lubricant for this type of massage.

Begin by having the woman breathe deeply and focus on her body. Let her know that she can begin getting in touch with any sensations she is having.

Begin by slowly and gently massaging around her entire vulva and her clitoral area. The key to this type of massage is to move very slowly and with intention. Begin to massage her clitoris slowly and do so without the intention of making her come. You are instead trying to give her subtle pleasure. Massage around her entire vulva slowly, including her labia. Do this for a few minutes, being sure to focus on the entire area and not just her clitoris.

When ready, and using lube, slide one finger into her vagina. Begin to gently massage the inside of her vagina.

By lifting your fingers towards the front of her body, you will find the location of her G-spot.

Encourage her to express herself vocally and to release any sounds she naturally makes as a result of this massage. Move your fingers in a circular motion slowly and with your other hand, massage her pelvic area, her vulva, and clitoris. Doing this serves to connect the inner with the outer.

Continue to massage her in this way and let the experience unfold with no end goal in mind. Let her know that if her body reaches orgasm, she should not fight it. If she doesn't reach orgasm, she can simply enjoy the pleasure that the massage is providing her with. As discussed earlier, this massage is intended to reconnect a woman with her pleasure and allow her to focus on herself and her body, so an orgasm is not necessary.

After this massage, she will feel more in touch with her body. If penetrative sex ensues, both of you will feel increased levels of pleasure, and your orgasms will be more intense because of how engorged and activated her vagina and clitoris will be after having been massaged.

The Male Erotic Massage

There are several different options for providing your male partner with an erotic massage. Firstly, you can massage their testicles. This is less likely to lead to orgasm than a penis massage, so it can be a great way to get a man relaxed and in the mood.
Another form of erotic massage for men, which is discussed in the Kama Sutra, is the penis massage. This type of massage can be tricky, as it could lead to orgasm quite quickly. The effectiveness of this massage will depend on the man's ability to last as his penis is being massaged.

The third variety of massage is the prostate massage. Since this type of massage requires the man's partner to insert a finger into his anus, some couples may be less comfortable with this type of erotic massage. If you do wish to try this kind of massage, it can be very pleasing for the man. The *prostate* is a small gland located inside a man's body between the base of his penis and his anus. It is accessed through the anus. This type of massage is similar to anal sex, but it is not the same, as the goals are different, and so is the technique. Keep in mind that this type of massage will require you to use lots of lube for maximum comfortability. Once your fingers are well-lubricated, you can slide a finger or two inside of the man's anus very slowly. As we discussed previously, you will have to go slow so as not to shock the anus into closing tightly. You will need to work your way in gradually. Once in, you will be able to find the prostate by feeling around on the upper (front) wall of the rectum for a small lump that is rough in texture a few inches deep. Once you have found it, you can begin to gently massage it. You can move your fingers in circles and apply light pressure to it. This massage has the potential to feel quite pleasurable for the man. Communicate while the massage is occurring in order to give him the most pleasure possible.

You can perform this type of massage in a number of different positions. The man could be lying down while you straddle his legs, he could be on his hands and knees while you sit or kneel behind him, he could lie across your lap while you sit on a bed, or you could do any position that is comfortable for you.

This massage does not need to lead to orgasm; at least that is not the goal. If it happens, that is fine; however, the aim of this massage is just to provide a relaxing and pleasurable experience for him.

That is the extent to which we will discuss the prostate massage, and we will now focus on the testicle massage. This type of massage is the most common and the most successful for relaxation and pleasure.

You can perform the testicle massage in several different positions. The man could be lying down on the bed, he could be reclining in a chair, be in a sitting position, or you any other position that is comfortable for him. This massage does not need to lead to orgasm- that is not the goal. If it happens, that is fine; however, the aim of this massage is simply to provide a relaxing and pleasurable experience for the man.

Remember from our discussion of the classic massage, if you have massage oil, that is preferable for this type of massage, but if not, you can use coconut oil. If you don't have either of those, you can use a sexual lubricant to lubricate your hands and avoid skin to skin friction. This is especially important when massaging the testicles. Before you touch him, warm your hands by rubbing them together. This will ensure that it feels nice and that it doesn't shock his testicles if you touch them with cold hands.

Begin by cupping your warm hand around his testicles. Gently move your hand in a circular motion. Be sure not to squeeze them too tightly, especially as you are beginning. Allow the testicles to warm up and relax. Massage them in a circular motion and apply gentle pressure to them. You can incorporate your second hand to provide him with extra sensation.

If he can handle it, you can gently touch his penis as you massage his testicles. If he becomes too erect and is about to reach orgasm, focus solely on the testicles. Massage the area around his testicles, including his inner thighs and his lower butt.
Let this massage flow and see where it takes you. Encourage him not to hold back and to let out any sounds that may find themselves escaping his mouth. Try to help him last as long as he can as you massage him.

After completing this massage, you may find that he is extremely horny, and this may lead to sex. If so, there is no problem with that. Enjoy yourselves and the increased pleasure that will come after such a sensual experience together.

Chapter 5: Kama Sutra Sex Positions

Today in pop culture, the Kamasutra's 64 sex positions are often discussed, making it seem like this book is a secret guide to penetrative sex. By this point in the book, you know that this is untrue. In this chapter, we are going to begin looking at some of the sex positions contained within the Kama Sutra to give you an idea of what exactly this book says about sex.

You may have actually performed one or two of these Kama Sutra sex positions without even knowing that they came from this ancient book. In this chapter, we are going to begin our discussion of the Kama Sutra sex positions by looking at the easiest and simplest sex positions that it contains. In the chapters that follow, we are going to look at Kama Sutra positions for intimacy, as well as some of the more advanced sex positions.

Many people wish to try these sex positions for themselves, and they have become quite popular in the mainstream media today. Many variations can be found, which have come as a result of tweaking the original positions of the Kama Sutra. People always push the envelope when it comes to sexual intercourse and physical pleasure, and many novel sex positions have come about as a result. Maybe you will recognize one or two of these!

Easy Kama Sutra Sex Positions

We are going to begin by looking at some of the easier Kama Sutra sex positions. These positions can be done by any couple, regardless of your strength or flexibility.

The Reverse Cowgirl

This position is quite a classic position, though it is one of the positions included in the book of Kama Sutra. This position is great for the female orgasm, as it allows the woman to take control since she is on top.

To get into this position, the man will lie down on his back on the bed. The woman will straddle him, but instead of facing his head, she will face his lower body, as depicted above. From here, the woman can lift her body up and down, using her legs at the speed and depth that feels best. She can also thrust at the angle that she enjoys the most, and she can feel the pleasure build as she moves her body. The man can sit back and relax, as the woman rides him sensually.

Below, you can see another variation of the Reverse Cowgirl Position, in which the woman opens up her body to allow for clitoral stimulation at the same time as penetration. In this variation, the woman will lie back so that she is lying on top of the man, facing away from him- his penis still inside of her. She can plant one of her hands back onto the bed to help hold herself up, while the other hand stimulates her clitoris. She can also use a vibrator on her clitoris in this position.

The Congress of a Dog

This position is called *The Congress of a Dog*. This is a position in which the man and woman are intended to emulate two animals having sex. In this case, they are intended to act as a male dog mating with a female dog. This is similar to the position above, but in this case, this position can be likened to the modern *Doggy Style* position.

This position is a favorite among men and women alike. Both women and men can get intense pleasure from this position because the angles at which their genitals come together creates harmonic pleasure for both parties.

To get into position, the woman gets on her hands and knees on the bed (or couch or floor, this position works anywhere really), and the man kneels behind her. He takes his erect penis and enters her vagina. He starts by slowly sliding it in and gradually begins getting faster and deeper. He does this by thrusting his hips and can control the pace in this way. He grabs onto her hips for a stronger thrust and pulls her body towards his to get himself deeper into her with each thrust. In this position, he has a view of her entire backside and can see it shake and bounce with each movement, making him hornier and hornier. He can talk dirty to her and grab her butt cheeks from here.

Doggy style is a position that women can get a lot of pleasure from. It is no surprise it is most often the favorite position, especially among young people, of both genders. Because of the curve of the man's erect penis and the angle at which it enters into the woman's vagina, her G-spot will likely be stimulated with each thrust. This G-spot stimulation means that it will be very likely that she will reach an orgasm from penetration. G spot stimulation can make a woman feel such intense full-body pleasure for quite a long time before she actually reaches an orgasm. Hitting her G-spot will continue to feel amazing for both the woman and man until finally, one or both of them cannot wait any longer, and ultimate pleasure is reached.

The Supported Congress

This position is a variety of the standing position, but it can be done with more ease than some of the other standing varieties.

To get into this position, the man stands in front of a wall with the woman standing in front of him, facing him. The woman lifts one knee and wraps her leg around one of the man's legs. The man can then slide his penis into her vagina; her leg raised to allow for deeper penetration and easier access. In standing positions, it may be more difficult to get the penetration right away, but with some maneuvering and adjustments because of height differences, you will eventually get into a comfortable rhythm.

This position is a midway point to another Kamasutra position called The Suspended Congress, where the woman has both legs up, and the man is holding them both under her knees and thrusting into her while holding her weight up. This position is quite difficult for the man, but if achieved, it can lead to very deep penetration.

The Supported Congress is a great place to start if you want to eventually try it with both legs up, as it is quite similar.

The Mare's Position

This Kama Sutra position is more of a sexual technique than a sex position itself. This sexual technique has the potential to change your sex life forever!

In this position, the man sits with his legs stretched out in front of him and his arms back, supporting his weight on the bed. The woman straddles him, facing away from him and lowers herself down onto his erect penis. Once inside of her, the woman uses her vaginal muscles to apply and release pressure on the man's penis, almost as if she is milking it. This makes for very pleasurable sensations on both the man's penis and the woman's vagina. This creates more stimulation on the man's penis, and also stronger sensations for the woman's vagina. This also strengthens her vaginal muscles, which in time will lead to stronger and more pleasurable orgasms for the woman!

Afternoon Delight

Afternoon Delight is a nice position to try on a quiet Sunday after a long work week when you are both feeling tired and want a bit of lazy sex. You can start this position off with some lazy hand and finger play and then progress it to penetration in the same position if you are already cuddling and don't want to move around too much. This position is optimal for stoners and sleepyheads.

The man lies down on his side, his erect penis poking out in front of him. The woman lies on her back at a 90-degree angle to the man's body, halfway down near his genitals. She then bends her knees, lifts her legs, and drapes them over the man's side, sliding her vagina towards him, so it is close to his penis. He can move forward to meet her and slide his penis in her vagina. The woman can lie back and relax while the man thrusts his hips. This position can be done while you watch a tv show, while you are reading or while you are both half-asleep and want a little bit of Afternoon Delight. If this inspires you to try something more involved once you get into the mood, you can easily transition to Missionary or Doggy Style from here.

The Lap Position

This next position is another that is best for male pleasure and the male orgasm. This position requires strength on the part of the man and the woman and is quite an athletic position, but this is why it is called an advanced sex position. Be careful when trying this one.

To get into position, the man will sit upright in a comfortable chair or on the edge of a bed with his feet planted on the floor. The woman will climb onto his lap and wrap her legs around behind the man or stick them straight out past him. Then, the man can insert his penis into the woman's vagina. From here, the woman will lean back until she is lying straight back, and her body is flat. While she does this, the man will have to hold onto her at her hips or her lower back, depending on your height variations. The man in this position will perform a combination of thrusting his hips into the woman from a seated position and pulling her onto his penis repeatedly. A high amount of upper body strength is required on the part of the man in this position. Place some pillows on the floor underneath the woman when trying this position, just in case. The woman can hold onto the man's arms for support as well here.

This position is great for the male's pleasure because it allows him to control the speed and depth of thrusting.

The Ascending Position

This position allows the woman to take full control of both her body and the man's penis and is good for women who have some trouble reaching orgasm in other sexual positions. The man takes a passive role in this position, with the woman's weight on top of him, which can be a huge turn-on. He can lie back and watch her take control and enjoy the pleasure he is getting from his penis inside of her and from watching the woman gyrate and find pleasure on top of him.

The man lies down on his back on the bed; he can prop up his head on a pillow if he wants a better view of the woman. She sits cross-legged on top of his genital area, her legs crossed over his waistline. She holds onto his penis and puts it into her vagina. She can wait to do this after oral or after giving him a handjob first, or she can get right to the penetration, depending on if they have already done foreplay prior to this. Once he is inside of her, she can lean back and rest her hands on his legs for support if needed. From here, she grinds her hips and can control her hip angles and control the speed of thrusting. In this leaned back position, her clitoris is perfectly accessible to be stimulated with her own hand. The man will be too far to do this for her as he is lying down, and her legs are holding his body down. The restriction of his movement by his naked woman will be sure to make the man so horny and frustrated that his penis will be rock hard. She can change the angle of her hips to reach G-spot stimulation by the man's penis. She may even be able to reach both clitoral and G-spot orgasms at the same time from this position.

The Cross Position

This position is similar to another position of the Kama Sutra, the Half-Pressed Position. If you like this one, you are sure to like the Half-Pressed Position too.

The woman lies on her back with one leg extended straight into the air. The man kneels in front of her, straddling her leg that is extended on the bed and holds onto her other leg, which is in the air. He can then move his body forward between her two legs until he is close enough to insert his penis into her vagina. He can hold her legs spread with his body, straddling one of them and placing the other one on his shoulder. By doing this, his hands will be free so that he can play with her clitoris, massage her breasts, rubbing his hands up and down her body or whatever they please. They can talk dirty to each other while looking at each other in the eyes and tell each other what they want to be done to them or what feels good.

Chapter 6: The Kama Sutra and Intimacy

For a book written so long ago, it is still quite relevant in terms of its discussions on ways to achieve intimacy and how to treat your partner well in the bedroom. In this chapter, we are going to talk about the best Kama Sutra sex positions for intimacy and what the Kama Sutra can teach you about improving the level of intimacy in your relationship or marriage.

What Is Intimacy?

Intimacy is very important between two people when part of a couple, especially in the bedroom. Intimacy is what brings you close and keeps you close. For this reason, we are going to address intimacy in this chapter before moving onto the rest of the concepts related to sex, sex positions, and techniques for you and your partner. Firstly, we will look at what intimacy means and the different types of intimacy that exist.

There are different types of intimacy, and here I will outline them for you before digging deeper into the intimacy that exists between couples. Intimacy, in a general sense, is defined as mutual openness and vulnerability between two people. There are different ways in which you can give and receive openness and vulnerability in a relationship. Intimacy does not have to include a sexual relationship (though it can); therefore, it is not only reserved for romantic relationships. Intimacy can also be present in other types of close relationships like friendships or family relationships. Below, I will outline the different forms of intimacy.

- Emotional Intimacy

Emotional intimacy is the ability to express oneself maturely and openly, leading to a deep emotional connection between people. Saying things like "I love you" or "you are very important to me" are examples of this. It is also the ability to respond maturely and openly when someone expresses themselves to you by saying things like "I'm sorry" or "I love you too." This type of open and vulnerable dialogue leads to an emotional connection. For a deep emotional connection to form, there must be a mutual willingness to be vulnerable and open with one's deeper thoughts and feelings. This is where this type of emotional intimacy comes from.

- Physical Intimacy

Physical intimacy is the type that most people think of when they hear the term "intimacy," and it is the kind that we will be most concerned with in this book, as it is the type of intimacy that includes sex and all activities related to sex. It also involves other non-sexual types of physical contact, such as hugging and kissing. Physical intimacy can be found in close friendships or familial relationships where hugging and kisses on the cheek are common, but it is most often found in romantic relationships.

Physical intimacy is the type of intimacy involved when people are trying to make each other orgasm. Physical intimacy is almost always required for orgasm. Physical intimacy doesn't necessarily mean that you are in love with the person you are having sex with; it just means that you are doing something intimate with another person in a physical way.

It is also possible to be intimate with yourself, and while this begins with the emotional intimacy of self-awareness, it also involves the physical intimacy of masturbation and physical self-exploration. I define sexual, physical intimacy of the self as being in touch with the parts of yourself physically that you would not normally be in touch with. If you are a woman, your breasts, your clitoris, your vagina, and your anus. If you are a man, your testicles, your penis, your anus. Being able to be physically intimate with yourself allows you to have more fulfilling sex, more fulfilling orgasms, and a more fulfilling overall relationship with your body. We will discuss this in more detail later on in this book. Allowing someone to be physically intimate with you in a sexual way is also an emotionally intimate experience, regardless of your relationship with the person. Being in charge of your own body while it is in the hands of another person is very important, and this is why masturbation is such a key element to physical intimacy.

You can think of physical intimacy as something that breaks the barrier of personal space. By this definition, this includes touching of any sort, but especially sexual intercourse, kissing touching, and anything else of a sexual nature. When you are having sex with anyone, regardless of whether you have romantic feelings for them or not, you are having a physically intimate relationship with them. The difference between a relationship that involves physical intimacy alone and no other forms of intimacy and a romantic relationship is that a romantic relationship will also involve emotional intimacy, shared activities and intellectual intimacy is that a deep and lasting romantic relationship will need to include all of these forms of intimacy at once. In this book, we are going to focus on how all of these types of intimacy come together to create a successful and deep romantic relationship between two people in love. We are going to begin by taking the next section to discuss how to maintain and increase the levels of intimacy in your relationship.

The Importance of Intimacy

Feeling awkward when it comes to talking about intimacy is one of the most human experiences a person can have. Sometimes, we fall into a sexual rut with someone, and then we realize that the fiery passion that used to burn at the base of your tummy has dimmed. The way to remedy this is to work on your intimacy.

When it comes to a long-term relationship, you likely have reached a high level of intimacy, and this is often what makes your sex life so rewarding. While you can achieve physical pleasure from having sex with anyone, or from masturbating alone, the connection that you feel when having sex with someone whom you are emotionally intimate with will lead your physical body to be in harmony with your emotions and this leads to great levels of both physical and emotional pleasure, which is exactly where the term "making love" comes from.

When you care about another person deeply, you care about bringing them pleasure in a variety of forms; sexual pleasure is one of them. When you bring two people together who are genuinely invested in the pleasure of each other, this forms a beautiful sexual bond full of pleasure in every sense. This is why intimacy is important in sex and why sex with intimacy is not only a physical act but also an emotional experience.

The Kama Sutra and Intimacy

The Kama Sutra has quite a few things to say about intimacy and how to maintain and restore it. As I mentioned, the Kama Sutra is a guide to love and to enjoy a pleasurable life with your partner. The Kama Sutra can serve as a guide for a long-term relationship or a marriage to keep sex interesting and to try new forms of intimacy. By keeping your relationship new and different, it will keep you both interested in what is to come, which will keep you both engaged in your relationship with one another.

The Kama Sutra text views sex as a spiritual act between two people that, with time, will increase a person's level of spirituality and sexual power. The book aims to help people to get in touch with their desires, which will aid them in reaching the full extent of their sexual power. It aims to liberate people in a sexual sense. These concepts were quite advanced for the time that the book was written, which is why this book is still so widely discussed to this day. Even though it was written so long ago, this book is still quite relevant for couples who wish to improve their relationship or their level of intimacy.

Sex is one part of a romantic relationship, but there are so many other aspects to achieving deep emotional closeness with another person, which can be learned through reading the Kama Sutra. The rest of this book will focus on discussing many of the benefits of the Kama Sutra and the ways that it can help you increase your level of intimacy with your partner.

For example, the Kama Sutra states that taking a bath together is a great way to build intimacy in a relationship.

Taking a bath together is a nice way to unwind after a long day and spend some time together on self-care. Doing self-care together is actually quite intimate, as this is something usually reserved for our time alone. Relaxing in a warm bath, either with bubbles or without, is a good way to set a mood. Sitting together in the closeness of a bathtub with the steam and the cleanliness will get you both in touch with your own bodies, but also in touch with their body. While this doesn't have to lead to sex, it can be a type of foreplay whether you intend for it to be or not. You may get in the bath together to spend some time to relax and share a few kisses. This may turn to making out and progress to much more. You may also get into the bath together to get yourselves in the mood for love and get naked while slowly easing into the sex. In Kamasutra, it is said that washing someone else's hair is a very intimate act. This may not be something that you have thought of before, or may not be something you are interested in. I assure you; it will lead to a greater level of intimacy with your partner if you give it a chance. When these acts of self-care that are usually done in private are shared with our partner, it can create magical moments of connection.

When you get into the bath, you can give each other head massages, back massages, or soap each other up. Begin kissing and making out and gliding your hands over your partner's wet body. Start with their back and arms and face. Let your desires take over both of you. As mentioned above, setting the mood like this will have you both focused on pleasure and touch and forgetting about all of your responsibilities and stressors in no time. This is good! We want to be focused when we have sex as a couple. Begin with one of you lathering the other with soap and shampoo in a slow and caring fashion. Rinse them off in the same way, taking care of their special needs and routines. Then, do the same the other way around. Take your time with this and enjoy the moment. You can do this as an act leading up to making love, or simply as a caring gesture for each other before bed.

It won't necessarily lead here, but a positive aspect of bathing together is that you will both be naked already for wherever you decide to take your sex from here. You will also both be clean, so any type of oral sex can be done without wondering when your partner last showered. As we all know, when we get comfortable with someone, we tend to put less into our image as we don't feel the need to impress them anymore!

How to Increase and Maintain Intimacy

Shared interests and activities are one of the forms of intimacy. This form of intimacy is less well-known, but it is also considered a form of intimacy. When you share activities with another person that you both enjoy and are passionate about, this creates a sense of connection. For example, when you cook together or travel together. These shared experiences give you memories to share, and this leads to bonding and intimacy (openness and vulnerability).

Being able to be vulnerable and open with your emotions is a requirement for intimacy. It is necessary to share oneself with the other person in a relationship. This mutual sharing of yourselves is what will lead to intimacy in the first place or an increase in intimacy.
Sometimes in a long-term relationship, you become so comfortable with each other that you don't have to communicate as much as you used to since you know each other so well. The key here is to continue communicating, even if you think the other person knows what you are thinking or feeling without you having to say it. By doing this, you keep the lines of communication open in your relationship. This avoids any chance of miscommunication or misunderstanding that would be perpetuated by a lack of communication. By having misunderstandings go unresolved, this could lead to resentment and an overall breakdown in communication, which can reduce levels of intimacy in the relationship.

This intimacy and vulnerability include being able to communicate about your desires- be they sexual desires or any other sort of desires. By sharing these with your partner, you will be able to ensure that they know how to please you in every sense of the word. This also leads to boundaries being set and upheld, since your desires include things you are comfortable and okay with, and this conversation will often lead to things which you are not okay with.

By learning these things about your partner, you can begin to work together to ensure each person's intimacy needs are met. For example, if your number one intimacy preference is for emotional intimacy and your partner likes to show their love in physical ways, you can discuss how they can begin to be more vocal about their love for you, and you can be more receptive to their physical displays of affection. Putting these things out on the table for discussion is the best way to learn about each other. You can never stop learning about your partner, and this will only strengthen your relationship.

It is important to communicate about your needs for intimacy regularly since people will grow and change over the course of a relationship. Especially in a long-term relationship, being aware of when a person's intimacy needs change is important to maintaining a good level of intimacy.

Another way that romance is shown and received is through gestures and gifts. This is probably the first thing you think of when you hear the term "romance" for example, bringing your partner flowers after they have a long day, or drawing them a bath when you know they are feeling stressed out. These gifts and gestures are ways of communicating that don't involve words. When you are in a long-term relationship, it is important to be able to show your love and adoration in ways other than saying "I love you," and gestures are a great way to do this. If you and your partner have gotten into a routine way of living with each other, try to spice things up by offering to cook them dinner or by changing something up in order to show them your feelings and bring about some extra romance.

This will help you to feel connected in new ways and will keep your spark alive, even if you are extremely comfortable with one another.

Kama Sutra Sex Positions for Intimacy

The Lotus

Arguably the most intimate position of them all is The Lotus. The Lotus position is most intimate because of the closeness of your entire bodies, infinitely pressed against each other at all points from head to toe, while being face to face.

The man sits on the bed cross-legged, his torso upright. His penis is erect and ready to get it on. The woman climbs on top of him and sits in his lap, wrapping her arms and legs around him. He holds her by wrapping his arms around her as well. With some shifting, they slide his penis inside of her. In this position, both people will be grinding more than they will be thrusting or humping. This is also what makes it so intimate. Grinding face to face while she is sitting on his lap with him inside of her, that is about as intimate as it gets.

In this position, you will not be doing any crazy thrusting, so it is ideal for a steamy make-out session, as your mouths will be so close that you can feel each other's breath the entire time. You can look into each other's eyes and whisper sweet nothings to them as you share this intimate experience.

The Position of Indra's Wife

To get into this position, the woman will lie down on her back, and she will bring her thighs to her sides. She will bend her knees so that her legs are bent at her sides. This opens up her entire vaginal area for intercourse. The man will lie on top of her and enter her from the front.

This position may take practice due to the flexibility is requires from the woman, but if she can accomplish this, it will be greatly pleasurable for her. This position opens up the woman to receive the man, which will result in deeper penetration, and thus, greater pleasure for both of them.

Half-Pressed Position

This position is another midpoint to a more difficult Kamasutra position requiring a lot of flexibility, but this one is quite good even at this midway point! The woman's legs are spread wide, and so it is very pleasurable for both of them.

The woman lies down on her back with her man kneeling in front of her. She stretches one leg straight out past him, besides his body and with the other leg, she bends her knee and places her foot on his chest. From here, he enters her vagina. The woman can move her hips up or down to give varying amounts of pressure to the man's penis for added pleasure for him. The stretching of her leg opens her clitoris up to potentially be stimulated by the base of his penis when he thrusts his hips and penetrates deeply into her. Having one foot planted on his chest keeps her legs open wide with every one of his thrusts in order to allow for deep penetration and clitoral stimulation.

The Hinge Position

You may have tried this position before, but may not have known that it was a Kamasutra position. This position is a spin on doggy style, so if you are a big fan of the classic Doggy Style position, give this one a try next time you want to experiment with something new!

The man kneels on the bed with one knee down as usual, and the other leg propped up at a 90-degree angle. The woman is on all fours in front of the man, supporting her weight on her forearms. The man slides his penis into the woman's vagina from behind. Both the woman and the man are able to control the depth and speed from this position as the woman can thrust herself back onto his penis, and the man can thrust his hips forward. With one knee bent, the man has more control over his thrusts and can hold onto his woman's hips for a quicker speed if they want a deeper thrust and a faster and more rough sex session. This is one of those positions where it makes a quick thrusting speed easy because his knee is propped up.

The Closed Door

This position is similar to the missionary position in that both people are lying down face-to-face, and the man is on top. The difference, however, and what makes this an advanced position is that the woman will keep her legs shut tightly the entire time. The man's penis can be inserted while her legs are open, and then once it is in, she will close her legs. What this does is constrict her vagina and make the canal tighter for the man's penis. In addition to this, if she is aroused, her vagina will be engorged, and the canal will be tighter already. Because of this, the man's penis will be hugged closely as it slides in and out of her, and this will make for extra pleasure for him.

The Lock

To get into this position, the woman will lean back and relax on the bed, getting ready to receive her partner. Her partner will then approach her from the front, placing her legs on his shoulders and lifting her buttocks onto his thighs, as he will be sitting on his legs, which are bent behind him. The woman will lift her upper body slightly so that she can wrap her arms around her partner's shoulders or his neck. The man will support the woman's lower back, and then he can thrust into her from his sitting position, and he can use his arms to lift and lower her body onto his penis.

Variation of the Yawning Position

Have you ever heard of the term 'balls deep'?
Have you ever wanted to try it?

The Yawning Position creates the deepest possible penetration of any sexual position. In the classic yawning position, the woman puts her legs in the air and spreads her legs with her knees straight, forming a 'V' shape. The man kneels in front of her and puts his penis inside her from the front. This creates an intense sensation for both partners.

The variation of The Yawning Position that we are going to look at can begin when the woman is fully aroused and wet. The woman lies on her back and lifts her legs into the air with her knees straight. The man lies on top of her in a missionary-like position. She places her straight legs on the man's shoulders. He can then enter her vagina with his erect penis and thrust his hips forward for the deepest penetration. As I said, this position makes for the deepest possible vaginal penetration of any sexual position, and if the woman can manage it, she can slide her legs to the outer edges of the man's shoulders which will make for maximum depth of penetration as her legs will be as far spread as possible.

The Standing Behind Position

In this position, the woman will stand facing a wall and will plant her hands on the wall in front of her. She will then bend her knees so that she can spread her legs. The man will come up behind and below her and come into her from behind. He can grab onto her hips or her shoulders so that he has something to hold onto, and he can use this to thrust deeper into her. This position is good in the shower or in any room of the house as having the woman planting her hands on the wall is both hot and safe when it comes to shower sex. This would be especially useful in the tight space of a stand-up shower. Just be sure to use lots of lubrication!

The Crab Position

In this position, the woman will lie on her back, and she will cross her legs. Then, she will hold her legs to her stomach. The man can assist by holding her legs there while he lies on top of her and enters her from the front. This position is quite intimate as it requires the man and woman to work together to hold her body in this posture. They are face to face while doing so, which makes it quite an intimate experience.

The Raised Feet Position

This position needs a little bit of flexibility, but it is also a sort of a stretch, so if you ease into it you should be able to reach it in a few minutes after your body is warmed up.

The woman lies on her back and brings her knees to her chest, wrapping her arms around them, her body forming a small ball shape. The man kneels near her buttocks and enters her vagina from a kneeling position in front of her. Her vagina will be quite easily accessible because her legs are lifted at her chest. If the flexibility is there, the man can now lean forward with his upper body, and with his own chest, he can hold her legs to her chest for her so that her hands are free. With her free hands, she can hold the back of his neck, pull his hair, or caress his face, depending on what direction you want to go with this sexual encounter. From here, the man's penis can very easily meet the woman's G-spot because of its curve, and this will make for an intense orgasm for both parties. The restriction of movement paired with the extreme closeness of their bodies is sure to make for some pent-up arousal that has no other way to be released than through a full-body orgasm.

The Waterfall

This position requires lots of trust between the woman and the man. The waterfall is a position in which the man has complete control. The man will begin by sitting in a chair with his feet on the floor. The woman will climb onto his lap and insert his penis into her. She can wrap her legs around his waist. Then, slowly she will lean all the way back until her head and arms are touching the floor (with pillows underneath). From here, the man will hold onto her hips and can move her body onto his penis at whatever speed and depth he wishes. He can also grab onto her breasts and massage her clitoris in this position if he wishes.

The Sitting Duck

Another position requiring complete trust is the sitting duck. This is a position that allows the woman to have complete control. The man will lie down on the floor on his back. The woman will straddle him and slide his penis into her. Then, one by one, she will cross her legs so that she is essentially sitting on his penis cross-legged. In this position, the man has no freedom of movement, and everything is up to the woman. She can even touch her clitoris in this position if she wishes.

Chapter 7: Advanced Kama Sutra Sex Positions

In this chapter, we are going to continue our examination of the Kama Sutra sex positions by looking at some of the more advanced positions. These positions will require more flexibility and strength from either the man, the woman or both.

While they require more strength and flexibility, they come with great rewards in the form of pleasure if you can get into them.

Advanced Kama Sutra Sex Positions

After reading through this list of advanced Kama Sutra sex positions, try some for yourself with your partner. Challenging yourselves to get into new sex positions will be an intimate and sexy experience that will benefit your relationship.

The Turning Position

The Turning Position is a fun one that you have probably never heard of before. It can add some fun into your stale sex life or some pizazz into a new and youthful relationship. This is one of the more challenging positions to master and requires quite a lot of communication from both parties. It will also require some practice to execute it seamlessly, but don't be intimidated; you will master it in no time and begin to wow all of your present and/or future partners! This position is well suited to couples who would like to try something different and explore new ways of reaching pleasure together at a point in their relationship when they are comfortable with each other and know how to communicate well.

The position begins in the classic Missionary position (as discussed previously in this book) with the man on top of the woman and both of them face to face. The man's legs should both be between the woman's legs, and his penis is already inside of her. This is where it gets more complicated, so listen closely. The man now lifts his left leg over the woman's right leg and then proceeds to lift his right leg over her right leg, keeping his penis inside of her, and continues by moving his upper body in a clockwise direction until he is at a 90-degree angle to her body, essentially lying across her (while still penetrating her). He will then move his legs over her upper body, one leg at a time, continuing to turn around in a clockwise direction so that his feet are at either side of her head, still maintaining the positioning of his penis inside her vagina. From here, he will complete the turn and come back to his starting Missionary position without ever removing his penis from her vagina. Doing this seamlessly and sensually without accidentally pulling out of her will require some practice and cooperation on both of their parts. When it is done well, it looks like he is turning in a slow and smooth circle around her body.

This position will lead to new sensations for both people as every single angle of his penis inside her vagina will be felt by both of them. It will lead to new challenges for both of them as it is a complex position to try. And it will lead to the exploration of new points of view of the other person's body, all three of these things leading to greater intimacy and closeness between partners.

The Scissors Position

This position is a little difficult to get yourselves into, but once you do, it will be well worth the effort. To begin, the man will sit on the bed with his arms behind him, holding his weight up but leaning back. Then, he will bend one of his knees, so his leg is bent. The woman will lie down on the bed face-down and with her head at the opposite end of the bed as the man. She will spread her legs and move her body toward the man's until their bodies meet. When they meet, their bodies will look like two pairs of scissors crossed into one another. From here, the man will insert his penis into her vagina. The woman can move her body up and down on his penis, and the man can thrust into her. It may take a bit of time to develop a rhythm in this position, but when you do, you will both feel intense pleasure.

The Plow

As the name suggests, this position is designed to make you emulate a human plow, but I assure you, this position is much sexier than it sounds. This position is a great introduction to some of the more interesting and difficult Kama Sutra sex positions. This is a great option if you wish to get acquainted with the world of Kamasutra for the first time and wish to challenge yourselves.

You, as the woman, lie face-down on the bed with your hips and legs sticking off the end and support yourself on your elbows. Your man stands on the floor beside the bed, his body positioned between your legs. He then lifts your lower half up by your hips and thighs and inserts his penis into your vagina, while supporting your legs the entire time. You can take a more passive role in this position, and he can adjust the angle he holds your legs at for maximum pleasure.

The Peg Position

The Peg has a sexy name that implies pleasure and may even have you turned on already. This is a more difficult position, certainly more difficult to get yourselves into, but it comes with the reward of a great all-encompassing orgasm for both parties if it can be done.

The man lies on his side, and the woman lies facing him on her side, with her head towards his feet. The woman will lift her knees towards her chest and place one of her legs underneath the man's legs and have the other on top of his legs. Essentially, she is hugging his legs with her entire body. She slides up so that her vulva is next to his penis. When aligned properly, he can penetrate her and can achieve depth and control as she is positioned perfectly for his penis to enter her. The woman wraps her arms around his legs, and he can use his hands and arms to help with his thrusting, or if she is comfortable, he can use his hands to stimulate her anal area with his fingers or a toy. The woman is positioned like this allows for all of her vulvae to be open and accessible once again, and this is what will lead to a stronger orgasm for her. The man being able to see all of her and to play with her anus will lead to a stronger orgasm for him.

The Posture of Splitting Bamboo

The woman will lie on her back and have the man lie on top of her, sliding his body in between her legs. The woman will lift one of her legs and put it on one of his shoulders, and the other will stretch out past his body. From here, he pushes his hips forward and can easily slide his penis into her vagina, which is open and in a perfect position for penetration. The man will do the thrusting here. After some time, the woman will switch and put the other leg on his other shoulder. She can continue to alternate as they engage in intercourse.

This position requires flexibility in the woman but gives a deep penetration once accomplished and almost rides that line between pleasure and pain due to the stretch.

This position allows for deep penetration as well as varied pressure on the man's penis, which will be extremely pleasurable for him.

If the woman is feeling flexible and wants to try a new position that will have both of them benefitting from a deeper penetration than most of the classics, this position will be a great choice.

The Suspended Congress

To get into this position, the man will stand facing a wall with the woman standing in front of him, her back to the wall. She will then jump into his arms and wrap both her arms and her legs around him. Once here, he can insert his penis into her vagina while holding onto her buttocks or underneath her knees. He can lean her back on the wall in front of him for support so that he does not have to support her entire weight in his arms. If he holds onto her underneath her knees, this will open her up so that her vagina is easily accessible. The fact that she is suspended coupled with this will make it so that there is deep penetration occurring, and this will be pleasurable for both the man and the woman. Deep penetration is great for the female orgasm because there are two places located deep within the vagina that, when stimulated, lead to a very intense orgasm for her. The penis must achieve continuous deep penetration in order for this to happen, and in this position, it is quite possible.

This position is great for the female orgasm because of the angle that the man's penis enters her vagina. It is also quite pleasurable for the woman because the man is in control in this position, so the woman can relax and enjoy the pleasure he is bringing to her body.

Crossed Keys

The Crossed Keys is a relatively simple position but makes for an interesting and new position to try if you have never done it before. This is a great introduction to the world of more complex and acrobatic positions. While this is not quite acrobatic, it will introduce you to this type of sex.

Have your woman lie down on her back at the edge of the bed with her legs sticking straight up into the air, knees straight. She then crosses one leg in front of the other, keeping them sticking straight up. Stand at the edge of the bed and grab a hold of her outstretched legs. Then, with your feet planted on the floor, slide your penis into her vagina and holding her legs as a stable base, you can thrust harder and faster as she likes it. With her legs crossed over each other like this, it tightens her vagina so that it creates a tighter and more pleasurable environment for your penis as well as creating more pleasure for her because the tighter vagina canal will mean more contact of your penis with the walls of her vagina and will lead to G-spot stimulation.

The Toad Position

This position is similar to The Toad (or The Frog) stretch that you may have done in a yoga class before. Facing the floor with bent knees spread wide to get those hips stretched. I bet you never thought that would help you in your sex life... But low and behold, turn that stretch over, and you have The Toad position! I will explain in more detail as follows.

The woman lays on her back, bending her knees towards her chest and spreading her knees open wide. This opens her body up for easy penetration, clitoris access, and maximum exposure of all of her pleasurable parts to her man's body that will be rubbing against them. The woman's entire vulva can be a pleasurable area if it is exposed to touch like the man's pelvis or hips rubbing it. This, coupled with the clitoris being rubbed at the same time, will drive her crazy. The man lies on top of her and slides his penis into her vagina, having lots of space for deep penetration. In this position, the woman's clitoris can easily be stimulated from the thrusting motion of the man's body on top of hers or from the base of his penis when he comes as close to her as possible with each thrust. If the woman wants to take more control, once he is inside of her, she can wrap her legs around his waist and use them to pull his hips towards her along with his movement to increase the pressure and depth of his penetration.

The Widely Opened Position

The name of this position means that the woman's entire body is widely opened to receive pleasure in the form of her man. Her body is in a position that says she is ready for this experience.

As the woman, lie down on a bed on your back with your man on top of you, both of his legs between yours. Have him hold his weight up, so he is hovering over you, allowing you to get into position before he comes into you. Proceed to throw your head all the way back so you can see your headboard and arch your back at the same time, pushing your breasts into the air. Use your elbows behind you to support you and lift your hips into the air to meet your man's body that is hovering over top of you. Hold onto this position and (in whatever sensual language you feel turned on by) invite your man to put his penis into you. While you hold yourself up in this position, he can then thrust his penis in and out with varying speed and force. If it proves to be too difficult for you to hold up your body weight the entire time, ask your man to help you by holding himself up with one arm, and by wrapping his other arm under your lower back to support you a bit.

So why hold your body in this difficult position you ask? The reason for this is that the woman's raised position allows the man to achieve deep penetration like the vagina is raised up and more exposed to the front where the man's penis is. Further, because she is pressed up in an arched-back position, her clitoris is lifted and exposed more than ever, which will allow for the friction of the man's thrusts against her body to stimulate the clitoris with each pump.

The Standing Position

The standing position may be a little difficult, but with practice, you might just add this one into your regular rotation. Many variations can be done with this position, depending on what feels best for both of you and how your stamina is.

To start, it may be easier to have the man standing against a wall so that he can lean his back onto it for support. The woman then will stand in front of the man, facing away from him. Now for the tricky part, you will need to play around a bit to find the right way for both of you to reach this. The man will now need to insert his penis into his female partner's vagina from behind. This will work best if the man leans back against the wall, lowering his body so that he can push his hips upward toward his partner's vulva. The woman can reach back and hold onto the man if she wishes.

The Fixing of a Nail

This is another position that involves the man on top of the woman in a position similar to the Missionary Position, but this is a more difficult variation.

In this position, the woman will place one of her legs on the man's head, and the other will be stretched out below her. The Kama Sutra states that this position will require a lot of practice to accomplish. Once you are able to do this position, you will benefit from a very deep penetration, as well as a high likelihood of G-Spot stimulation for the woman.

The Pressed Position

This position is a little challenging, but it has great benefits for those who can achieve it. This position requires a little bit of flexibility, but it also acts as a stretch, so if you ease into it you should be able to reach the full position within a few minutes after your body is warmed up.

To get into this position, the woman lies on her back and brings her knees to her chest, wrapping her arms around them, her body forming a small ball shape. The man kneels near her buttocks and enters her vagina from a kneeling position in front of her. Her vagina will be quite easily accessible because her legs are lifted at her chest. If the flexibility is there, the man can now lean forward with his upper body, and with his own chest, he can hold her legs to her chest for her so that her hands are free. With her free hands, she can hold the back of his neck, pull his hair, or caress his face, depending on what direction you want to go with this sexual encounter. From here, the man's penis can very easily meet the woman's G-spot because of its curve, and this will make for an intense orgasm for both parties. The restriction of movement paired with the extreme closeness of their bodies is sure to make for some pent-up arousal that has no other way to be released than through a full-body orgasm.

The Sphinx Position

The Sphinx gets its name from the ancient Egyptian sculptures of women in this type of position, although without the man penetrating her. These sculptures and statues were not erotic! But you can make your own erotic Sphinx at home after you read on about this position.

The woman lies face down, supporting herself on her elbows. She stretches one leg out behind her and bends the other out to the side of her body to spread out and open up access to her vagina. The man lies on top of the woman, and his penis enters her vagina from behind. This may be hard if he has a smaller penis, but he will need to get as low as possible, and it should still work! The weight of the man lying on top of the woman makes for added pleasure for her because it spreads her legs further apart so that her pleasure centers are more accessible. It also increases pressure on her pelvis, which will help in leading to an orgasm, and when it does, an even stronger and better orgasm because the pressure from the outside meets the pressure from the inside and voilà! Full body bliss.

X-Rated

The X-Rated is a position that the man will love if he has not already suggested it sometime in your relationship! You can probably glean this from the name though.

If you are the man, lie down on your back, and the woman will lie on top of you, facing down your body with her head at your feet. She will wrap her arms around your legs and spread her legs so that they are on either side of your hips. She can then slide up or down your body to adjust for ease of inserting your penis into her. If it is easier, start in reverse cowgirl (like we examined earlier in this book) and have her lie forward after you penetrate her so that she is lying on your legs. She can wrap her arms around your legs after this. Either you can pump your hips into her with her lying on your penis, or she can lift her hips up and down on your penis for the magic to happen. She can be in control of the depth and speed of penetration by doing this if you wish. You as the man in this position, will likely want your head propped up by a pillow or three so that you can take in the full view of your woman below the waist with her naked bum in the air, gyrating on your erection in all her beauty.

This position is loved by many men, but also by many women for the same reasons that they love reverse cowgirl. Deep penetration, the ability to be in control of the humping and G-spot stimulation. The trifecta of female pleasure!

Chapter 8: Other Kama Sutra Techniques

Now that you have gained a solid understanding of the sex positions that are included within the Kama Sutra, we are going to look at some of the other topics that the text discusses.

Techniques That Do Not Involve Penetration

As I mentioned in the first chapter of this book, the Kama Sutra contains much more than a list of sex positions. In this section, we are going to look at some of the other demonstrations of love that the Kama Sutra teaches.

These techniques are said to be intended for foreplay. They will help you and your partner to get in the mood by touching and kissing each other. They can also be done anytime that you wish to share some intimate moments with your significant other.

Kissing

The Kama Sutra discusses kissing as one of the many ways to connect with your partner, aside from having sexual intercourse. The Kama Sutra mentions kissing as a way to connect with your partner before sex, during sex, or any other time you wish.

There are numerous places that the Kama Sutra deems the "places for kissing." They are as follows;

- Forehead
- Cheeks
- Eyes
- Throat
- Bosom
- Breasts
- Lips
- Interior of the Mouth
- Joints of the Thighs

- Arms
- The navel

There are also different techniques for kissing. They are listed below.

1. The Normal/Nominal Kiss

A young girl kisses her partner with a small peck on the lips.

2. The Straight Kiss

When two people make contact with their lips.

3. The Turned Kiss

One partner holds the head and chin of the other partner and kisses them.

4. The Throbbing Kiss

When a young girl kisses her partner and moves only her bottom lip.

5. The Touching Kiss

The man and woman touch each other's hands, close their eyes, and the girl touches her partner's lips with her tongue.

6. The Bent Kiss

When the two kissers bend their heads and kiss.

7. The Pressed Kiss

When one partner kisses the lower lip of the other partner with force.

8. The Greatly Pressed Kiss

When one partner takes the lower lip of the other between two fingers and then touches the lip with their tongue using great force.

9. Kiss of the Upper Lip

When a man kisses the woman's upper lip, and she kisses his lower lip.

10. A Clasping Kiss

When one person takes both of the other person's lips with their lips. It is stated that a woman should only have this kind of kiss with a man who has no mustache.

11. The Kiss that Kindles Love

A woman looks at her partner's face while he is asleep and kisses it.

12. The Kiss That Turns Away

When a woman kisses a man while he is fighting with her, or while he is busy with business. This kiss happens when his mind is "turned away."

13. The Kiss That Awakens

When a man comes home late, and his wife is already asleep, he kisses her.

14. Kiss Showing The Intention

When a person kisses the reflection of their lover in a mirror or water.

15. The Transferred Kiss

When a person kisses a child, who is sitting on his lap or a picture while his lover is in the room.

16. The Demonstrative Kiss

When a man kisses a woman's finger if she is standing up, her toe if she is sitting down or while a woman is shampooing her lover's body.

Scratching and Biting

The following list includes several forms of biting which are done to show your partner that you love them. It can also be done as a type of foreplay if this person is turned on by biting.

- Swollen Bite
- Hidden Bite
- Point
- Line of Point
- Coral and the Jewel
- Line of the Jewels
- Broken Cloud
- Biting of the Boar

Striking

The Kama Sutra also talks about something called striking. This may come as a surprise to you, but striking is something that many people find pleasure in. Striking is a form of rough sex, but one that does not involve anything too serious in terms of the acts that it calls for.

Striking can be done in a gentle way, or in a firmer way, depending on what the couple themselves prefer. This can be seen as an introduction to rough sex. In today's world, rough sex is also sometimes referred to as BDSM. BDSM stands for Bondage, Discipline, Dominant and Submissive, Sadism, and Masochism. The four letters in this acronym overlap to mean a wide variety of things. Under this umbrella, there is something for everyone and probably many things that you didn't even know about that turn you on. It is all about finding pleasure without restrictions or judgment and letting yourself explore a different world of sex.

When comparing the striking techniques of the Kama Sutra to modern-day BDSM, many similarities can be drawn. More specifically, this technique could be compared to S&M. Sadism and masochism, commonly known as S&M, is the addition of pain play into your sexual experiences. The thin line between pleasure and pain is ridden here to give extreme pleasure mixed with a little bit of fear. The sadist is the person who gets pleasure from inflicting pain on their partner or rather is turned on by the power it has. The masochist is the person who gets pleasure from being in pain at the hands of their partner and riding the line between pleasure and pain.

Places You Can Strike

When it comes to striking, the Kama Sutra mentions six places that you can strike. They include the following;

- Head
- Shoulders
- Back
- Sides

- Between the breast
- The Jaghana (the buttocks)

The Ways You Can Strike

There are also 4 specific ways that you can strike. They include the following;

- Back of the Hand
- Fingers spread out
- With Open Hand
- With Fist

A Note on Sexual Compatibility

Concerning the techniques above that involves scratching, biting, and striking, one topic that this brings up is sexual compatibility. Firstly, what is Sexual Compatibility?

Sexual compatibility between people means that they share the same beliefs, values, preferences, desires, and expectations related to sex. This can include things like what sex acts you prefer the most, your level of sex drive, the type of sex you wish to have, including any fetishes, and so on. For example, if you have a very high sex drive, meaning that you need and expect to have sex every single day, you will be sexually compatible with someone who also has a high sex drive. If you were in a sexual relationship with someone who had a very low sex drive, this would be incompatible as you would likely become frustrated by their low need for frequent sex. Another example is if you desire a lot of oral sex and you require this in order to become fully aroused during sex, you would be sexually compatible with someone who also enjoys oral sex, especially giving it. If you were with someone who did not feel comfortable with oral sex at all, this would not make for a sexually compatible match.

Your preferences and values do not have to be exactly the same as the person you are in a sexual relationship with, but they must be able to fit together (like yin and yang) for a sexual relationship to be compatible. An example of this is if you enjoy slow and tender sex, but your partner enjoys rough sex. This could mean that you are sexually incompatible, but it could also work if you are both able to meet in the middle. You could start off by having slow and tender foreplay while your arousal builds, and when you are both ready for penetration, the sex can begin to lead towards a rougher style. As long as both people are comfortable with this, this sexual relationship could work.

When it comes to kinks and fetishes, sexual compatibility is quite important. For example, BDSM, including dominance and submission. If you have one partner who is sexually dominant and the other who prefers submission, this works out very well. If, however, you prefer dominance and so does your partner or if both prefer submission, you may have some trouble reaching a place of agreement when it comes to your sexual encounters. The dominant person will not usually become turned on by being told what to do, and the submissive person will usually not be too excited by telling someone else what to do. While these can work on a spectrum and people can enjoy a bit of both, many people are either dominant or submissive.

Taking this into account is important because when trying new things in the bedroom, it is important to ensure that you and your partner are both comfortable with the new techniques that you are introducing.

Double Oral Sex Technique: The Roll

This position is a wonderful oral sex position. Remember, as I mentioned that the book of Kama Sutra includes a variety of oral sex positions, not only positions in which to have intercourse. This is one of those positions.

In this position, the man will be stimulating the woman's anus and/or vagina orally while she gives him oral sex at the same time.

To get into this position, the woman will lie on the bed on her back, and she will hold onto her ankles, spreading her legs out to the side as much as possible. The man will come over the woman, facing her feet, and he will place one of his knees on either side of her head, and one of his hands on either side of her hips. He will then lower himself down so that he can stimulate her orally. The woman will pull her ankles toward her head so that her body rolls up into a ball, giving the man more ease of access. She will then take his penis in her mouth and stimulate him orally. This position allows both people to benefit from oral sex at the same time. The man can also use one of his hands to stimulate the woman anally, vaginally, or clitorally while he gives her oral.

Oral Sex for Men

This position is done when the man is standing up, and the woman is on her knees in front of him, giving him oral sex. You may be thinking that this is not an advanced sex position because you have done it many times, and it is quite common. Here, however, we are going to make it an advanced position.

To make this into an advanced sex position, while the woman is kneeling in front of the man and giving him oral sex, she can use one of her hands to hold onto his testicles and gently massage them. This will add to his pleasure quite a bit. She can also (or instead) use her other hand to reach around behind him and stimulate his anus with her finger. She can move her finger around the outside of his anus, stimulating the sensitive skin there, and this will make him feel immense amounts of pleasure. Doing both of these at the same time will make it virtually impossible for him not to orgasm very quickly.

Oral Sex for Women

Similar to the previous position, this one may seem as if it is common and has been done a million times, however, with this position as well, we will be adding some elements that take it from an easier position to an advanced one.

To get into this position, the woman lies down on her back, and the man will lie down as well, but instead of lying down parallel to her with his mouth at her clitoris, he will lie down with his mouth at her clitoris but his body perpendicular to her. This way, their bodies form the letter 'T.' Lying like this makes it so that the woman can have the most pleasure possible from oral sex because it makes it easier for the man to stimulate her clitoris for a longer period without becoming fatigued. It is easier to move your tongue in an up and down motion than in a side to side motion, and when forming a T with their bodies, his tongue can move up and down (side to side on the clitoris) and give her the most pleasure possible. This is because stimulating the clitoris in this way is the most likely to lead to orgasm, whereas moving over it in a top to bottom motion will not lead to as much pleasure or as much chance of orgasm. When lying in a classic oral sex position of the man between the woman's legs, it would be hard for him to move his tongue in a side to side motion for a long time as it would become very fatigued, but if he moves his tongue up and down, it will not be as pleasurable for her. For these reasons, this T position is the best choice for oral sex for a woman.

Chapter 9: The Kama Sutra Theories of Romance

In this chapter, we are going to look at the Kama Sutra in terms of the way it discusses romance. There are a variety of tips that the Kama Sutra contains, which are related to romance, including tips for cuddling and embracing. We will then look at some Kama Sutra theories of relationships. The Kama Sutra outlines various relationships that we will look at in this chapter.

Kama Sutra Cuddling and Embracing

The first embrace we will discuss is called *The Milk and Water Embrace*. This position gets its name from the idea that the two people in this position are enmeshed and become so close that they lose themselves in the other person. Interestingly, this position can be used as a loving embrace after sex or a cuddle before sex.

The man sits on the edge of the bed, his legs planted on the floor. The woman approaches him and climbs into his lap, her face to his. She wraps her legs around his waist and her arms around his neck. He holds onto her by wrapping his arms around her back. The woman is pressed against her man, and this is a great position for cuddling, or she can keep both arms around his neck for a closer embrace.

This position is quite easy to get into and only requires a bit of strength from the man. Both of their bodies are supporting each other in this position, which is what makes it so intimate. Their bodies are touching at every point from head to toe, and they can breathe together and feel each other's heartbeat. This is why this position is said to be two people becoming one, like mixing milk and water when you can't tell where one ends, and the other begins.

From here, if they wish to transition in this position to penetrative sex, the woman can position herself so that her legs are open wide and receive his penis. To begin thrusting, they can work together, with the man using his feet on the floor as support. He can move his hips up and down, and the woman can grind her hips on his lap for pleasurable clit stimulation. If she wants, the woman can touch herself during this movement for extra pleasure.

The Kama Sutra also mentions several positions for cuddling and embracing aside from the Milk and Water Embrace. These other positions can be included after sex or during a time when you and your partner wish to hold each other and share an intimate moment.

Each time you make love with your partner, it is a bonding experience resulting in increased closeness. Each of these experiences of lovemaking contributes to your shared moments and your intimacy. Because of this, post-sex behavior is very important.

After a great orgasm, you probably collapse on top of each other, short of breath and muscles tired. Having made love, you are probably feeling quite close and romantic with each other since you have made each other feel warm and pleasured like no other. Therefore, after collapsing into each other, you will likely want to be as close as possible. We are going to look at some of the closest and romantic positions for that after-sex recovery cuddle.

First is the *head on chest* cuddle. Lie down on your back with your partner lying beside you on their side, their head resting on your chest or in the crook of your neck. In this position, you can hold each other with your arms wrapped around their body, and you can give your partner soft forehead kisses.

Second is the spooning position. Both of you will lie on your sides facing the same direction, with your bodies pressed against each other. Spooning is a position in which you can have sex as well, with the man behind the woman. This position is good for a lazy Sunday morning when you are both sleepily horny for each other. If you have just finished having sex in this position, you can nicely transition to cuddling in this same position right after he pulls out of her. When he finishes, he can then wrap his arms around her and kiss her softly on the cheek.

These cuddling positions are perfect for the after-sex whispered conversation that often happens when you have sex in a relationship. You can tell the person that what they just did to you made you feel amazing, or that they were so sexy when they did that certain thing. You can share words like "*I love you*" and gentle kisses.

If you want a position that allows you to share kisses on the lips and gazes into each other's eyes, this next position will be best for you. Lie on your sides facing each other with your legs intertwined and your faces just inches from each other. From here, you can romantically gaze into their soul and enjoy the after-sex glow on your partner's face.

A common practice after sex is that you may also want to share the intimacy of a nap together. Any of these cuddling positions previously mentioned will be perfect for a post-sex nap. The tiredness that you feel after an orgasm is best accompanied by a cat nap with your lover. The vulnerability of sleeping naked together is something you don't share with just anyone and is a special moment with the person you love.

We are all busy people in this day and age, and sometimes we won't have time to lie around with our partner after sex. So how do we maintain that intimacy of a post-sex cuddle if we have just squeezed in a quickie before breakfast and the kids will wake up soon? The deeper idea here is the connection and making time for our partner. Spending time after sex is a way of showing each other that despite the busy lives we lead, we are still doing life together and share a bond with them that we don't share with anyone else. There are other ways to show this post-sex if you simply don't have time for a cuddle. However, I would encourage you to try to set aside even two to three minutes after sex to get into a close embrace with your partner and to just enjoy their presence without the distraction of life or even of the act of sex. To come together without any sort of action and get quiet together.

Kama Sutra Theories of Relationships

There are a variety of different relationships that are discussed in the Kama Sutra. Some of these relationships are between a woman and a man who are married, some are between a man and his mistress, and others involve group relationships. Below I have outlined some of the different relationships that the Kama Sutra talks about, including how the Kama Sutra says that these individuals should interact when it comes to sex.

Before moving on, note that Kama Sutra discusses sex using the term *Congress*. You will see examples of this below.

The United Congress

The United Congress refers to a sexual encounter involving one man and two women. The Kama Sutra mentions that a man should enjoy sex with two women at the same time, both of whom love him equally.

When a man is having sex with two women at once, this is called the *United Congress*.

The Congress of the Herd of Cows

The Kama Sutra also mentions group sex, though it may not be the type of group sex that you would expect. The type of group sex that is discussed in the text involves many women and one single man.

When a man is enjoying sex with many women, this called *Congress of the Herd of Cows*.

The Gramaneri

Another form of group sex that is discussed in the Kama Sutra is something called *The Gramaneri*.

This kind of group sex involves many men that are having sex with one woman. The woman involved is usually married to one of the men who are present in this group sexual encounter. In this scenario, there are two options. The men could opt to have sex with the woman one at a time, each of the men taking a turn.

Alternatively, all of the men could have sex with the woman at the same time. For this option, the Kama Sutra specifies the following arrangement; One man holds the woman, another man penetrates her vaginally, another man is given oral sex by her, and another holds her "middle part." Then, they will alternate and continue to "enjoy her" in all areas, taking turns at each part of her body.

Keep in mind that the Kama Sutra was written long ago. It was written to be read by men. Further, it was written in a time and place where a man could have multiple women at the same time, even if he was married.

Conclusion

The hope is that this book has given you the tools you need to keep your sex life fresh and ever-changing by introducing you to the world of Kama Sutra. Maybe you have tried some of the positions from the Kama Sutra before, and you needed help to learn more. Maybe you are new to sex, and you wanted to study up on different positions to try for beginners. You now have a whole arsenal of positions to try. Maybe you have tried all of the classics and are looking to get into something completely new and adventurous. Whatever experience you came with, I hope that you are leaving this book having learned a few new things to take with you into your sexual adventures from here forward. I hope this serves as a tool for you to explore and discover yourself and your future partners.

What to Do Next?

As you go on in your sexual life, stay open-minded, and never stop listening to your body. People change, and you will likely change as well. By being open to these changes and being receptive to them in yourself and your long-term partner, you will be able to ensure you are always getting the most out of sex. Don't forget to communicate with your partner to better understand them and sex in general, all communication leads to learning, and this is a great thing when it comes to sex and relationships.

There is something for everyone in this book, so continue to pass it on to your friends and your partners so that we can live in a world of educated and informed sexual beings. The Kama Sutra is a guidebook for love and everything involved in loving another person. It is more than just a book of sex positions, but these days most people only know it for its complex and flexibility-requiring positions for intercourse. The book of Kamasutra includes a general guide to living well in ways other than through sex. It includes a guide to foreplay, a guide to kissing and touching, as well as other ways to achieve intimacy with your partner, such as bathing together and giving each other massages. I hope that after reading this book, you understand and can appreciate this text in a new way.

In addition to the positions enclosed in these pages, I hope that you learned how to focus on your pleasure and the pleasure of your partner, how to be present during sex, and how to become more sexually intuitive, to feel the most pleasure possible. What a waste of pleasure it would be to always have sex in the same positions over and over and never fully reach your potential for orgasm! If you haven't already, try some of the things you've learned through reading this book, and I assure you that your sex life will be much better for it!

You are now ready to go off into the world of sexual exploration and have great orgasms from here on out. Stay curious and keep learning!

How to Benefit from the Kama Sutra for Life

1. New Sex Positions

After reading about the sex positions of the Kama Sutra, you can now incorporate them into your own sex life. Read back through the chapters on sex positions with your partner and try these new positions with them. This will make for a fun and interesting experience for the two of you. Who knows, you may even find a new favorite position for intercourse.

2. New Relationship Dynamics

As I mentioned previously, though it is an ancient book, the Kama Sutra mentions same-sex relations. Within the book, same-sex relations are referred to as *the third nature*. As I mentioned, it also talks about group sex and group relationships. What this means is that although the Kama Sutra was written so long ago, in some ways, it has become more and more relevant over the years. As our modern-day relationships have shifted and changed, the Kama Sutra has stood the test of time. In some ways, it can be said that this book has aged well.

3. New Fantasies and Kinks to Explore

In addition to talking about group sex and same-sex encounters, the Kama Sutra also recognizes that there are many different ways that people find sexual satisfaction. The Kama Sutra allows for the exploration of a person's *kinks*. For example, the Kama Sutra mentions rough sex and how it can bring sexual pleasure and satisfaction to some. As kinks and fetishes have become more widely accepted in our world, this book has begun to show that it has aged well in yet another way.

This book is here to provide you with everything you want to know about the Kama Sutra and so much more! Do yourself a favor, your partner a favor, and everyone that you will ever have sex with favor by reading this book and teaching yourself as much as you possibly can. Give your partner the gift of informing yourself about how to please them like never before using these ancient but ever-relevant positions. All you have to do is click that download button, and you will be able to begin your journey to becoming the best sexual being you have ever been!

Taboo Sex Stories:

Erotica Seductive Sex Fantasies for Adults. Threesome, GangBang, BDSM and Femdom

© **Copyright 2019 by CHASECHECK LTD - All rights reserved.**

The content contained within this book may not be reproduced, duplicated or transmitted without direct written permission from the author or the publisher.

Under no circumstances will any blame or legal responsibility be held against the publisher, or author, for any damages, reparation, or monetary loss due to the information contained within this book. Either directly or indirectly.

Legal Notice:

This book is copyright protected. This book is only for personal use. You cannot amend, distribute, sell, use, quote or paraphrase any part, or the content within this book, without the consent of the author or publisher.

Disclaimer Notice:

Please note the information contained within this document is for educational and entertainment purposes only. All effort has been executed to present accurate, up to date, and reliable, complete information. No warranties of any kind are declared or implied. Readers acknowledge that the author is not engaging in the rendering of legal, financial, medical or professional advice. The content within this book has been derived from various sources. Please consult a licensed professional before attempting any techniques outlined in this book.

By reading this document, the reader agrees that under no circumstances is the author responsible for any losses, direct or indirect, which are incurred as a result of the use of information contained within this document, including, but not limited to, — errors, omissions, or inaccuracies.

Table of Contents

Blind Pleasure

Variety Is the Spice of Sex

Clara's Experiment

Amelia's Punishment

Unwrapped Gifts

Closer to the Edge

Shut Up and Fuck Me

Blind Pleasure

Catherine, a hesitant wife, gives in to Rich, her husband's greatest fantasy: He wants to see her fucked by other men. Yes, men—as in plural. He wants to watch her gangbanged while he enjoys watching every single moment of it, but she's not so convinced. She is nervous about what to expect but soon finds that she doesn't have to be so afraid of what is to cum, over and over again. She goes off to the local swinger's club with him for a night she will never forget—and may even want to repeat some time.

"Catherine."

The sound of my husband's voice sent a shiver down my spine, and the skin on my arms began to prickle into goosebumps. I knew what he wanted. I kept my eyes planted firmly on my reflection as I finished getting myself ready to his standards. Eyeliner, heavy and winged into the perfect cat-eye. Black, smoky shadow was blended onto my eyelids. My eyes, the most indistinctive shade of flat brown, looked bigger, and I could see my own hesitation in them.

"Catie."

His voice was quieter and more urgent. More needing. I felt his hand on the small of my back, and it sent a quick shock shooting within me. I loved his touch—I couldn't deny that. It was everyone else's that I was hesitant about. Still, I kept my gaze planted on myself, putting the finishing touches on my face. My lips, a deep pink, almost red against my naturally pale skin. My brown hair was straightened and lay almost pin-straight down to my shoulders, curving in just slightly toward my cheeks to frame my narrow face.

"It's time."

His hand slid off of my back, leaving the place that he had touched, feeling almost uncomfortably cold, vying for his touch again. His fingers wrapped around my wrist and pulled, beckoning me to turn, and I did to look at him.

My husband, Rich, was conventionally attractive. Between the two of us, he blew me out of the water. He had a perfectly sculpted jawline, strong and masculine, with just a hint of 5-o-clock shadow across it, and a strong brow. His eyes were bright blue and his hair, almost black and trimmed to create a taper cut. He was wearing a tight, black t-shirt and a pair of tight jeans that betrayed his large bulge in his pants. I looked over him and couldn't help it. Just the sight of him, all ready to go was enough to make me wet. He smirked at me as I looked him over, satisfied.

He grabbed my hand and took me outdoors to the car. We drove in a heavy silence to the club we were going to. We had never done anything like this before, and while I had agreed to do so, it was more because he wanted to than anything else. He wanted to see other men fuck me; he had said one day when we were showering after a night of X-rated passion. His cock had quickly hardened at the suggestion as he watched me, slowly washing away the sweat from the night. I had agreed to do it for him, but I couldn't say that I was particularly excited about it.

"You'll change your tune real quick, hon," he had replied when I shrugged my shoulders. "Think of all the men that are there—to please *you*. They're there to have fun with you." And so, here we were, preparing to enter a swinger's club for the first time. Rich had figured everything out on his own; he arranged for the night, for the reservations that we apparently needed, and for the people that would be there.

Before I knew it, we were parked outside of a nondescript building. I never would have guessed that inside was a club, apparently full of people that wanted to trade partners. It looked like a simple brick building without a sign, and if it weren't for the cars parked all over it or the fact that I saw another couple entering the building, I'd have assumed we were in the wrong place. I was expecting something a bit... More flashy? This was certainly not.

Rich squeezed my hand and brought me back to reality. I turned to look at him and was immediately met with his lips on mine. His tongue danced over my bottom lip, waiting for me to open mine, and I quickly obliged, feeling his tongue against mine. His hand slid up my arm and to my breast, giving it a quick squeeze. When he came up for air, breaking the kiss, he smirked at me again. God, I loved that smirk. "Don't sweat it, hon. You're going to love it; I know you will." He kept massaging my breast, playing with it, but this time, he let his finger linger over my nipple, pressing in.

I gasped, feeling myself begin to get wet, and my clit twitched, beginning to swell, and I leaned in for another kiss. My hand snaked around to feel his cock, so big in his pants and so trapped that I just *had* to free them from their cage. I unbuttoned the pants and undid the zipper, reaching in to pull it out. It was at full attention and ready to go. My hand ran over it, and I felt his body tense as he moaned against my lips. This time, it was my turn to smirk as I slowly rubbed his cock, up and down. Up and down.

He reached down to touch my pussy, slipping underneath my little black dress and right past the little black thong that I had worn to match, his fingers expertly finding my clit. He rubbed on it, and my legs spread open for him, granting full access. I ran my hand over his cock, feeling the shaft get harder. The car smelled of our passion as I quickly undid my seatbelt and leaned over to take him in my mouth, but he protested, quickly pulling his hand away from me and leaving me wanting.

"Slow down," he said with a dark chuckle. He was watching me with amusement as he took his fingers into his mouth, sucking off every bit of liquid that I had left on him. "We have plenty of time for that later."

So off we went, into the club, and we picked up a few shots, followed by a cocktail each, on our way, to "ease our nerves," Rich had said, but I knew he just meant mine. I was watching the way that his clothes clung to his body, and especially to his crotch, watching that bulge that remained there. No one batted an eye as we walked through the club. There was music, low, pulsing, but nondescript in the background to fill any silence, and couples and groups were talking quietly amongst each other as they sipped their drinks and looked at each other like chunks of meat. It almost made me nervous until I realized that I was looking at my husband in exactly the same way. With our drinks in hand, my husband led me to a private room in the back. When we entered, I saw that it was decorated like a hotel suite; there was a bathroom connected to it and a queen-sized poster bed.

The lighting was dim, and I finished my drink, placing the drink on a nightstand. The alcohol left me pleasantly buzzed, and Rich grinned. He could see the flush on my cheeks, even in the absence of light. He made his way over to me and roughly pushed me onto the bed, gripping at my breasts with both hands for a moment before they both slipped into the top of my dress, His fingers pinched at my nipples, delicately at first and then with more fervor as he nibbled at my neck before slamming his lips against mine. I could taste the alcohol on his breath and it just made me want him more. I spread my legs and thrust my hips against his, rubbing myself on his hard cock. I reached my hands down to undo his pants, but he stopped me, grabbing my wrist and then attaching a strap around them. I stopped, blinking in surprise. We had played with the restraints every now and then at home and I recognized them as the ones that we used. The restraint went around one of the posts on the bed and then another came out for the other hand.

Before I could protest, he had pulled out a pocket vibrator, placing it against my clit first and then teasing the slit of my pussy. My hips bucked upwards at the jolt, and a moan escaped my lips. He left it there as he placed a tie around each of my ankles as well, leaving me spread-eagle on the bed. I was enjoying the vibrator so much that I hardly noticed.

He reached back up for the vibrator, taking it slowly from its position and back up to my clit and then turned it off just as I was really starting to get into it. I could feel myself starting to drip, and I was certain that I had already left a wet spot on the bed. Before I could beg for more, I felt Rich's lips kissing me. His tongue flicked across my clit, making me gasp and shudder. He licked with a bit more force, one hand snaking up to grasp my chest. He pinched and pulled at my nipple as he licked, his tongue expertly tracing my clit until he moved downward, licking at my opening as well. He let his tongue tease the entrance just a bit longer with a quick "Mmm…" against me.

"Rich, fuck me," I managed to moan out as I felt my body flex. I tried to reach down to grab his head, but the restraints held me back. I felt him laugh against me. I was desperate to get that cock inside me, and he knew it. He knew how much I longed for it. He climbed atop me in the bed and pressed himself against me. He smelled like me, a faint, almost pungent scent, and he looked down at me. I leaned up to rub against him some more, but he pulled away.

"Oh, believe me, you'll be fucked plenty," he practically purred as he pulled something else out of his pocket. It was a black blindfold, and it was very quickly wrapped around my head. I couldn't see anything, and for a moment, I felt a hint of anxiety, but that was quickly forgotten when I heard a zip and felt his cock enter me.

It was slow at first, just the tip, and immediately, my body tensed up in pleasure. I felt every inch of him as he slid into me, and I squeezed against him, moaning softly. I tried to reach out for him, but my hands were restrained. "Good girl," he said softly as he thrust harder and harder. His balls bounced against my ass, sounding like slaps, and my pussy got even wetter than I thought was possible. I felt his hands clawing at my chest as if trying to tear away the dress that I was wearing. The restraints held me back, and it was almost hotter that I couldn't see what was happening. I was in total ecstasy as he rammed into me and I heard him grunt in equal pleasure.

"Fuck me harder, Rich," I moaned out, and he obliged, but just as I was about to orgasm, he stopped and pulled away. I was left in shock and utter silence. "... Rich?" I called out, only to hear him chuckling from across the room.

"Have fun," he said, and then I knew it was beginning.

Within seconds, I could smell a new man near me; he smelled of aftershave, woody almost. My heart was pounding in my chest, and I was almost afraid to speak when I realized what was about to happen, but all apprehension melted away as soon as I felt another vibrator rubbing against my clit as a finger slipped into my pussy.

"Mmm... Nice, wet, and tight," the voice said, almost breathy as the man that I couldn't see felt me up. He felt good. Maybe it was the alcohol and lack of inhibition, or the fact that Rich had been driving me crazy all night, or the fact that I had complete permission to fuck a strange man with him watching, but those first seconds were better than I expected.

Before I could say a word, I felt his fingers probe into me again, holding the vibrator in place with what I assume was his palm as his other hand squeezed my ass, pulling at my cheeks. His fingers teased my asshole, and my entire body tightened up in pleasure. I moaned as the vibrator was replaced with a face that felt clean-shaven—there was none of the prickling I usually felt with Rich. I felt him sucking, kissing, and licking at my clit, slowly at first, tantalizingly teasing me. "Such a bad little girl, look how much she wants it," he murmured between my lips. The feeling sent shivers down my spine. "Do you want it, you hot little slut?"

I moaned again, practically unable to speak as he continued to suck away. I felt him pull away and heard another zip as he undid his pants and the rustling of clothing. His cock felt different—it was wider than Rich's as it rubbed at my slit, teasing my swollen lips as he did so. I thrust my hips up, trying to get him to enter, but he pulled back, laughing. "She's ready to go, Rich!" he called out, and I heard Rich chuckling. I could hear the pleasure in his voice—it was low and almost urgent. He was enjoying every moment of this, so why shouldn't I?

I heard footsteps approach me as the strange man's cock continued to tease me, moving up and down, sometimes, sliding across my clit and sometimes circling my asshole, leaving me breathless with anticipation. My senses were on overdrive; I could hear his own breathing change as he enjoyed himself as well. Suddenly, I felt a mouth on my neck, and I smelled another scent—this one was citrusy.

"She's definitely a looker, isn't she?" said another voice, and I felt his hands lightly brushing over my arms. I shivered at the touch, moaning as the first man, the one who smelled of sandalwood, finally thrust into me. His cock was longer than Rich's too, it felt like, as it slid deeper and deeper, slowly penetrating me until I felt his balls against my ass. He held it there as I felt the other man pull down my dress, leaving my breasts bare. I knew my nipples were perfectly erect at that point, and I could feel a faint breeze over them. It was warm. Was it his breath? His head must have been awfully close to them, and citrus man gently touched each one. Then, he pinched a bit harder, leaving me moaning again. I couldn't do anything; I was stuck exactly in place, but I really just wanted to ride the cock that was inside of me.

I felt the man who was next to me lower his head down to take my nipple into my mouth, and he bit down on it, hard enough to send a shiver down my spine but not so hard to hurt. The cock that was in me thrust harder, and I cried out, but not in pain. I felt the man inside of me squeeze at my ass and then suddenly smack it hard enough to sting. I cried out but felt myself get wetter against him, and I clenched against every inch of his girth, feeling it fill me. His cock pulsated against me as he pulled it out, never quite all the way, before slamming back into me, all the while I felt the man's fingers clawing at my ass more and more.

"I want more," I managed to gasp out, and in response, I got another slap across the ass, a bit more forceful this time, and I yelped in response. This brought another slap quickly, followed by another.

"You want more, you little slut?" Sandalwood said, his breath starting to hitch as he kept slamming into me. I moaned in response as I felt another slap. I'm sure my ass was red by that point, but I was too lost in passion to care.

"Yes, please give me more," I managed to moan out between breaths.

Then, I felt another hand on me suddenly. This hand was different. It was rougher. Stronger. More confident as it caressed over my body. Three. There were three pairs of hands on me now, and strangely, I didn't mind. In fact, I loved every moment of it. One pair held me in place as Sandalwood continued to thrust with as much force as he could muster, and I lifted my hips so that my clit would rub against his pelvis. Citrus continued to knead and suck at my breasts and nipples, and this new pair of hands was slowly exploring my body with his hands. I heard more zipping, and very quickly, a rock-hard cock was shoved in my face.

"Open," I heard a gruff voice command, and I did so, turning my head toward him. He shoved himself into my mouth so hard that I gagged at first, tears springing to my eyes. I let my tongue roll over his dick, lingering on the frenulum before pushing it deeper into my mouth.

I could hardly take it. Every nerve in my body felt like it was on overdrive as I was pleasured from three different men, and I could hear my husband's own breathing, almost ragged in the corner. Was he jerking himself as he watched? The thought of Rich's face, enjoying watching his wife become a toy for all of these men, was enough for me, but he loved it.

I knew I wasn't going to be able to last much longer. I could feel my own pleasure building and building until I could hardly take it anymore. My own moans had grown louder, and I could feel my body taking control, moving and grinding into Sandalwood harder and harder. Citrus was sucking harder than before, so hard that it would have hurt, but in the moment, I loved it.

Right as I was about to cum, I felt Sandalwood pull his dick out of me and leave me thrusting my body upward, searching blindly for him. He wasn't there, but I could hear him chucking. I could feel the warmth of his body radiating off of him, just outside of my reach.

"Beg for it," he said.

My mouth was full of another cock, licking and sucking on it, and I whined. I tried to open my mouth to pull away to speak, but the man held me in place roughly, twisting his hand in my hair to keep me right where I was. I got it then—I wasn't going to be allowed to finish until they were each satisfied. I sucked on his dick with as much passion as I could muster. I could feel his shaft twitching and bulging in my mouth as I continued to slurp at it. He held me in place and slammed himself into my mouth, letting himself go down my throat to make me gag. He didn't let up, going harder and harder until I tasted him. The salty, hot liquid shot down my throat, burning and making me gag as I felt him cum into my mouth. His cock twitched and pulsated in my mouth as he held me there to his own pleasure, and when he pulled out, I moved to spit, but he held my mouth shut.
"Swallow it," he told me. I did, shuddering as it went down my throat, leaving its aftertaste in my mouth. I wasn't normally a swallower, but nothing about this situation was normal. It was strangely erotic to be ordered around, and at this point, I think it would have been impossible for me to get any wetter. I could feel my own juices dribbling down to my ass as I was spread out, and the sheets right underneath me were soaked. The whole room smelled musty, of sex and men, and I *loved* it.

"Please," I said breathlessly, thrusting my pelvis up, looking for Sandalwood. He had to have been there somewhere. But then, another dick was shoved in my face. I sucked it in greedily and tasted myself all over it, and that woody smell of the man who had, only moments prior, been thrusting into me was standing over me. He shuddered as my lips wrapped around his shaft, licking myself up and savoring the taste. He was so hard, and he was so wide that my jaw was opened up almost uncomfortably far as I took him in, gently, slowly, sensually using my tongue to caress his head and shaft.

Then, I felt something else beneath me. Was that Citrus? I couldn't smell him near me anymore, I realized, and that must have been why. He was underneath me now, rubbing his own cock against me. He started up on my clit, making me moan against Sandalwood's dick as he did. It was a gentle touch, but it was enough to drive me crazy with desire. I wanted him, and I wanted him *then*.

I thrust my hips up just right, taking the cock into my body as I continued to suck on the first one. I groaned in ecstasy as I felt the length of him enter me. He pulled my legs up as much as he could with the constraints and thrust his way into me as hard as he could. I cried out, only to have my head thrust back onto the cock in my mouth, and I continued to suck on it.

Citrus was a much more sensual fucker than Sandalwood had been. He entered me and gyrated his hips, allowing himself to touch more of me. He angled himself just right to shoot toward the top of my vagina, rubbing against the walls and leaving me hotter than before. As my body got closer, and I felt more of my own wetness dribble out and down onto Citrus, I felt him pull away, just like before. I wanted him so badly, but I knew what was happening. I needed to finish off Sandalwood first.

I sucked on Sandalwood harder, craning my neck as far as I could until he pushed himself toward me. My nose was against his groin. It was unshaven; I could feel the hairs tickling against my face as I took as much of him in as I could, letting my lips tighten around him before pulling away. "That's right, you little slut," he managed to hiss out as I pulled away, letting the tip of my tongue trace along his shaft as I did it. I smiled until the next thrust from Citrus made me moan, almost losing myself in the pleasure. Sandalwood's hand, yanking my hair, brought me back to reality, and I repeated that motion, again and again, getting quicker and quicker until he was shaking. I teased his head with my tongue. I could feel his dick getting firmer. He was getting close, and I could taste the precum on the tip as I flicked it with my tongue. I shoved him down my throat as hard as I could manage without gagging and sucked, and then I felt him jolt, thrusting himself into my mouth as again, I was rewarded with the taste of cum shooting down my throat. His was slightly less pungent than the first man's, and I sucked it down greedily, licking along his shaft as his body continued to be rocked with enjoyment. I grinned. Mission accomplished. Now, there was nothing standing in my way.

Citrus slammed deeper than before into my body, and I felt his weight atop me as he climbed into the position that he wanted. I could smell him as he fucked me, and I moaned out, craning my head to kiss him as he continued to slam into me. I was searching for him, yearning for his mouth, but before I could find it, it was back on my nipple, flicking it with his tongue, sending my whole body convulsing. I was so close. "Fuck me harder," I managed to whisper between gasping breaths, my mouth now gloriously free from cock as I leaned up, placing my head into the crook of his neck.

He obliged instantly, shoving his dick harder into my body, and I lost myself in the moment. I cried out and rubbed myself against his pelvis as he continued to thrust, and almost immediately, all of the frustration and tension was released in ecstasy as I *finally* got the orgasm I had been waiting for. I felt my pussy clench around his dick harder and harder as he thrust, cumming within me to the feeling of my walls tightening. It was so intense that I lost myself, unaware of everything in that instant. I collapsed against the bed; all energy thoroughly drained from my body. I couldn't keep going even if I wanted to.

When I regained my wits, I realized it was almost silent, but I could hear someone shuffling around. I sat there in my post-sex haze, utterly exhausted and uninterested in what was going on around me, and I suddenly felt the restraints loosen and fall off and then felt my blindfold removed.

The room was surprisingly empty. I could see Rich staring at me with a look of arousal, admiration, and satisfaction all in one. He was thrilled to have seen me do what I had done. I was totally exhausted on the bed, and even freed up, I was not sure that I wanted to get up and do anything.

Rich smirked at me as I laid there in my post-sex high. "You ready for another round?" he murmured, running his hand up and down my body, sending a shiver down my spine.

I laughed as he got on top of me to kiss me unabashedly, his tongue dancing in my mouth as he savored the taste of others on my lips. His own cock was pressed against me, bare and rubbing against my thoroughly fucked, swollen pussy. I kissed him back. Surely, round two wouldn't be so bad. It was the least I could do to repay him for the fun I had.

Variety Is the Spice of Sex

Lindsey loved fucking new people. For her, fucking was something exciting and new, and while she loved fucking her husband, she wanted more. She wanted the act of exploring new bodies and getting new sensations and new connections. Her husband, Matt, has always seemed uninterested in the threesome or open relationship life, but for his wife, he's willing to try anything once. They open up a to their neighbor, sexy Delilah for some threesome fun to try to accommodate Lindsey's needs, and spend a day fucking harder than they have ever fucked before, leaving both Matt and Lindsey thoroughly satisfied.

I was bored.

I was being fucked by my husband, but I was completely bored out of my mind. Sex had grown dull. Sure, we could bring in toys. We did that a lot—I had toys of every kind imaginable. Rabbit vibes and cock rings and dildos galore, but none of them could keep my attention for very long at all. I wanted *more*. I wanted something else that would keep me happy. I wasn't sure what I wanted yet, but I knew that whatever it was, it wasn't this.

I pinched and kneaded at my nipples as my husband fucked me from behind. He grunted and groaned and unleaded within my pussy, collapsing onto me as he did. I could feel his heart pounding in his chest as he rested there for a moment before he turned his head to kiss me. He smiled at me, but it quickly faltered. "Again?" Matt asked with a hesitant frown.

I averted my gaze, almost ashamed that I was unable to enjoy the moment. We had tried everything that I could think of. We had done some of that teacher-student roleplay. It wasn't for me. We tried some light bondage, but I didn't care for that, either. I was just *bored*. This was the first relationship that I had been in for longer than a few months, and I almost thought that what I needed was something fresh. Fresh meat to enjoy or something. It was exciting to explore new bodies sometimes, and I felt like I hadn't been able to do that. I loved my husband, sure, but sexually? I was an explorer. I wanted to get out, fuck my brains out, and fuck as many people as I could. I had given up that life when I got married, but a part of me couldn't help but think that that was what I was missing.

"Is there anything I can do?" asked Matt.

I shook my head. It would be another night for the vibe in the bath with a glass of wine for me. I didn't need to make him feel worse or more inadequate about it.

"Do you want to fuck other people?" he finally asked me. I could hear it in his voice. It was almost breaking him to suggest it, but he loved me, and he wanted me to be happy.

I hesitated, but he must have seen the excitement that I tried to hide in my face. I saw his shoulders fall.

"What about a threesome?" I suggested suddenly.

He looked at me, confused.

"I don't want to fuck someone on my own," I told him. "I want you to join in. Wouldn't you want another toy to play with?" I winked at him and slapped his ass, enjoying the quick bounce as I did, squeezing and kneading the muscle. His ass was firmly toned. He, for one, did not skip leg day, that was for sure.

Matt sighed. "Lindsey, I don't know…" He looked at me with mixed emotions swirling in his green eyes.

"You'll love it," I promised him, giving him a quick kiss and nibbling on his lip. "It's fun."

He shrugged his shoulders. I was his only partner that he had ever had; he had wanted to save himself for marriage. He wasn't religious or anything, but he hadn't wanted to, shall we say, play the field; he wanted to keep sex something special for himself. But let's be real—a quick fuck is so much fun.

I grinned. "Trust me?"

He sighed again and nodded his head. "But no dicks. I'm firm on that one."

"Fine by me!" I said with a grin. I slapped his ass again, giggling as it bounced. There was a pink print on his cheek now as I clenched. I saw dick start to harden again as I did it, and I smiled at him, genuinely excited. I pulled him forward, kissing him, and he kissed back, ready for round two.

I did all of the work from that point on. I screened out options that would be interested in a bit of rough fun with us. I looked for women only, knowing Matt's stance, and I didn't mind myself. Sometimes, all you want is an extra pair of tits to fondle that aren't your own. Eventually, I had found the perfect person: The young neighbor that had just moved into the apartment next door.

Delilah was a perky, young 19 years old. Perfect tits, double-Ds on her hourglass figure. Her skin was a deep olive color, and her hair was down to her waist, black, thick, and I could only imagine pulling it myself as I played with those perfect little nipples that I made sure to check out and sample before choosing her to be the perfect partner. She was *gorgeous*. She was kinky, too—she had shown me her collection of restraints and even a few leather floggers, and I knew that we would be in for fun.

She knocked at the door, and when I opened it, she looked shy; she was almost too nervous to enter. I grabbed her wrist brusquely, immediately feeling a thrill as I pulled her in. This would be fun, and I was determined to enjoy each and every moment of it. The thought of a fresh, new body made me wet; I could feel my pussy twitch as I led her in. She looked at Matt and blushed a bit, but it just made me want her more.

Matt was sitting on our bed, naked and almost lazily stroking his own cock, displaying it for Delilah to see. He seemed a bit hesitant but was willing to give it a shot.

I took off my robe that I had been wearing to open the door, revealing that I was perfectly naked underneath and looked at Delilah. She was eyeing my husband's cock with a mixture of being impressed and desiring to get her own hands on it. I could see that look in her eyes—the look of lust. The look of her lips parting slightly as she inhaled. The shine of her eyes dilating as she looked at him. She wanted him, and that was enough to make me happy.

"You ready?" I purred as I reached over to pull Delilah's shirt over her head. She nodded her head and turned her eyes to me, taking in every inch of my body. I instinctively straightened out, pushing my chest outward more, and Delilah reached up to grab them. She ran her fingers over my nipples, pinching and rubbing at them, and I gasped at the feeling. Her fingers were so soft and warm as they worked their magic, the touch of a woman who was clearly experienced with the female body.

I leaned in to kiss Delilah, watching Matt's reaction as I did. He watched us intently, and I could see the way his cock twitched when I did it. I smiled against Delilah's lips as my tongue parted them and made its way into her mouth, tasting her. She tasted sweet, almost like a cup of wine. Had she had to drink a glass of wine to loosen up? I chuckled as I nibbled on her lips, and I led her to bed to join Matt.

Matt grinned as we did and opened his arms to us. I settled in on the left side of him, and Delilah was on the right. I pulled her in again to kiss, both of our breasts resting against Matt's chest as we did so. I moaned as I kissed her, and I felt Matt reach up to grab my breast and touch it. He touched my nipples with his own fingers. They were rougher than Delilah's; I immediately noticed. He flicked his fingers over them and was just a bit tougher than I was.

I reached down for Matt's hand on my breast and removed it, guiding it over to feel Delilah's as well, and I immediately felt him tense up, his breathing picking up. Then, I pulled away from Delilah's lips, pushing her down to kiss Matt as well.

He reciprocated, his cock twitching as he did. I reached down to stroke it, running my nails gently up and down the shaft, making him shudder as he continued to kiss Delilah, with more fervor as I continued to play with him. He bit her lip, and I could hear him groan as I lowered my head down to lick him. I used just my tongue at first, running it up and down just as I had done with my nails. I saw his hips shift upward as he sought out my mouth, or any other wet hole he could get his cock in, and I obliged, taking it between my lips and hearing him moan against Delilah. After all, this had to be just as enjoyable, if not more so, for him than for me if I wanted him to feel like he wanted to do this again. I was in for the long haul, and I didn't mind sharing my new toy.

I turned to look at Delilah, who was shifting to straddle him now, his hand both reaching for her breasts, kneading, tugging, and rubbing them between his hands. I could smell her wetness between her legs as she continued to kiss him, and I shifted down a bit to let her make her way downward. I pulled her hips, guiding her perfectly round ass down to him. I lined her up and took Matt's cock, still wet with my saliva, and put it into her. As soon as it felt her lips, it thrust upwards, and she moaned, throwing her head back.

Then, he thrust again and again. He was watching her intently, watching those perfect breasts bouncing on her chest, nipples pointed out, and still shimmering with saliva. He turned his attention back to me then and reached out with his hand to grasp my breasts as well. Mine were just as big, but age had already started to weigh them down. He didn't seem to mind as he greedily tugged and squeezed at them. His fingers glossed over my nipples, and I felt myself get wetter, my own clit starting to swell in anticipation of my turn for fun.

I watched as Delilah rode Matt harder and harder. She started to really moan and whine. "Oh, Matt!" she groaned, her head thrown back. "Fuck me harder!"

I slapped her ass, seeing the red mark appear almost immediately, but she only moaned louder. I grinned and slapped her again and again. I could feel myself starting to drip down my legs as they continued to fuck, and before they could get too into it, I interrupted the fun. I pulled Delilah up and off of Matt, pushing her down next to him. She gasped, looking up at me, almost in surprise. I could see the wetness from their fucking glistening between her thighs. Her pussy was perfectly waxed and hair-free. Perfect.

I looked over my new toy and forced her legs open. She was caught off guard, but she obliged, and I quickly buried my face between her lips, feeling that one little nub that seemed so hard for so many men to find. She gasped and shuddered as my tongue ran over her. I positioned myself just right on my knees, head down, and ass raised. Matt watched as I continued to lick at Delilah and seemed to get the idea as I shifted. He could enter from behind.

Matt quickly got into position and slammed into me quickly. "Lindsey, you're so wet," he groaned as he slid all the way, stopping only when his balls slapped my ass. I chuckled at him as I continued to lick Delilah's clit, feeling her shift at the feeling. She moaned as she continued to get licked. As I felt her getting closer to cumming, I slapped her ass suddenly. It surprised her, judging by the yelp, but judging by the gush of fluids in my face, she loved it. I slapped her again and reached up to take her breast in my hand.

Matt continued to fuck me from behind, and I kept my composure, sucking on that little nub. I slide my fingers into Delilah, one at first, then another. Then, I angle them just right, reaching around to get to that magical g-spot, and as soon as I reach it, I hear her moan, her hips shooting up as soon as I touch it. I grin to myself, knowing that I have reached it.

I played with that little spot inside of her a bit longer, listening to the change in her breath and feeling the fluids soaking my hand as I continued to lick her. Within seconds, I could feel her whole body spasm, and her vagina tightened and clenched on my fingers over and over again.

I pulled my hands away from her, knowing that she'll be far too sensitive for the next few moments to be of much fun. Instead, I turned to look over my shoulder at Matt. He was watching us intently as he thrust deeper. He had kept pace deep and slow while I tongued at Delilah, but now that I was done with her, he sped up, harder.

"Spank me," I managed to moan as he pushed deeper and deeper into me. I reached down between my legs to touch my clit, swollen and soaking wet, as he obliged, pulling out just long enough to slap both of my ass cheeks in quick succession. The sting felt so good, and just as quickly as he had stopped, he slammed himself into me again and again. I felt his hands tangle into my hair and pull my head back—it was uncharacteristically rough for him, and when I looked up at him, I could see his gaze fixated on me. He was completely in the moment, enjoying it.

"Play with her again," he said gruffly, shoving me down toward Delilah, who was watching us with heated passion.

I grinned, feeling wetter at the thought of my husband, my usually so sweet and gentle husband, getting rough and hot and bothered by the idea of me fucking another woman. I could live with that. "My pleasure," I told him as he slowed down his fucking to let me keep my own balance.

I pulled Delilah closer to me, and she smiled up at me, her eyes begging for round two. I lined her up underneath me so that I could grind on her pelvis while I leaned down to kiss each of her perky little perfect nipples before taking one in my mouth.

I heard Matt's breathing pick up as he watched me, and I knew I needed to put on a show. Arching my back just right to bring my ass up for him, I leaned in to tug on Delilah's lips before I reached over to the nightstand next to our bed. I pulled out a toy—a large vibrator, which I quickly placed against Delilah's clit before settling my own right onto it as well, starting it on low. I gasped at the feeling, gliding my clit atop it as I watched Delilah's delicious expression on her face. It was perfect in that moment—she was so hot with her fuck-me eyes as she leaned up for a kiss, moaning against me. Matt's own tempo increased a bit, and I could feel his desperation as he fucked me harder. I heard him getting closer and closer and I pulled away from Delilah's mouth just long enough to look over my shoulder at him, making eye contact as he watched me. I turned away to suckle at Delilah's nipple again, but just as my lips grazed over the tiny little nub, he yanked my hair back.

"You'll look at me now," he practically growled, and I smirked at him. He thrust into me again, and my mouth opened, head back as he took me harder. I pushed harder against the vibrator that was underneath me, reaching down to turn up the speed.

Immediately, Delilah cried out in pleasure, and I pinched her nipples a little bit harder that time, never looking away from Matt as he continued to fuck me. Any time I started to close my eyes to enjoy the moment, he pulled my hair harder and forced me to keep my eyes on him. My pussy clenched his cock tighter as he forced me. Who knew I was into him being more dominant. It wouldn't be long—I knew I wouldn't be able to last out much longer as he continued to ride me.

"You don't cum until I tell you to cum," he told her, never letting up the intensity in his gaze or his fucking. All I could do was nod in response as another wave of pleasure threatened to throw me over the edge. The vibrator was too strong for me to be able to resist for too much longer, and I shifted off of it, leaving it in place for Delilah, who was practically in her own little world, enjoying herself. As soon as I was off of the vibrator, she took it with her free hand and plunged it into herself with a moan, her back arching, and eyes closing tightly.

Matt let go of my hair, and I looked down at Delilah, grinning at my handiwork, but before I could do much more, he thrust into me again, so hard that I could hardly stand it. I whined as he got deeper and deeper, and I knew he was challenging me. He *wanted* to make this hard for me, and could I really blame him? He was reclaiming his confidence—he *needed* to do this.

I tried to fend off the impending orgasm, but before I knew it, my vagina was tightening in waves of pleasure all down his shaft, and I felt him thrust harder into me and groan as well. I rode the waves of pleasure before collapsing onto Delilah, who smiled knowingly at me before she reached up to toy with my sensitive nipples.

She didn't get to for very long before I felt Matt's hand wrap around my arm, flipping me over. "You didn't listen," he told me, his eyes shining in dark amusement. I couldn't quite tell what he thought as he looked down at me.

"Sounds like I'm in need of a punishment," I replied coyly.

"Someone's a bad girl," purred Delilah with a giggle as she gently rubbed the vibrator along my clit. It was almost too sensitive to be enjoyable in the moment.

"Are you going to help me punish her?" asked Matt, looking at Delilah. "You'll get your reward when you're done."

This new side of Matt was so incredibly hot, and in that moment, I realized that this is exactly what we were missing in our own sex life. We were missing that carnal, intense, uninhibited pleasure that we were enjoying right that moment.

Delilah giggled sensuously as she lowered herself. "It's my turn to do the licking, I think," she murmured as she ran her tongue from my nipple all around my areola before lowering herself to lick at my stomach as well. She was so gentle, and her face was so smooth, in stark contrast to the looming form of Matt as he looked over his handiwork. My entire body was glistening with sweat, and my hair, once perfectly put in place, was tousled and knotting. He loved ravaging me and he loved looking at the ravaged body he left behind.

As Delilah slowly worked her way right back up to the other nipple, I moaned in pleasure. I could feel myself getting primed for another round already. My clit was twitching to attention, and my pussy ached to be filled again. I wanted this—I wanted to be dominated and controlled.

Matt watched as Delilah played with me. He watched the young woman's perfect figure move to straddle me, placing her clit against mine before rubbing. He watched as I gasped at the sudden shift and as my back begin to arch. His own cock was already hard and ready for round two, and he rubbed it slowly to keep his hands busy as Delilah's danced all over my skin. She was everywhere as she touched me; her hands never lingered too long in any place as she rode me, watching me. I felt myself getting wetter and more eager to continue playing the more that she rode me. I felt myself vying for her, and my own hips thrust upwards to meet her.

"No," Matt said.

I looked at him in surprise. No, what? He answered my silent question almost immediately.

"Don't move, or I'll have to tie you up."

I was shocked at what he said, but it only made me hotter. It only made me want to move to make him do it, but I found myself obeying. I didn't move as Delilah continued to ride me. I fought the urge to move, and she seemed to take it as a challenge to make me fail. She removed herself from me and lowered herself down to lick my slit, tasting the amalgamation of our juices that coated me as she did. Her tongue penetrated into me, and I gasped, but still managed to avoid moving. She licked me harder and harder, quickly taking the vibrator and turning it on as well, placing it against my clit. Her other free hand squeezed my ass, her nails digging into my skin just enough to pleasantly sting as she did so.

"Mmm..." I heard myself moan, and I looked at Matt in the eyes. He admired the work that was being done above me before lowering himself down. He took Delilah in front of him, positioned her just right, and thrust into her. The motion pushed her deeper into me and I could hear her gasp as he took her. I looked up and saw them fucking. He pulled her hair back, just as he had pulled mine, exposing a neck that he leaned down to nibble on before he sucked deeply onto it. I could hear the slurps as he sucked on her neck, marking her. I took a moment to catch my breath and reached down for the vibrator.

"Don't move," he repeated as he pulled Delilah back and fucked her harder. I obliged and sat there, watching him thrust his cock deeper into her, watching his balls bouncing and watching the ripples in his thighs as he held himself up and balanced them both. He was on his knees, as was she, her back arched so that he could reach her chest and her neck all at once. She moaned, eyes closed as she enjoyed the moment, and Matt maintained perfect eye contact with me as he took the vibrator that I had tried to use, turned it on, put it in place on Delilah, and finished the job.

Her head was thrown back in pleasure, mouth wide open and eyes squeezed shut. I could see her thighs tighten and contract as she came, and as soon as she was done, Matt let her go, shifting right back over to me without missing a beat or breaking eye contact.

"Don't move," he reaffirmed one last time as he watched me. "And you don't cum until I tell you to. Do you understand?"

"Yes," I breathed, watching him. My legs were quivering on their own, aching for his touch, and as soon as he spread my legs himself, I felt my breathing quicken almost immediately. I didn't move, and he thrust into me with abandon. He did not look away as he continued.

Before long, he yanked me up. "Turn around," he commanded, and I did so immediately. He pulled me into that same position to take me from behind, and got in deeply, pushing and thrusting as hard as he could into me. He pulled my hair and bit at my ear as he did so. I felt my breath gasping and felt his hands around my throat, not hard enough to completely cut off breathing, but just enough to put some pressure down as his cock reached deeper than ever before into me.

He grunted as he thrust, quicker and quicker, his shaft pulling out all but the tip of his head before thrusting it back in. "You're mine," he whispered into my ear gruffly as the pressure on my neck suddenly loosened. I had completely forgotten all about Delilah at this point, and quite frankly, I didn't care whether she was there or not. Matt shoved me down on the bed, slapping my ass with actual force behind it, so hard that I yelped, but that yelp of pain very quickly became a moan of pleasure as he buried his cock in me again, all the way to the balls. At this angle, they slapped against my clit just right, and he slammed into me, quicker and quicker.

"Cum for me now, or not at all," he told me suddenly, and he didn't have to say anything twice. As he buried his load in me, I felt myself clench all around him. I felt each thrust as he came before collapsing against me in a sweaty, exhausted heap. He pulled himself out of me and looked me over. My ass was red from the slaps, and my hair had gotten even worse. Delilah had apparently taken her leave while we were in the throes of abandon, but I was pretty sure she looked almost as disheveled as I did. I sighed, thoroughly fucked, thoroughly satisfied, and thoroughly ready for a nap.

"So, when's the next time?" Matt practically purred, running a hand up and down my arm, watching as I shivered in response. All I could do was laugh in response.

Clara's Experiment

Clara has never known what she wanted out of life. She was never very satisfied, and even though she always tried to enjoy herself, she decided that she wanted to try something new—she wanted to be dominated, and she wanted to do it with someone that she would never have to see again. Armed with the power of the internet, she finds someone to dominate her and goes for a night that she will never forget, meeting sexy, alluring Anthony in the penthouse suite of a hotel for a night of dark passion and submission that introduces her to a lifestyle she's not likely to forget anytime soon.

I looked down at my phone and saw an unbelievingly handsome face looking back at me. It was the profile for the man that I was heading to meet that evening, and I felt a pit of apprehension in my stomach. He looked like he was... Well, experienced, and it made me nervous. I had spent the night prior looking into doms online. It turns out; there are dating apps just like that. I'd never tried anything like that before, but a quick one-night stand seemed like an ample opportunity to get to know whether I'd like it or not.

The man's face was very serious. His skin was tanned, but not dark, and his gaze, intense. His profile picture showed that he meant business, I noted—it was that of someone who knew what he wanted and was not willing to let anyone else prevent him from getting that, and that was exactly what I wanted. I was curious, vaguely, about the sub life, but had never had the guts, or the opportunity, to experiment with it myself. That was, until that night.

I stood at the bottom of a tall hotel, looking up at it, my phone still in hand. It was maybe 9:30 pm on a Friday night, and I was all dressed up. My makeup was expertly applied, and I wore red pumps with a short, form-fitting red dress that was stretched practically taut over my body. Underneath, I wore nothing—no bra, no panties, just as I had been told to do. I had to be careful when I leaned over or sit down or I'd run the risk of flashing someone, but that was a small price to pay for the pleasure I hoped to get that night. I was eager to give this a shot, that was for sure. I just had to get out and make it happen.

I took a deep breath. "Clara, get it together. You can do this!" I told myself, tightening my grasp around my phone before I stepped into the building with purpose. My head was held high and confident, despite feeling the exact opposite. I went up to the penthouse. I typed in a quick message into the dating app, informing him that I was on my way up, and I marveled at the fact that I would be setting foot into the area that would be deemed "high-class" or whatever else people say of the presidential suites in hotels. I had no idea what to expect as I made my way up the elevator to the room.

The elevator doors opened and revealed the man, Anthony, staring back at me. He was leaned against the wall, arms crossed casually, head back, and eyes glancing up and down as if trying to determine if I was worth the effort on that very night. He must have decided that I was, as he straightened up as soon as I stepped off the elevator. Did he think that I'd chicken out, maybe? Maybe he thought I'd just get right back on it and leave. Who knows? Whatever it was, though, I knew that I was in for a unique time. I had never seen anything like him before—his gaze was intense, but something in it was reassuring. I immediately felt at ease, something I had never experienced with a man before, certainly not a strange one that I had never met.

He looked at me and smirked. I was no longer standing tall—I was standing with my body relaxed as we walked. My arms were pulled in slightly... Almost submissively. He placed a hand on the small of my back, and I felt a thrilling jolt through me. I hadn't expected that at all, not that I could complain. It was nice.

Very quickly, we were inside the room, behind a closed door, and I stood, not really sure what to do next. I wasn't sure where I should be, and I looked around myself nervously. Thankfully, I didn't have to bring myself to ask. We hadn't yet exchanged a single word.

"Sit," he said. It wasn't a request—I could hear that. He wasn't yet looking at me, too busy rustling through a few things. I nodded my head to myself before moving to sit down on the bed. My head was spinning, but I obediently sat there without a care in the world. I was almost shocked at the fact that I was there without a protest, but I chose not to say a thing.

"Did you prepare yourself?" he asked. Anthony had given me several instructions—I was to be clean-shaven and without underwear when I arrived. Again, I nodded my head without a word.

He looked up to me briefly, almost questioningly. "I didn't hear you, Ellen."

Hearing my name on his lips brought a quick shiver down my spine. "Yes," I replied quietly. My voice quivered.

He stood up to full height as he looked over me, his dark eyes almost disapproving for a moment. "This is your first time," he said suddenly.

"Yes." I turned my gaze away from him.

He blinked, clearly taken aback by that. "You're... New and you were looking for partners on a dating app?" Something about the way that he said that made me feel a bit embarrassed. Had I made a mistake already? I had hoped to get everything just right.

"... Yes?"

He ran one hand through his hair, his gaze lifting off of me and focusing on something behind me as if considering something. "Look, had I known..." he began before I had to interrupt him.

"I want to learn."

"You need to learn some manners," he said with a smirk. I could see his hand tense at his hand, as if he had resisted the urge to smack me across my face. I shrank back slightly at the thought, but at the same time, I felt myself starting to get wet. I hadn't expected that, at all, but I was interested in seeing where things would go.

"I'm sorry," I told him contritely, looking at him.

"Look away," he commanded me, and I obeyed. "You have a lot of learning to do. Are you sure you want this?" In the corner of my eye, I could see that he was hard. He wanted to punish me. He wanted to discipline me and teach me what I should and should not do. But, he also didn't want to get me in for more than I expected. After all, from everything I've read, this is about consent. Consensual abuse, basically. Or at least, that's how I understood it.

"I do want this," I told him, keeping my gaze planted firmly on his feet. It felt comfortable to look there, and I was looking at his brown shoes. They looked like leather, quite nice from what I could see.

"Okay," he replied simply after a pause. "Then let's begin. Safe words…"

With all of the niceties figured out, he grinned at me. It was a dark grin on his face, one that showed that he's more interested in using me than anything else. "Strip," he told me.

I nodded my head and grabbed the hem of my dress to pull it up. As soon as it was over my head, he swatted my now-bare ass swiftly with his hand, and I yelped at the sting. It started, but it was almost… pleasant? "What's that?" he practically purred, "I can't hear you."

"Yes, sir," I told him quietly, using the manners that he had just gone over with me.

"That's better."

He watched as I removed the dress, tossing it onto the bed. I was standing there, bare naked, aside from the red heels I had on. Red was his choice—he liked his gifts wrapped in red, he had told me. I looked at his feet a bit longer, watching as they walked in a circle to get a good look at his prize for the night. I got the feeling that I was being hung up for display, like a piece of meat, but somehow, the thought of being used like that only made me even more eager to please. He pushed me over the bed to take a look at me and pulled my lips and cheeks apart, viewing my pussy. He must have grinned—I couldn't see his reaction, but he gave each cheek a slap.

"Such a naughty little whore you are, aren't you," he practically purred, running a finger over my little nub, trailing down the outside of my lips and back again.

I gasped at the touch. I hadn't expected it so quickly, and yet, there it was. His fingers were gently, delicately, tantalizingly rubbing along my inner lips, careful to avoid the slit itself. He didn't want to move too quickly. I could feel myself begin to leak more, and he chuckled behind me. He was clearly fully satisfied, and he gave me another slap on both cheeks, harder this time. I yelped, and he let go. The sound of his footsteps said that he was leaving the area and I looked tentatively over my shoulder to see what he was doing.

Anthony had gone over to get something from a drawer, and I had to admit, I was a little afraid to see what he'd bring back. Quickly, I found that he had brought back a little riding crop. It smelled of leather as he put it down next to me. "You are to obey me and only me," Anthony said as he put down what looked like a strand of beads as well, and a toy that I couldn't quite tell what it was for. He grinned, but I hesitated to make eye contact with him.

"On your knees," he said suddenly, and I obliged. "Lean forward," he demanded.

I sat on the bed, on my knees, leaning forward so that my head rested against the bed. My ass was up in the air, and I felt the beads teasing at my pussy, a little at first. "Mmm," I purred as he let them go in, one at a time, inside of me. He let them all enter me and then quickly pulled them out. The feeling was shocking and unexpected and almost as good coming out as going in. I felt my pussy clench between my legs at the sudden absence of stimulation, but before I could protest, I felt him probing my asshole, gently at first.

"Have you ever had anything up here," he asked as he used what I assumed was his finger at first to poke at me. I was tight and clenching it in nervousness. I shook my head no, biting my lip and squeezing my eyes shut in anticipation for what I assumed was about to happen. "I don't hear you, slut," he said with a quick slap against my upper thigh.

"N-no, sir," I replied through clenched teeth. That had hurt, and yet, I felt myself grow wetter. I wanted this, I realized.

"Do you want it?" he asked me, and I saw him reach for the leather crop next to me.

"Yes, sir," I told him, and he snapped the crop against me. It stung, but just as quickly, he gently pulled it across the reddening skin, almost delicately, and I felt myself gasp. It moved slowly, moving to tenderly trace the outsides of my lips before gently tapping at those too. It was just enough to bring feeling there, barely brushing over them and I gasped at the sensation.

"Good," he growled, leaning over me to cup a breast that was hanging down on the bed. My nipples were brushing the sheets as he did it, and he reached up to bring them between his fingers, rolling them about until I moaned my pleasure. I loved it. I wanted it. I wanted more, and without saying a word, he obliged. He placed a couple of nipple clamps onto me, bringing a sudden gasp out of me. It was borderline painful, but another few traces around my lips and clit were enough to make me forget the pain in the moment.

He pulled my hair back, and I could see him watching me from the corner of my eyes. "Is this what you want, bitch?" he asked her, and I could see the steely amusement in his eyes. It was exactly the look I didn't know I wanted to see from him.

"Yes," I told him. He gripped my head harder. "Yes, sir!"

Anthony then took a moment to shove those beads, the beads that I had all but forgotten, into my ass, one at a time. Each bead that popped in made me gasp and shudder. Two... Three... Four... Five... My thighs were quivering, and I was barely holding myself up. The feeling was so foreign, but the weight within my ass was pleasant. I clenched around it.

"Good girl," he said with a slap, sending me gasping again. He flipped me over to look at his handiwork, and I laid there, palms up and at my head, turned to look at him from the side, and he grinned. "Good," he said, watching as my breath heaved in and out rapidly. My mouth was agape and I could feel the pressure within me building.

Without a word, he plunged his fingers inside of me, reaching up to find my g-spot, pressing against it. I shut my eyes and whined at the feeling, unable to help it as my thighs shot upwards in response, begging and pleading wordlessly for more than I had already gotten.

He chuckled darkly at me. "You think you're ready for this? For me?" he purred, leaning closer. He swatted at me with the crop just under my rib cage with a smirk. He was enjoying every moment.

"Y-yes, sir," I managed to just barely breathe out. I couldn't help it. I was spilling all over his bed; I could feel the wetness when he pushed me right down onto the mattress roughly. The sight only made him hotter, and I could see his dick hardening in his pants. He released it, revealing a solid seven inches—larger than average but not overwhelming. He rubbed it along my lips, his head tracing them, but never diving into the opening.

The feeling was enough to make me shudder and hitch my breath in my chest. My nipples were aching wonderfully under the weight of the clamps, and I reached toward his hips without thinking about it, preparing to pull him in.

Anthony pulled away, swiftly swatting both hands with his crop, leaving me crying out as pain met pleasure. "You do not touch me unless I tell you to," he told me curtly. "Do you understand, slut?"

"Yes, sir," I squeak out, rubbing my hands.

"Since you can't control your hands, I'll have to control them for you. Over your head, slut," he told me, and I obeyed as he walked around me, unwilling to give me the pleasure of feeling him against me by reaching over. He clenched both of my wrists and bound them together, putting them above me and into a bond to keep them from moving. The bond clipped to something on the headboard—I couldn't quite see it, but I could feel that it pulled my arms tightly. I tried to shift up to relieve some of the pressure.

"You stay here," he told me as he walked back to the other side of the bed and between my legs, pulling my hips back down toward him. I winced at the feeling of my wrists being pulled tightly but resisted making a sound. "Good girl."

As a reward for my obedience, he shoved his dick right into me, just as I had been waiting for. He pushed every inch in quickly, not giving me the chance to adjust to his length or his girth as he slammed against me. I caught my breath in my chest and whimpered as he did it again. His balls slammed into the beads in my ass, and I couldn't help but pull away a bit, only to meet his hands roughly holding me in place.

"You will stay here and take my cock like a good girl, do you understand me?"

"Y-yes."

"Good." He pushed in harder and harder, lifting the crop to tap it against each of the nipple clamps, evoking a scream from me as my hips slammed up to meet his as he thrust again. "Good, slut, take every inch of me."

"Give me every inch," I mewled in reply, breathing heavily. I was in heaven—I could feel the pressure of the beads within me rubbing pleasurably against the pressure of his cock as he continued to whip along me. It was so good... I was getting wetter within him, and I felt myself clench up around him.

"You are not to cum yet, do you understand?"

"Yes..." I breathed out between moans of pleasure. My head was back, eyes short, but I could hear him grunting as he sped up. He kept the rhythm, hard, fast, and deep, for a moment, his own breathing starting to hitch within him as well. He sounded so sexy in the moment as he used me like the toy that I knew I was meant to be. I wanted him to have me, and I let him pound me so hard that I thought I might tear under his pressure.

He groaned in pleasure as I felt his hips buck against me, leaving his load inside of me. He remained there, pushing against my hips for a few moments before he finally decided to pull away, looking at me like a piece of meat. He took a moment to catch his breath, his cock half-hard still, and shining in the dim light.

Wordlessly, he climbed up over me and dropped his balls in my face. "Lick them clean," he told me, and I obliged immediately.

I licked up every last drop of me from his balls and from his shaft, slowly and tenderly removing it. He was fully hard again by the time that I was done sucking on it and playing with it. "You have five minutes, suck me off, or you will be punished." Without a word, he set a timer and removed the restraints that had held me against the bed, though my hands were still together.

I obliged immediately, leaning down and taking as much of his girth as I could into my mouth. I lingered on the tip for a few moments, sucking it until I felt it twitch, and then I moved on to the shaft. Without my hands, I'd have to make do with just my mouth. I ran it into my throat as deeply as I could manage without choking and let my tongue squeeze against it, quickly pulling it out of my mouth and licking it from the balls up to the tip again and again.

The more that I sucked on him, the more I felt him twitching in my mouth and tried my best, but the timer came and went, and he flipped me over onto my back. He swatted me with the crop four times, hard this time, and I cried out at the feeling dancing. I was certain that the skin was welted at that point. "Nice try, but you failed," he told me as my eyes watered from the smarting welts underneath me.

"I'm sorry, sir," I told him, wincing. All I wanted at that point was to finish. I was going insane, feeling the weight of the beads within me, and I was getting desperate.

"Your punishment," he told me, "is that you will be fucked without being allowed to cum, do you understand me?"

"Yes, sir," I said back, despite feeling like I wanted to protest. It was almost like my body and mind wanted two different things. He slammed his cock into me again, once again hard, and he worked me up, slamming in harder and harder. He could feel me getting close and pulled out just before I was able to cum, leaving me collapsing against the bed, frustrated.

"What's wrong?" he asked, leaning over me with that same smirk on his face. "Frustrated?"
"No, sir."

"Oh, I see," he said, prying my legs apart. He lowered his head to lick at my clit, his tongue dancing gently around the protected little nub. He licked up and down it slowly, sensually, watching as my body tensed up in response. He lowered his tongue to dance on the outside of my lips, teasing the entrance just barely with a flick of his tongue before bringing it right back up to the top again. He sucked on the little nub, his tongue dancing on and around it as he did. His finger snaked up to penetrate me, slowly pushing into me as he did. He looked up at me from his place, eating at me and watched as my back arched and I moaned loudly in pleasure. I couldn't take it... I felt the pressure building up, and I didn't think that I could hold it back anymore...

And he pulled away. He looked at me from his position and stood up over me.

"The little slut doesn't deserve to finish tonight after failing me," he told me with a quick swat of the crop against my skin, leaving me wanting desperately without anything to relieve myself. I groaned as I fell down onto the bed, and he smirked again.

"Then again... You are a new little slut, aren't you? Do you want to beg for release?"

"Please," I said suddenly, my voice pleading. My pussy was dripping and empty, and I wanted something—anything—in it.

"Please, what?"

"P-please fuck me," I cried out in desperation.

"What's that?"

"Sir, please, fuck me sir!" I moaned, fighting the urge to reach for him. My body couldn't take the buildup any longer, and before I could say another word, he pushed himself into me again. I gasped, shuddering at the feeling. It was exactly what I needed, and I writhed on the bed, thrusting my body against his.

"Cum for me, slut," he commanded firmly.

I felt my body oblige immediately. I felt the clench of pressure in my pussy as it gripped against his dick. I felt the waves of release that I had been waiting for all evening, giving way around him, over and over, for what felt like forever as he finished within me. I felt his release alongside mine, and he pulled himself out of me.

My breathing was heavy, and I was exhausted beyond belief, eyes still closed. My whole body ached pleasantly under the strain and release. I felt the nipple clamps release off of me, and I looked up to see Anthony watching me. He smirked self-satisfied. "Now, get out of my sight, you slut. I'll see you tomorrow."

He didn't even have the courtesy to ask—just assumed that I'd be back again. He wasn't wrong.

Amelia's Punishment

Amelia is a housekeeper that has a strange job. Every week, she's asked to come over and clean, wearing a skimpy outfit for a man that rarely ever says more than a word or two to her at a time. She cleans the spotless surfaces for the money but finds herself getting paid more than she ever thought she could ask for when she accidentally drops a crystal glass and needs to be punished for her transgressions by her sexy boss, Mr. Erikson, who wants nothing more than to rip her skimpy little outfit off of her and ravish her body.

Even though the area was always immaculately clean, I was still always asked to come over every week to dust, wipe, and polish anything that I found on the shelves. It was mildly humiliating; Mr. Erikson required me to wear this skimpy little maid's outfit that barely covered my ass cheeks, but let's be real here for a moment—I *loved* having my cheeks hang out. Sometimes, if Mr. Erikson, the fine specimen of a man that he was, was looking my direction, I'd intentionally stand up on my tippy toes to reach out to some imagined hard to reach area *just* to give him a flash of my ass. No panties. That part was all me, not him. I imagine that he'd get hard at his desk, hidden behind the wooden surface, as I reached up. I imagined that he'd let his eyes slowly take me in as stretched. I imagined that he was an ass man, based on the fact that mine was just barely covered, but to be fair, my dress barely covered my tits either—it pushed them up, almost uncomfortably tight, to create a huge cleave down my front as they were smashed together. I looked good, that was for sure, and I always had to wonder if he only wanted me here so that he could have some eye candy. After all, there were rarely any real messes for me.

I was busy scrubbing some invisible splotch on the wall, over and over, slowly just rubbing my towel on the wall. Sometimes, I'd sit there and sensually begin to clean objects, suggestively running my fingers up and down the length of an ornate crystal decanter filled with amber liquid. It was rum, maybe, or brandy or whiskey. I never opened it up, but I did know that the amount of liquid in the bottle was always changing from week to week when I did my rounds, so it must have been for more than just decoration.

That day, I could feel Mr. Erikson watch me with mild disinterest as if I weren't there. His gaze would drift over to me, and I'd feel tension in the air, but he must have been distracted. It was like he saw right through me as his eyes caressed my legs, lazily going up and down their lengths, but his mind was clearly elsewhere. I'd have to try harder if I wanted him to actually look at me. The idea of a challenge made my pussy twinge in anticipation. We never fucked or anything. In fact, we never even touched or said more than just a few terse words to each other, but the tension in the air was palatable. I bet Mr. Erikson could have cut the tension with his dick. I knew he liked watching me; the bulge that he had in his pants the few times he walked by, unabashedly unconcealed, told me that much.

I'd have to try harder; I told myself if I wanted to win that day. I wanted that sexual tension to build up so much that I could hardly take it. I'd never actually initiate; the job paid too well to just be eye candy. But, I'd be lying if I said that I didn't regularly think about throwing myself on the desk and begging him to take me on more than one occasion.

As I worked on cleaning up the wall, then, I let the rag slip out of my hand to the floor. Honest mistake, right? I bent down, keeping my knees straight, revealing myself to Mr. Erikson. Considering the clattering of his pen that I heard, he must have seen it all, and I smirked, feeling another twitch in my pussy. My clit was starting to swell, and I could feel the fluids beginning to soak everything. Slowly, I straightened up without a word, discarding the rag and getting a clean one, and I moved on to polishing the glasses that matched the decanter. They were smooth and felt hefty in my hand, the cool crystalline surface shining brilliantly in the light of the office. The office was kept dark most of the time, curtains drawn and warm lamps on creating just enough light for Mr. Erikson to do whatever it was that he did at his desk. I wasn't sure what he did—I had never thought to ask him, nor did I really care. We didn't talk much. My job was to clean everything and I was not allowed to leave for the whole two hours that I was paid to be there to clean it. At first, the two hours seemed to drag on forever, but our unspoken game made the time fly by when I wasn't paying attention to it. I gently placed the glass back down and picked up the next one, polishing that one as well. I would imagine that they were his cock, hard and smooth in my hand, as the towel rubbed up and down, polishing even the bottom of it. My fingers would linger, rubbing sensually on the crystal surface. I'd do them one by one before putting them perfectly down where they had been before. As I reached to put the last glass down, it slipped from my hand and clattered as it fell onto the ground, thankfully onto a rug. I froze when I realized what happened.

"Amelia?" I heard him speak—he never spoke if he could avoid it.

"Yes, sir?" I managed to force myself to say, my voice shaking. I was shocked that I had made such a mistake—I was usually so careful with what I did. It was highly abnormal for me to make mistakes like that. Everything was calculated and planned out, but I had gotten careless.

I heard Mr. Erikson's chair move out from behind his desk, and I could hear the rustling of his clothing as he stood up. He was looking right at me, but I couldn't bring myself to even look at him. I had done it now! I knew I'd be fired on the spot—I'd heard rumors in the house that he was always firing the house staff if they didn't exceed his expectations! I groaned inwardly.

"Amelia." He was firmer this time as my name escaped his lips, sending a shiver down my spine. Despite the concern for being fired, I *still* wanted him. Hell—half of me hoped he'd bend me over the desk and spank me for my punishment and let me get back to work.

I forced my eyes to slowly shift over to him; my gaze slowly drifting across his body from the ground up. When I made it to his cock, my eyes widened, seeing it swollen and bulging against his pants, threatening to destroy the zipper if it wasn't freed soon. His pants were black, crisply ironed and somehow, without a single wrinkle in them, despite working at a desk. He was toned—or at least, I assumed he was toned by the shape of his arms when he'd work, bulging and rippling. He clearly exercised regularly. When I finally raised my gaze to meet his own icy cool one, I was greeted with the sight of a barely perceptible smirk. If I didn't know him better, and to be frank, I barely knew him at all; I'd say that he was giving me bedroom eyes—you know the kind that says that you're ready to throw the person onto the bed and fuck their brains out kind of eyes.

And it made me so hot.

"You've been a naughty girl, Amelia," he said, his voice quiet and in control as he looked me over. I was shrinking into myself, making myself as small as possible. My arms were crossed in front of me, pushing my breasts up further in their skimpy little covering that could hardly be considered covered in the first place.

"I'm sorry sir," I managed to squeak out in response.

And he chuckled. It was a dark chuckle, sensuous as he looked me over like he was considering something. "You better be." Something about the veiled threat sent a thrill running down my spine. "Do you know what we do to naughty girls around here, Amelia?"

"N-no sir." I had some high hopes, though.

"They are punished according to their crimes. Do you know why that glass is always here?"

"No..."

"No, what?"

"No, sir."

"Good girl." He smirked, one brow raising up as he did. He was checking me out. "That was my late father's set. It is irreplaceable."

I hadn't realized, and suddenly, I felt bad. It wasn't broken; somehow, it had managed to land on a rug and didn't break, thankfully, but I still felt *awful*. "What is my punishment, sir?" My gaze was firmly on his feet at this point. I couldn't explain it, but all of my confidence that I had had just moments prior had all melted away.

"You need a spanking, Amelia." I heard him cracking his knuckles then, and I looked up at him in surprise. His dick was harder than ever, judging by the fact that his pants had somehow become even tauter than they had been just moments prior, and I looked at him in awe. Was he going to fuck me? I kind of hoped he did. My fear melted away as he beckoned for me to move closer to him, and I did it without a single protest.

Suddenly, I felt his hands wrap around my wrist and pull me close. I could smell his aftershave; he smelled clean and strong with a hint of subtle spiciness, and I loved it. His fingers on my skin were strong and warm, firm, but not painful, and he placed his other hand on the small of my back, wordlessly telling me to bend over, and I did, my body resting atop his desk. He was strong and firm; I couldn't help but want to obey, even as I felt the first sting of his strong, warm hand hitting my bare ass. I squealed in surprise, bucking back at the sudden surprise of the movement, sending a pen holder clattering to the ground. I tried to pull away, but he firmly pressed into the small of my back. He wanted me to stay there.

"You've been such a naughty girl," he practically purred in my ear, his voice low and husky. I could hear the desperation in it. He wanted this just as much as I did. I didn't protest as I felt his hand slowly rubbing over my ass, giving it a firm squeeze as he did. Then both hands groped at me, pulling my cheeks apart. "You have such a tight little ass," he marveled under his breath. "I'm going to make it mine."

I gasped as he pressed his cock against me. It was hard and larger than I had thought in his pants. He leaned over me, letting his hands slide up my whole body from my ass, up my back, and sliding around my waist and up higher to grasp my tits, squeezing them tightly. He fondled them, letting his hand squeeze a bit tighter than I had expected. With the weight of him atop me, I felt my heart pounding in my chest, and I gasped. I fought the urge to turn my head to kiss him. I was so wet at that point. I'm sure it was soaking through his pants as he continued to grind his cock against me. I could feel myself practically dripping between my thighs as he kneaded at my nipples, slipping his fingers into the tight top of the dress. He didn't even bother fighting with it; he just tore it off, literally tearing down the front, and I didn't say a word. It was almost hotter to see the display of strength as he did it.

With my breasts free, he pulled at them before pulling back. Then, unexpectedly, I felt another slap against my ass. It was strong, and it was painful, almost immediately. I cried out at the sudden impact, but it was more in shock than anything else.

"What a naughty, dirty little slut you are," he breathed in my ear as he leaned over me again. "You're dripping." His breath on my neck sent shivers down my spine, and I turned my head just slightly, granting him access to do whatever he wanted to it, and he obliged. His lips fell on my neck and I felt his tongue dance across my skin before he nipped and nibbled. He wasn't rough enough to hurt, but I was sure I'd need to wear a scarf for the next few days.

He pulled back, and again, I felt another slap on my ass, but this time, he didn't pull his hand away. He let his hand linger against my skin. "Do you like your punishment?" His fingers slid closer to my slit, close enough to feel my wetness all over them.

"Yes, sir," I breathed out, tensing up and pushing my ass out just enough to try to encourage him to enter me. He pulled his fingers away from me, teasing the lips with the lightest of touches. He wasn't going to let me enjoy things that easily.

"Good. I don't tolerate little dirty sluts that don't know their place. You're going to learn your lesson tonight, do you hear me?"

"Yes, sir." I felt him let go of my ass and slap me again, and I cried out at the strange immersion of pain and pleasure as he did it.

Mr. Erikson flipped me over onto his desk and lifted me up as if I weighed nothing, setting me down atop it to get a full view of his handiwork. He looked at my breasts, no longer covered up by the black fabric that was in tatters around my waist, as if considering something, and then tore it all the way off. "You don't need this, do you?"

I shook my head breathlessly, in awe at the strength of the man in front of me. He leaned over me, his hands resting on either side of my legs, his nose so close that I could have touched it just by leaning forward. The urge to kiss him grew harder, and I leaned in to do it, only to feel his hand pulling my hair back to stop me. I squealed and looked up at him.

"You do not touch me. I touch you. You are here for me."

"Yes, sir," I said, trying not to struggle against the tugging on my hair.

He released my hair and pushed me down onto the desk, unzipping his pants and releasing the largest cock I had ever seen. No wonder his pants looked so tense against the heft of it. He pushed it against me, and I could feel it, hot and pulsating against my thigh. He rubbed it on me, up and down, and I could feel it gliding over me. The rubbing on me seemed to turn him on more, and he suddenly rammed it straight inside of me without hesitation.

I felt his big cock fill me up until I felt like I couldn't possibly expand any further, and yet, he kept pushing it in, forcing it deeper until I wondered if I would split in half. He held it there, tense and deep within me, and I realized he still hadn't gone all the way.

"Your wet pussy is so tight," he growled in my ear. He gyrated his hips just enough to press against my inner walls, and I moaned in pleasure. It was a tight fit, but that made it even better. I clenched against him as he slowly pulled himself out, and he thrust in again and again. "I will ravish this pussy tonight, do you hear me?"

I could barely manage to speak at the feeling of his cock rubbing against me. It was like a dream come true—I had fantasized about this moment so much, and here it was, happening.

"Amelia. Do. You. Hear. Me." He thrust in deeply between each and every word he said, making me moan every single time. I was breathing heavily, looking up at him, my mouth agape. I could hardly control myself enough to speak.

"Y-yes, sir," I managed to breathe between thrusts. His cock was better than I could have possibly imagined.

"Do you want me to take this pussy?"

"Yes!" I cried out, throwing my head back, bracing myself against the desk. He reached out and grabbed my breasts, weighing them in his hands. He was rough, but not hurtful as he ran his thumbs over my nipples, tracing circles right around them with the pads of his thumbs resting right onto them. My eyes were shut, enjoying the sensations of my body as he continued to thrust within me. I could feel the tension building up in pleasurable waves as he occasionally flicked and twisted at my nipples between thrusts.

I could feel myself getting close, and my breathing hitched in my chest as he continued to thrust inside of me. He would go faster and slower. Sometimes, he would almost tenderly and slowly pull it out and push it back in, other times, he would thrust his cock into me so rapidly that he had to hold me in place so I wouldn't fall off of the desk.

More items clamored to the floor, landing near the torn and discarded maid's costume. Just when I thought I wouldn't be able to take it any longer, he pulled out of me, looking at me in dark amusement. He was enjoying taking charge. "You're not cumming 'til I tell you that you can," he informed me as he flipped me over and pushed me back. I was standing on the floor now, on my tiptoes, and my arms and torso were stretched out across the surface of the desk. He spanked me again, hitting atop an area that had already been swatted earlier, and it stung enough to make me hiss in pain, but before I could protest, his cock was right back inside of me, making me forget all about the stinging.

He stayed there for just a moment or two, and as soon as I could feel myself getting close again, he stopped. "You're such a dirty little wench, aren't you, getting close already? Control yourself." He took my hand this time and led me to a door in the back of his office that I had never entered before. As soon as he opened the door, he revealed that there was a large, walk-in closet, but it was entirely devoid of any hangers or jackets, or even office supplies. Instead, there was a large, thick pole that went from wall to wall, and there were restraints suspended for it, thick and black and appearing strong enough to hold someone up. I hesitated, looking at it, but felt Mr. Erikson's cock against my back, wet and chilled by the ambient air. It pressed against me firmly, ushering me to enter, and I did, slowly turning around to look at him. Now we were in uncharted territory for me, but I wasn't sure that I really cared. I wanted this man's cock in me as hard as it could be to get me off as soon as possible and he seemed to sense that based on the fervor with which he wrapped his fingers around my delicate wrists and tied me up. It wasn't so bad; I told myself as I felt the restraints. They were tight against my wrist, but they didn't hurt. They held my hands right above my head and kept me from being able to move them too much, but it was okay with me. I didn't mind—until suddenly, he tightened the restraints and I felt my arms being yanked upward. I had to stand on my toes to keep the pressure from getting to be too much for me.

Mr. Erikson looked over my body carefully, eyeing my tits and my hips and the dip between them. He spread my lips between my legs and smirked as he did. "You've quite the body here. Why have you teased me so much with it?" His gaze flitted to mine for a fleeting instant, and I saw that intense desire burning within them. I smirked back, but just as quickly as I did, I felt a quick stinging across my thighs as he slapped them. I could see the handprints welting immediately.

"Did you want me?" he asked me after a moment.

"I did, sir," I replied, licking my lips slowly. I could see him watching me do it. I wanted him to want me right that moment so that we could fuck more. I stood up taller, thrusting out my chest, hoping that he'd give in and take me right then and there.

He ran his fingers up and down my thighs before slipping them between my legs, reaching up to touch that tiny nub folded away in my lips. He touched my clit, and I felt my legs immediately begin to quiver. I moaned softly at the contact, my hips thrusting. I felt his fingers trail further downward, and he traced my slit, pushing against it, but never actually penetrating me. His fingers slid further back than that, too—his fingers danced around my asshole, pressing on it. His finger, still wet with my juices, penetrated just slightly, slowly making its way into me. "Have you ever been fucked here before?"

"N-no sir," I gasped out as he pushed his finger deeper into me. I felt my muscles contract around his finger, and he put a second finger in as well, moving it in and out. After a few moments, he added in a third as well, gently penetrating just enough to get the muscles used to it. I felt myself starting to relax as he continued, and the sensation excited me further. The feelings of pleasure bloomed, and I found myself loving it, and then his fingers pulled out altogether.

I felt a dildo, larger than his fingers, thrust into my slit, pushing and twisting it deeper and deeper, and I felt the pleasure begin to build up even more. My pussy was swelling with anticipation as the sensations grew stronger, and he pulled the toy out, immediately pressing it against my ass again before slowly easing the toy in. "We'll have to work up to my cock. I wouldn't want to tear you in half," he said with a smirk as he slid the toy into me. I was on my tiptoes still, desperately trying to keep my legs from giving out underneath me as the pleasure threatened to overcome me, and just as quickly as it had started, he pulled it out and removed the restraints. I practically collapsed under the weight of myself, but he caught me and lowered me to the ground, positioning me on my hands and knees with my ass in the air. He pumped his cock into me a few times, lubricating himself with my own fluids, of which there was no shortage, before easing himself into my ass. His cock was massive, and I didn't think that it would fit, but still, it plunged deeper and deeper. I threw my hand backward with a moan of pleasure, and he wrapped his hand around me, reaching for my throat. He put pressure on it as he fucked me harder, not enough to cut off my windpipe, but just enough to elevate the sensation as he continued. He thrust harder and harder into my ass, and I could feel him getting harder inside my tight ass until finally, he groaned in pleasure, thrusting deeply and holding me there as he released his cum into me before pulling out slowly.

"Hold that cum in you. Don't let a drop fall out," he told me as he stood up, straightening out his tie and fixing his pants. I stayed on my hands and knees as he cleaned himself up, clenching my ass and feeling endlessly frustrated. He flipped me over. "Now, I can see that the dirty slut didn't finish with my cock, is that so?"

"Yes, sir," I told him, feeling the ache growing more than before. I wanted to fuck still, but he had other plans. He smirked at me. "Make your dirty pussy cum for me, but don't lose a drop of what I left in you," he commanded, crossing his arms and leaning back. I was taken aback by the command, but it wasn't the worst thing in the world. It would be the perfect way to entice him back for another round later. After all, I worked there several times a month.

I reached around, still on my hands and knees, using one hand to gently touch myself. I felt just how wet I was; I was practically dripping. My ass was still up in the air, and Mr. Erikson got the full view of my fingers, gently caressing my lips and rubbing on my clit as I did. I ran my fingers over the opening slowly at first, then pressed them in, one at a time, moaning sensually as they penetrated me. I reached in deeper, angling my fingers upward, touching at my g-spot within me, and I felt my hips thrust themselves in pleasure. I ran my fingers in deeper and deeper into myself, feeling every clench of my inner walls, every time I tightened and every shudder, and finally, within moments, I felt the pleasure welling up within me. I could feel the climax peaking, threatening to erupt, until it finally exploded, sending my hips and my vagina into spasms around my fingers, tensing up tighter and tighter, over and over again.

As the pleasure subsided, leaving my body pleasantly buzzing, I slowly pulled my fingers out from within me and looked at Mr. Erikson, who was watching with great interest, and I slowly licked my fluids off of myself. I sucked them clean, never breaking eye contact with him, even when I could see his pants start to tighten around his crotch again. "I can't wait for you to punish me again. I might have to even do some naughty things on purpose next time," I practically purred as I stood up to look at him.

He smirked back at me. "I'll just have to punish you harder next time."

Unwrapped Gifts

Nora loves her boyfriend and wants to give him a present for his birthday that he'll never forget, so she wraps herself up with her best friend for as long as she can remember, Becca, and sets herself up for some steamy action for Jared, happy to give him a day that he'll remember for years to come. Together, the naughty women enjoy themselves a little too much and leave him aching for more and looking for as much of a fuck as he can get. The lucky guy gets to unwrap two presents at once and enjoy every moment of it.

It was Jared's birthday, and I had a big plan in store for him. It was going to be the greatest birthday of his life, and he had no idea yet. I grinned at my friend, Becca, who was next to me. She was drop-dead gorgeous. She had naturally auburn hair that fell in waves and the greenest eyes that I had ever seen, and her lightly tanned skin was dusted with freckles right atop her perfectly sculpted cheekbones that sat high. She was wearing sultry makeup that day, her eyes shadowy and perfectly done, and she had a skintight, short dress with a deep v plunge, showing off the perfect cleavage she had.

Becca was my best friend and had been for years. She was someone that I was willing to share just about anything with—and I mean *anything*. As we smirked at each other, we knew that we were in for quite the night. I reached out to touch her arm, and she looked at me for a moment. "Are you sure about this, Nora?"

"Of course! It can't be too bad, can it? Besides, don't you remember our experimental phase in college?" It was true—we had been quite willing to explore each other's bodies and the wonders that they brought with each other when we were roommates, especially after a few nights of too many drinks.

She smiled widely, her eyes sparkling. She knew I had a point, but it wasn't every day that you fuck your best friend with your boyfriend. She put a hand on my back gently, and I hugged her. We would have a good time, that much I was sure of. I just had to be willing to actually do it, and I was sure that, in the moment, the look on Jared's face when he realizes that his birthday gift is literally his dream, being able to fuck two women at once, he would love every moment of it.

"What do you say we pre-game a bit?" asked Becca, looking at me through her lashes, her lips tugging upwards just slightly. She raised one brow as she did, waiting for my response. That didn't sound like that bad of an idea, I told myself. Besides, watching me get it on with a girl was another one of his biggest fantasies, and he was due to be home any time now.

I leaned in toward Becca, planting a kiss on her lips gently, and as I pulled back, she dove in for more. She pulled me in greedily, savoring the taste of my lips as she bit onto them, her tongue skating across them as she sucked. Her eyes were closed as she enjoyed herself, moaning against my lips. Her hand snaked around my neck, wrapping itself into my hair to hold me in place tightly in her passion. We weren't in love or anything, but who said a couple of girls couldn't platonically enjoy their body together in peace?

I reached up toward her breasts, feeling them gently with my palms. Her nipples hardened underneath the weight of my hand, pressing against my skin, and I could tell that she liked it by the way she kissed harder. Her hands twisted in my hair and one of her hands dropped down to rub on the outside of my own dress, right on my crotch area. We were careful not to mess each other up too much—we were all dressed up for Jared to unwrap. But, we could still tease each other and that we were doing.

Becca's breasts were so soft under my hand. Seriously, women's tits were like nature's greatest stress balls. The more I played with her, and the more she rubbed up against me, the less nervous I became. I found myself stroking her thighs, up and down, letting my fingers skate across the smooth, perfectly waxed surface. I was on her inner thigh, feeling the softness and the warmth emanating from just above. I could smell her moistness, soft, sweet, feminine, and carnal all at once, and it just made me want to play with her more. I let my fingers sneak their way up her dress to rub against the thin fabric of her panties. They were lace, and they weren't doing much at all to contain the juices that were beginning to flow. They were damp already, and I was able to slip my finger around them to touch the waxed pussy that was waiting for me. She was so warm and so soft under my fingers, and as soon as I let them graze over the lips between her legs, I felt Becca's kissing grow more desperate. Her pelvis tensed and her hips thrust forward, and I felt her legs spread apart just enough to let my had have more access. I reached up to touch her clit, rubbing it gently and tracing circles around it. I could feel it twitching and throbbing under my finger, telling a tale of how much she was enjoying the moment. Her breath caught in her chest and suddenly, she was practically silent and still, feeling my touch.

I reached my other hand to knead at her breast, rubbing it in between my fingers as I did. She loved every moment of it, and she couldn't hide it, even if she wanted to. I smiled as I slammed into her lips again, letting my tongue slip between her lips to taste hers this time. My fingers rubbed up against her over and over again before finally slipping inside of her. Her pussy was so tight against my fingers as I pushed in, feeling her inner walls clench against me. She wanted me to push into her, and I did, over and over again. I pushed harder and harder until I could feel her practically writhing underneath the weight of my hand.

She was so tight with my fingers in her, and I plunged deeper, twisting my fingers within her. I could feel her body begin to tense up more and more until I made her cum with a loud moan, head thrown back and hair draped down, exposing her long, slender neck as the waves of pleasure shook her body.

I kissed against her neck as I waited for the waves to subside, and when they did, she looked at me lustily, grinning. Her hair was mussed, but it just made her look hotter. She leaned over me, pinning me to the wall, ready to return the favor as she pushed her fingers around the tiny black thong I was wearing and stroking my clit. The sensation zapped throughout me, earning a throaty moan, and she pressed harder. She was touching me harder, tugging at my hair with her other hand so that she could wrap her lips around my neck and suck on the skin.

Her fingers expertly stroked over my clit as it swelled and pulsed until a finger slid into me. She curled her fingers up, and I felt myself tightening up as she stroked the inside of my pussy walls. I felt myself gyrate my hips, pushing her hand deeper. "You feel so good," I whispered to her between deep breaths as she teased me more and more. I wanted her deeper as I pushed against her hand, and she obliged, reaching her other hand to grope at my breasts instead, teasing my nipple underneath her fingers. I was practically whimpering at that point as she continued to fuck me with her fingers. Her mouth nibbled and licked at my neck and my ears as her fingers continued to knead me through the cloth. My body was shaking underneath the weight of her body and before I knew it, I was cumming around her fingers, feeling the pleasure overcome me for what felt like forever.

When I finally regained my senses, I opened my eyes to look at Becca, only to see Jared with an awestruck face right behind her. He had dark hair and skin, and his eyes were nearly black, but in the moment, he was slack-jawed, and I could see the erection growing in his pants. Who knew how long he had been watching, but he had certainly liked what he had seen enough to let us continue, completely uninterrupted.

Becca, seeing my focus shifted somewhere else, turned around to see what had caught my attention and smiled her sexiest smile, leaning forward and putting her hands in front of herself, clasped together so that her breasts were squeezed and pushed up. "Happy birthday, birthday boy!" she purred as she leaned over to run a hand up and down his chest, just as we had planned.

"We've got a great day in store for you," I chimed in, leaning over and planting a kiss right on his face, letting my hands slide down to rub against his hard cock in his pants. I unbuttoned him right there.

"I'll unwrap you first so you can unwrap your gift." His pants were quickly discarded, as was his shirt, leaving him there, naked and wonderfully toned, not unlike a Greek statue—the ones where every single bulge is in the right spot. But this statue had one extra part—a long, rock-hard cock that was ready for action. I touched it, feeling it twitch underneath the touch.

He looked at me and then at Becca, and it finally seemed to register. "Really, babe?" he asked, and I nodded in response with a sly smile. I was glad that he seemed eager to enjoy his gift, and I took him by the hand and led him to our bedroom. We had a king bed so there was plenty of room for anything that we wanted to do. We could both lay together there no problem, even with Becca. We weren't exactly big women by any means; we were both maybe 5' even and petite, in perfect contrast to Jared's 6' and muscular build.

As we got into bed, I felt Jared's hand slap my ass, and I squealed and giggled in response. We were definitely in for a fun time. "What do you want us to do?" I asked him in my sweetest voice. "We'll do *anything*." I really emphasized that last word, letting it hang with a suggestive waggle of my eyebrows that got him to chuckle to himself.

"Anything?"

"Anything," we both replied, hoping that he wouldn't come up with some off-the-wall answer about what it was that he actually did want. We waited for him quietly, looking at each other.

"Striptease," came his reply after what felt like forever.

We grinned. We could do that. And so, we did. I reached over to Becca, letting my hand rub along her neck as I grasped the lining of her dress before pulling it over her head, revealing her naked body for Jared to see. I looked at her—she had gone braless, which explained exactly why I had been able to feel her nipples so easily, and I tossed her shirt aside, looking at the beautiful, pink circles in the center of her breasts. I wanted to suck on them, and I leaned in to plant the lightest of kisses on each nipple, watching them stand to attention after doing so before letting Becca do the same to me. My dress was also discarded, but my thong and bra were left on.

"Remove her panties with your teeth," Jared told me suddenly, and I'm not going to lie—that caught me off guard. But, I did it anyway, leaning in closely to Becca's leg and sensually rubbing along the skin before reaching up with my mouth to wrap myself around the lace. I could smell her arousal; she was dripping even more now than she was before as I pulled the panties down carefully with my teeth, getting a glimpse of her perfect bare ass. Seriously, Becca was a goddess of a woman.

"Play with each other some more," commanded Jared, and we both obliged immediately. After all, he *was* the birthday boy—what he wanted, he would get. We just had to be willing participants for his every whim. Becca took charge first, leaning over me on the bed. Her perfect, perky tits hung over my face, tantalizingly teasing with every movement she made. I reached up to caress her nipples, and she leaned down to remove my bra, tossing it to the floor with abandon. She leaned down, looking up at Jared and holding his gaze as she kissed each of my nipples and let her tongue snake out of her mouth, licking the areolas, careful not to ever touch the nipple itself. She teased around the nipple, leaving it erect and longing. It felt good, but I found myself desperate for her touch, my own arousal growing with each and every lazy circle around the top of my breast. She moved to the other, slowly circling around the nipple again, leaving me breathless. She let her breath linger over it, watching as Jared stroked himself to us.

He loved his private show, his cock hard and long in his hand as he slowly, almost lazily, went up and down its shaft. I watched him touch himself and felt myself get wetter at the thrill of knowing that we were driving him crazy with every movement we made.

Becca slid down, kissing my taut stomach as she made her way down to my crotch little by little, she kissed the mound at the top.

She let her tongue taste me, but only tracing the outer lips of my labia, driving me insane. I felt my hips thrusting of their own accord, silently betting her to touch, and I could feel the wetness beginning to accumulate, and then be licked up greedily by Becca's swift tongue.

She teased me up more and more, knowing that she was driving me crazy. I always loved being licked up and down, and she knew that more than anyone else—but I still was denied.

And just as quickly as it began, it stopped as Jared came over to get between us. His cock was hard in his hand, and I could see the desire in his eyes as he looked at both of us, almost as if choosing which one of us he wanted to get to fuck first. His eyes rested on me as if waiting for my approval, and when I nodded my head, he turned to Becca and grabbed her shoulder, spinning her around. Her eyes widened for a moment, but she didn't protest as he pushed her to the bed.

He rubbed his cock on her clit, and I could see her pleasure clear as day as she moaned, head back before he pushed deep into her with a hard thrust. He was quick with his thrusts, going as deep as possible. His balls slapped against her ass over and over, and he let out a groan of pleasure as he reached forward to greedily paw at her breasts, holding them in his hand and squeezing.

Just as quickly as he started fucking her, he reached over to grab me and pull me over next to her. He pushed his hands inside of me as well, letting his rough fingers penetrate deeply and stroke my inner walls as he tried to please me as well. He had one hand on Becca's breast, his cock deep in her, and his other hand inside of me as I reached down to touch my clit as well, with another hand on my breast, tugging at my nipples.

He fucked harder and harder into Becca until her moans of pleasure became cries of utter ecstasy, so loud that if we had been in an apartment, I would have worried about neighbors hearing us. He fucked deeper and deeper into her, focusing on the sensation, his fingers slipping out from me and shoved into her face, which she happily lapped up, taking my taste into her mouth and sucking on them. He groaned again with one last thrust, shaking as he came deep in her. Judging by her face and sudden silence, she finished as well.

Jared pulled himself out of her and turned to me. "I'm not done with you yet," he told me with a sound that told me that he was serious. He leaned over me, towering over my small body. He grasped my breast and let his fingers return to my clit, gently grazing over the swollen little nub that was desperate for attention and release. My breathing got quicker as he touched me, and my hips thrust into him. I wanted him—bad. I pulled him against me, and he lowered his head to lick at my clit instead, first circling around it before finally flattening his tongue and pressing against it, rubbing and licking it until I couldn't take it any longer.

Just before I could get over the edge, he pulled away, leaving me ultimately disappointed as I looked up at him. He smirked. "Not so fast. I want to really enjoy my gift," he told me as he let his cock just barely touch the outside of my slit, driving me wild. I pushed up, hoping he'd give in, but he pulled back even further. He flipped me over onto my back and positioned me just right so that he could slam in from behind.

He thrust deeper and deeper into me, pushing further from behind. He was rubbing up against my inner walls. He pulled my head back, hooking my mouth with his fingers. I could taste myself on him, or maybe it was Becca on his fingers, either way, I let him pull me further and further back against him, letting myself get lost in the moment. I loved every moment of the fucking as his cock went deeper into me than I thought was possible.

"Do you like that?" he grunted as I moaned in ecstasy, pushing my ass up and slamming it against him to get him in me as deep as possible. I wanted him to fuck me harder.

"Yes," I gasped out between moans of pleasure. "Harder," I told him, and he obliged instantly. He let go of my head and slapped my ass, yanking my hair this time as he rode me. I felt him getting harder within me as he grew rougher. "Harder!" I cried out again.

He stopped and flipped me over again, looming over me, his cock ready for more action. He slapped at my thighs, leaving red welts on them before turning to slap me across the face. "I'll fuck your cunt harder," he told me as he thrust in deeper. I was in total ecstasy, feeling the waves of pleasure continue to rise up. He fucked and fucked until the lines between pain and pleasure were blurred, and I found myself succumbing to another wave of pleasure overcoming my whole body. I convulsed against his cock, once, twice, three times, and tightened up around him, moaning loudly. I could hardly think in the moment, and he pulled out.

"Done already?" He shoved his cock in my face. "Suck it."

I obliged, still trying to catch my breath. I sucked his cock into my mouth, tasting my cum all over it as my tongue slid down the shaft. I forced it down my throat deeply and sucked and sucked. I looked up at him and moaned against his cock, letting him feel my tongue near his head, and lingered on the frenulum. I lifted my hands to his cock and rubbed with them too, pulling down with my hands as I pulled my head and tongue back. I used the tip of my tongue to swirl around the head of his cock as I sucked, letting him hear my slurping.

He seemed to be loving it, as pretty soon, I could feel his hips starting to tense up. He wasn't going to last much longer. I watched him watching me and then reached over for Becca to get involved. I reached for her, beckoning her closer as I stopped sucking. I made space for her, and she quickly obliged, turning to lick his cock with me. We were on either side of his cock, sharing it as we licked, one at a time, on either side. I grabbed his balls, giving them a quick fondle and pressed against the perineum behind them, pushing up. His moans betrayed his pleasure and we could feel his cock starting to pulse against us harder. He was building up that fluid; he wouldn't last for much longer.

"How do you want to cum, birthday boy?" I purred for him, looking up with my best fuck-me eyes, and he smirked.

"On both of you," he said matter-of-factly between his breathing. His voice was low, husky, and sensual as he demanded it. He pushed against us with his cock, and we both started to lick at it again.

I sucked on his cock as Becca moved down for the balls, licking and sucking on them gently. We both kept going, feeling his cock swelling even more. He was just about to cum—we could both feel it as we tried to suck even more on him. It wouldn't be that much longer.

I felt his hand roughly grab the back of my hair, and I could see that he grabbed Becca as well, holding our heads steady as I kept sucking. His eyes were closed, head back as he thrust deeper and deeper into my mouth before he finally pulled himself out of my mouth, shifting to his hand.

He used his hand to keep jerking himself off, aiming his cock at both of us and finally, the strings of fluid came out of his cock, first on me and then onto her as well, spurting out in several streams as he groaned his pleasure, watching both of us as he did. He slowed to a stop after and looked at his handiwork. Both of our faces had strings of cum all over them, and the sight must have pleased him based on that satisfied smirk.

"Clean it off," he demanded, holding his cock to me, and I put the whole thing in my mouth, sucking and pressing my tongue against the bottom of his shaft to get the rest of that fluid out of him, swallowing it. "And each other, too," he told us.

I looked at Becca closer this time; she had it all across her lips and her cheek. Her tongue was already making quick work of the cum on her lips, but she couldn't reach on her cheek. I leaned forward and gently licked it away, letting my tongue linger as I did. When she was clean, she returned the favor, licking along my face as well. He chuckled to himself at the sight. "Good girls," he said huskily as he collapsed onto the bed, thoroughly spent.

"Happy birthday," we both told him as we curled up on either side of him without a care in the world. I didn't mind sharing with Becca at all, and in fact, it had actually been far more fun than I expected to share with her, and I wasn't quite sure that we'd never attempt that again. In fact, I would have loved to do that again in the future. It would be absolutely thrilling to get to fuck each other again, but not quite yet. I had had my fill. It was absolutely time for a nap before we decided on a round two.

Closer to the Edge

Erin is *frustrated*. She just wants a quiet home and a good, hard fuck that will leave her satisfied, and unfortunately, luck is not in her favor as she finds herself lacking both of those. She's woefully single with little desire to go out and find a one-night stand, and her neighbor loves to blast loud music to hide his own actions on a regular basis. Confronting her darkly sexy neighbor, Damian, to turn off his music, she finds herself tangled up in some sexy playtime that may be more than she ever bargained for, and she can't get enough of it.

I could hear the loud music pulsing against my wall in the apartment. It was loud and annoying, and I never wanted to hear that same bassline again. Of course, the neighbor never cared when I complained. I had tried telling him that his constant thundering about made it impossible for me to do my studying, and he laughed at me. I told him once that I couldn't sleep when he was listening to that loud music all night long and he told me to wear earplugs. When I tried telling him that he needed to learn to respect the people around him, he told me that all I needed was a good fuck because I was too uptight.

Now, I'll be honest; I hadn't had a good fuck in a while. But, that didn't mean that I couldn't think about things clearly. Besides, that's what my toys were for. I didn't need a dick to have a good time. And I clearly didn't need a dick to enjoy myself. I tried to ignore the music that was playing and went about my day. I couldn't read my book. I couldn't focus on the games that I was playing. I could even hear their music through my headphones, and no matter how hard I tried, I couldn't get away from it.

I tossed and turned around in my bed, desperate for some sort of relief; I couldn't get away from the noise, and eventually, I had had enough! I took my robe, tied it up around me, and stormed over to his door. I pounded on it and waited. Of course, no response. The neighbor had given up answering the door to me long ago, no matter how much I tried to knock. I ended up pounding again.

"DAMN IT, DAMIAN OPEN THIS DOOR RIGHT NOW!!" I shouted, slamming my fists against the door. "I'VE HAD ENOUGH WITH THIS MUSIC ALREADY! TURN IT OFF AND GET OUT HERE!"

I raised my fist to slam against the door again, but as I swung, he finally opened the door, and my hand connected with his chest. He stood there with a cocky grin on his face, one eyebrow, pierced, raised up, and arms crossed in front of him.

"Can I help you, Erin?"

I stared at him in shock. I hadn't expected him to open the door—and yet here we were. He was looking right at me, face to face, and I couldn't figure out what to do next.
"Erin." He repeated himself. "Please take your hand off of me."

I realized that my fist was still against his chest and pulled away, embarrassed. "S-sorry. But seriously, Damian! I can't think with your music so loud! What is wrong with you?!"

"Nothing's wrong with me; I'm just having a good time. It sounds like you need some practice learning about what a good time means," he replied. He held the door open wider, inviting me in, and I hesitated, not totally convinced that I wanted to enter.

Damian was the stereotypical bad boy neighbor. He wore all black, and his current tank top was skin-tight and taut, revealing the abs underneath. He wasn't a bad guy—I knew that much. I saw him occasionally carrying up groceries for the elderly neighbors and saw him feeding a stray cat outside once. But, he was also highly annoying. He lived in a corner unit, and I had the only unit that connected to his, so lucky me, I got to hear all of his music in all of its annoying blaring that I desperately wished I could make go away.

"Don't be a buzzkill, Erin. Get in here," he told me with that trademark smirk.

I huffed but finally went in. Why not? Maybe, if I talked to him like a normal human being, he'd actually shut up and let me live in peace.

We went into his home, and thankfully, he *finally* turned down the music to a tolerable level. It was still annoying, but at least it was no longer unbearable as the bassline continued heavily, punctuated by all sorts of drums. I had never been in his home before, and looking around, I could see why. It was clean, but at the same time, I had not been prepared to see what was in there.

The living room was lined with sex objects. There was no shortage of beads and dildos lining up and down the walls, and there was what appeared to be a bunch of restraints in there as well. I looked around at everything and turned to look at Damian with a look of mortification on my face. He must have caught onto it because he smirked at me. "Problem?" he asked.

"N-no..." I managed to squeak out, feeling my face flush. I looked around for somewhere to sit, unsure I really wanted to sit down in the first place. Did I really want to touch anything in here?

"Do you like what you see?" His voice had a hint of edge to it, and he looked at me with that look I hadn't seen from someone in a long while. It was the look of someone wanting to consume what was in front of them. He was loving every moment of this, and honestly? The sound of his voice kind of got me going almost immediately, and I suddenly became aware of the fact that I was really only wearing a robe with just my underwear underneath it and I flushed even brighter.

His cock was hard in his pants, and he didn't seem to care about it at all. He simply walked over to me to usher me to his couch and sat me down. I wasn't sure what I was thinking when I agreed to come in.

"So, Erin," he said, looking at me. He stood in front of me, and I was at eye level with his hard cock. "What is it that you came over here for?"

"Your music was too loud," I told him, trying hard not to look at his cock in my face. But, the harder I tried to resist from looking at him, the more that I really just wanted to. I was wet underneath my robe, and I prayed that he wouldn't be able to tell or smell it or anything else. I hoped that I'd be able to just sneak out and enjoy the rest of my quiet night.

"Really," he said, leaning in toward me. His face was right next to mine now as he leaned, and I could feel his breath on my skin. I wanted to slap him and kiss him all at the same time, and I could feel my clit at attention, ready for some loving that it had been so denied lately. It wanted to be touched. *I* wanted to be touched, but I didn't want him to know it.

"I can see how turned on you are right now," he whispered. "Your eyes... Your lips... I can smell it on you." He looked at my lips and bit his own, looking like he was ready to take them for his own. "You need to learn to lighten up, Erin," he purred to me. He looked at me closely, as if trying to discern my own interest. I could feel my own breath hitching as he looked at me, and I couldn't lie; the sexual tension was palpable between us. "I can teach you to lighten up."

"Really." I looked at him and scowled, crossing my arms in front of me.

"Yes, Erin, really," he told me. "Give it a shot. Besides, what's wrong with a little night of fun every now and then? Want a drink?"

I hesitated. Even though my mind wanted to say no, my body was begging me to give in. My body was begging for that connection and human touch. I needed it more than I have ever needed anything in my life, and I desperately wanted to accept in that moment. So I did something unexpected.

"Sure."

"Are you a wine kinda girl?" He looked me over as if trying to figure out my drink preference on his own.

"Whiskey, neat."

"Oho, big taste for someone so small, huh?" He smirked. "Coming right up."

He returned a few moments later with the drink in his hand and handed it over for me to sip at. I downed it, the whole two shots worth and handed him the cup back, proving the point. I wasn't some delicate flower, a special snowflake that wanted the world to cater to me. I just wanted some peace and quiet.

"So, Erin. Let's talk about boundaries."

"What kind of boundaries?" I glanced around his room and realized that we were in what was probably some sort of sex playroom, and suddenly, the loud music made sense. Was it there to drown out the sounds of fucking? That was honestly kind of hot, I realized, and my mind started to wander. Was every time the music got blasted a time when he was getting fucked? Was it possible that he was just enjoying the moment, or was he trying to hide the sounds of passion from me?

"What are you willing to do, and what are you not willing to do?"

"We'll get to that when we get to it!" I insisted, deciding to rush past that. I didn't want to talk about what I wanted and what I didn't.

"Fine, let's at least set up a safe word," he told me, and I started to worry a bit. Should I be concerned about what was going to happen? Safe words made it sound like it would be almost... violent. "Yellow for you're approaching a boundary. Red if you need to stop. I will respect those safe words. You can beg for me to stop, but unless you say, 'red,' I'm not stopping."

I nodded.

"Repeat the safe words to me, Erin."

"Yellow for slow down, red for stop."

"Very good," he replied. "Now, are you ready?"

"Yes." I looked at him and actually made eye contact without feeling feelings of rage for a moment. It was totally different than when we were fighting. I felt a strange mix of arousal, anticipation, and a bit of nervousness as well. What did the night have in store for me?

"Take off your clothes," he told me.

"That's rather forward, isn't it?"

Damian's hand wrapped around a flogger that he had in his back pocket, and he pulled it out. "I punish dirty little girls that don't listen to me," he purred, his eyes shining with arousal. He watched me closely, waiting to see if I said the safe words that we had talked about. I almost did, but I wanted to see where the night could go. Instead, I stripped as asked.

His eyes betrayed the surprise that I had only been wearing a bra and underwear underneath the robe, but he grinned at me, a dark, almost sadistic grin as he looked me over. "You've got quite the hot body, you little slut," he told me as his eyes rested on my breasts. "Take the underwear off, too. I want my toys to be completely naked. I'll be patient with you this time since you're new to being my little plaything, but I expect compliance."

Wordlessly, I started to drop the clothes onto the floor, and he suddenly swatted at me, making me squeal and pull my hand back in shock. I hadn't been expecting that. My hand, where I had been swatted, was already bright pink.

"You will respect me when I talk to you," he demanded. "You will say, 'yes, sir' when I tell you to do something. Do you understand?" His cock bulged and twitched in his pants.

"Yes, sir," I managed to say, rubbing my hand.

"Good. Now, strip."

"Yes, sir."

He tossed my clothes to the floor and inspected my completely naked body, nodding his approval. "Now, turn around. Bend over."

I was kind of shocked at the suddenness, but for some reason, I complied. "Yes, sir." When I bent over, he got to see my ass and lips in full view, and he chuckled to himself.

I couldn't see him, but I could feel his breath on my skin as he inspected my body. "It looks like you're already raring to go," Damian commented offhandedly, as matter-of-factly as you would expect someone to be over the weather. His finger traced the entrance of my pussy, picking up the liquid that I had already started to leak before sucking it off of himself. "This poor little pussy looks like it was neglected.

To be fair, it had been and hearing him say that only made me hotter for him. I felt my clit twitch, and he chuckled, putting his finger on it, rubbing it gently in soft circles that felt so good that I moaned. It had been so long since I had been touched by someone else that way. He continued to circle around it, watching my reaction as I sat there and let him have his way with me.

"Today's an exercise in patience, do you hear me?" he growled at me as he continued to rub along my clit. "If you are patient, you will be rewarded. If you get impatient or you're a naughty slut that can't control that sloppy pussy of yours, you will be punished. And trust me, I don't take my job lightly. I hand out punishments that I intend to keep."

"Yes, sir!" I squeaked as I felt his finger penetrate into my slit, stroking the inner walls. I felt the flogger that he had used on my hand dangle above my back, tickling and exciting the nerve endings in my bare skin as he did. The leather was cool and soft to the touch when it was not swung to sting, and it further excited me. I felt myself clench around his finger, and just as it did, he pulled his finger out from inside of me. "Slow down there, little slut. Enjoy the ride. You need a lesson in patience." He swatted my ass with the flogger, and I cried out as it stung against me. It had caught me off guard, but after the initial shock, it wasn't so bad after all.

"I'm sorry, sir," I gasped out. I didn't want to tell him the truth—that I was just a desperate, lusty slut that hadn't been fucked in far too long, so instead, I remained silent. I didn't say a word beyond that; I just looked over my shoulder, giving him the best fuck-me eyes I could.

He flipped me over and took my hand, leading me over to a bed, which he promptly pushed me onto. He was rough, but not hard enough to scare or worry me, and I went down as he wanted. He walked over to a drawer and pulled out a few different things, and when he came back, I saw this strange collar and a blindfold. I balked at the sight, and he hesitated for just a moment, giving me the chance to use those safe words if I wanted to, but when I didn't say a word after a few beats, he moved forward and got to work. He wrapped the restraint around me and before I knew it, my arms were tied to my neck and torso, and my legs were spread open. If I tried to move too much or if I tugged the leg restraints to put my legs back down, the restraint would tighten around my neck, forcing me to stay put, and the blindfold was added as well.

I couldn't see anything at all, but I could hear Damian moving around the room, and suddenly, there were headphones placed firmly over my ears, and the music was turned on. It was quieter music at the very least, but it was the same bass-heavy music that he normally listened to. I groaned my displeasure, but before I could remain irritated for long, I felt his cock at long last finally slide into my pussy and bring me that joy that I had been missing in my life. He slid right into me and I was shocked at how large he was. Holding my legs up at that angle actually made it better and the occasional tightening around my neck actually elevated the sensations of being fucked as Damian continued to go at it.

I felt myself starting to tense up, my poor, neglected pussy too weak to resist the desire to cum, and before I knew it, I was exploding with pleasure. It must have been just four or five thrusts before I had already finished, moaning out loud and momentarily forgetting the order that I had been given. As the orgasm ended, I felt Damian's flog hit against my ass again, stinging and making me yelp in pain. He drew back and hit again and again, and I whimpered. The music stopped suddenly as the headphones were removed from my head. "You're in for a punishment now, Erin. You were a selfish girl and selfish girls get punished." And just as suddenly as the headphones were removed, they were replaced and the music was turned up a notch or two, growing more intense. I was a bit concerned when I realized that I wasn't feeling anything at all. I couldn't feel him moving around and obviously couldn't hear or see him. It made me nervous, but there was nothing that I could do, other than maybe saying the safe word, but that would be admitting that he won.

My legs were starting to burn with the effort to keep them up, and I could feel them trembling. I swear, Damian was laughing somewhere nearby, even if I couldn't hear him, and suddenly, I felt him approach. The air shifted and I knew he was coming. I expected to feel another lash of the whip, but instead, I was pleasantly surprised; a vibrator was placed against my clit, and it was happy to jump right back to action. I felt it stirring to life again, willing to go for a round two. It had been so long that I may as well enjoy it again. My clit twitched underneath the weight of the vibrator and I moaned, feeling my hips lift of their own accord as it rested against my body. I grinded against it, enjoying the moment, but just as I started to really get going, feeling my pussy starting to soak itself, I felt the vibrator disappear.

I gasped as it was pulled away, and instinctively, I looked around, only to be reminded that I couldn't see or hear anything. I sighed to myself. Was this my punishment? Was he just going to be a tease? At the very least, it would still be fun, I told myself.

Next, I felt his mouth on my nipple, going around the tip with his tongue gently and carefully, not willing to do anything too intense. He danced about my nipple, making me wetter than before. I moaned, my pussy feeling achingly empty, and there was nothing for me to push up against. I couldn't even clench my legs together to try to make myself feel better—all I had was waiting for him to come back to me and who knew when that would be? His tongue spun about my nipple again before letting go. He hovered just above it. I could feel his breath on the wet skin with every breath, driving me madder than before.

He moved to the other nipple then, but never quite touched it, keeping his lips tantalizingly above my skin so close that I could touch it, but not close enough to bring me to any sort of release. I could feel him, and it felt good, but it was making me desperate. My pussy was sopping wet now, and I could smell my fluids all throughout the room. I could feel the slight vibrations on the bed—he must have laughed at my expression of sheer indignation at the deprivation that I was facing.

Damian moved away; suddenly, the air was colder around me, and he left me there for a few minutes. All that I had to keep me company was the throbbing of the bass in the song, throbbing much like my swollen, tortured pussy that wanted to be filled up, and when I finally felt like I couldn't take it anymore, I felt his tongue on me. It was flat and hard as he pressed it against my clit, letting his tongue caress the little nub while his fingers danced just outside of my slit, greedily touching everything that they could.

He plunged his tongue into me, and I moaned, back arching as he did it. He was getting more and more creative with what he was doing to me, and he was making it perfectly clear that he had no intention of ever actually letting me get off. As I'd start to tense up again, he pulled back, just long enough for my aching, quivering pussy to slow down before starting up again. Just as he'd get a rhythm, sensing the impending release, he'd change it up completely, sending me crashing back down and needing to be worked up again.

I felt like crying with desperation as this continued. He shifted from his mouth to his cock for a while, fucking me deeply and hard, only to stop when he thought that I was getting too into it. He teased me silly, and the whole time, I couldn't do anything. I was at his utter mercy, and there was no way for me to do anything but sit there and take it and hope that maybe, he'd show just a bit of compassion and let me get off.

Of course, that never happened as he expertly played with my body like it was made just for him. Maybe it was with how well he was able to turn it on and keep it going—all I knew was that I wanted to fuck him silly, free of the restraints, but I knew that if I said the safe word, it would all be over.

He pulled out again, this time, squirting his load all over my chest as he did, leaving his sticky cum all over me as he licked it up, little by little off of me. He rubbed around my breasts, but never touched the nipples as he ran his hands over me. And finally, he lifted up the headphones, making it possible for me to hear his voice in my ear.

"You have something to be mad about now, you dirty slut," he whispered as he released the bonds and removed the blindfold.

I sat there in shock as I looked at him. He looked satisfied with himself as he looked at the massive puddle that I had left on his bed. He looked over me as I stared back at him, and he waited for me to do something.

"That's it?" I finally managed to say, frustrated.

"That's it," he confirmed. "Naughty girls aren't rewarded in this house. You didn't hold out for me, and you didn't get rewarded any further." He leaned over, planted a kiss atop my head, patted my frustrated pussy, and handed me my robe. "Don't worry, Erin, I'll keep the music down lower for you," he said with a wink as I picked up my clothes and put them on, in shock. As frustrated as I was, I had to admit that he had been the best lay I had had in a very long time. When I was ready to go, he held the door open politely. "I'll see you again very soon," he murmured as I walked by, smirking.

I scowled, both frustrated with the end result of our encounter and the fact that he was right—he *would* be seeing me again in the near future. There was no way I could resist that cock again, and I'd have to be more disciplined next time to actually enjoy it.

Shut Up and Fuck Me

Krissy is a secretary that often feels like she doesn't get appreciated enough. She hates when she is stuck working late on Fridays when she's waiting for her boss to finish working so she can wrap everything up, and so one day, she decides to spice things up. Horny and with nothing else to do while she waits for her boss, the CEO of a financial institution, to finish up, she fantasizes about fucking him, or rather, him fucking her, while she has some fun with herself. Is it possible that the fantasies could become a reality when he walks out to her with her fingers inside of her?

I closed the laptop in front of me and sighed to myself. I had all this work to do, but I only had one thing on my mind: Hard, thick cock. More specifically, hard, thick cock slamming into me over and over again to get me off. I was so wet and horny as I sat there at my desk. I was all alone in the office, save for my boss, Mr. Roberts, in the room behind a closed door. He didn't like to be bothered while he worked, and he was scheduled to be on a conference call for another twenty minutes or so. I sighed again, letting my hand slide over my arm as I did. I wanted that release—no, I *needed* that release, and I didn't know how I could expect to get it. I needed to find some way to release all of that pressure that had built up within me, but it seemed so indecent to do it at work, knowing that my boss could open the door at any point in time to ask me to do something.

But for some reason, the idea of him opening the door only made it seem hotter than before. The idea of getting caught actually made me hotter than anything else. I imagined the scenario out in my mind. I was touching myself, probing at my innermost bits and feeling my wetness, groping my breasts, hair askew, and nipples poking out of my shirt for easier access for my wandering hands. I was moaning to myself in joy, and the door opens. Instead of getting up or apologizing or trying to cover myself up, I would stare my boss in the eyes as I continued to finger fuck myself, giving him those eyes that would dare him to come over and get involved as well.

He would get involved in that scenario in my mind. He would be so overcome with desire at the sight of his secretary fucking herself that he would throw himself at her, putting her up on the table and fucking her silly. His cock, I imagined, would be long, hard and thick, and it would fill me up so much that I would worry that I would tear. His hands would be needy as they ran over my body, tugging desperately, and his breath would be heavy in my ear as he whispered into it that he wanted to fuck me more than anything else.

The image of him plunging himself into me over and over again was almost overwhelming. I found myself gasping at the sight, and I realized that my fingers were wet—I had already slid down my skirt and was fingering myself. I glanced at his door—still locked, and I could hear his occasional roaring laugh as someone that he was trying to woo into a business deal said something that was probably not the least bit funny, but he laughed anyway in hopes that it would lighten the mood. I imagined the look on his face if he were to walk out right that moment—it would be shock and instant arousal as he did and I imagined the bulge in his pants that would grow as he did. It made me hotter to think about all of this, and I felt myself get even wetter as my fingers touched my insides. I rubbed against my inner wall almost lazily as my mind wandered.

What if instead, he threw me over the desk and fucked me silly from behind? His cock would be so hard and so satisfying as it pushed within me, deeper and deeper, as he demanded that I let him ravish my body, and I would not have a care in the world. I didn't care that we were at work and that he, or I, could lose a job over it. I imagined the sheer carnal pleasure at fucking someone without inhibitions, just enjoying each and every moment as it happened. I imagined the joy that I felt, letting him slam into me. It was so hot.

I felt myself let out a little whimper, biting my lip as I let my fingers dance around my clit. I felt myself feel a bit more desperate for that release, but I also didn't want it to end so quickly. I wanted to savor the moment. I wanted to live vicariously and dangerously, and right now, sexually explicit behaviors right in front of my boss's door seemed like a great way to make that happen. Maybe I was fucked up, I thought if I thought that the idea of potentially getting caught fingering myself was hot, but I didn't care, not in the moment.

My other hand reached over my breast, tantalizingly stroking the smooth skin. I reached down my shirt and let my fingers graze over my nipple. It felt so good as my nipple immediately responded, hardening underneath the touch. I licked my lips as I let my fingers trace the slit beneath the clit, but never entering me. Fuck, I needed to bring a vibrator to hide in my desk, or even in my purse, I told myself. It could be hot having someone find it in my desk, or having the security officer that has to check our bags make eye contact with me, blushing when he realizes that I'm carrying around a sex toy. It's not illegal, so he can't confiscate it, but he can think all about what I'm going to do with it later on.

I let myself tease myself a bit longer, running along the inner labia before I finally plunge my fingers in to rub at my inner walls. They are tight now from all of the buildup and tension that I have made as I continued to play with myself, and I looked over to the door. Still nothing, but he had to be getting close to wrapping up that business call now... and sure enough, I saw the light on the office phone turn off, signaling that he had hung up.

It was now or never, I told myself, looking at the door. Did I stop, or did I push my luck and see what would happen next? I decided to take my chances, drawn by the heady hormones coursing through my body and the feeling of excitement that was growing more and more tantalizing by the second the longer that I touched myself, and sure enough, I heard the click of the lock and the door handle opening up. I looked away from the door, throwing my head back in pleasure and pretending that I didn't see him coming out.

The door opened as I continued to finger fuck myself, and there was a moment of silence. I realized that touching myself was feeling even better, but it was not a cock in my vag—that's what I wanted more than anything else.

"Krissy?"

I heard his voice. It was bewildered at the sight. It was shocking, and possibly even a little turned on by the waver that I heard as if he was hesitant to stop me from the sexual release that I was so clearly enjoying. Head still tossed back in enjoyment; I opened my eyes to meet his gaze, slowly pulling my fingers out of my mouth and licking my fingers, one by one. I watched as his eyes widened slightly in response, but he never looked away. I could see his pants tighten, and I smirked. Instead of waiting for him, I stood up and walked toward him.

"I need you to fuck me right now," I told him in a low voice, looking at him through my eyelashes and pushing out my chest. One of my nipples was poking out for him to see, and I picked up his hand in my own, placing it on my chest. I pushed my hips against him, grinding on his rock-hard erection in his pants, and I pushed him toward his office without another word. He shockingly didn't fight back, considering that he was so much larger than I was. He seemed willing to comply with whatever I was going to ask him to do.

He probably thought that it was his lucky day; I told myself with a satisfied smirk as I felt the ache in my pussy grow more intense. I pushed him toward his chair. "I want you to do exactly what I say, do you understand me?" I told him without waiting for much of an answer as I pressed against his chest, urging him to sit down. He did, and I straddled him, rubbing myself against his cock that was still trapped in his pants. It was about as big as I had been hoping, I realized, and that was absolutely fitting for a man of his stature. I whined to myself as I felt his hardness underneath me and I grinded against it harder.

"I'm going to tie you up and have my way with you. I need your rock-hard cock in me so bad right now. You don't even know how badly I need to feel you within me," I told him, looking around for something—anything—that I could use to secure him behind me. I settled for some zip ties that I found in his drawer and put them on him, just behind the back of his chair. It wasn't much, but it would be enough for me to have my fun. A part of me was shocked that he was not protesting, but that only made it better in my book. I felt myself getting wetter, and I looked my boss over. He was the CEO of a major financial firm, and here I was, tying him up and getting ready to fuck both of our brains out, totally in control of every single moment of it.

Satisfied with how secure he was, I looked at his face. He was silent and watching me, but I could see the pleasure shining in his eyes. Did he get off on being dominated? I smirked, unzipping his pants and releasing his cock. It was still just as rock hard as it had felt inside of them as it sprang to attention, and I ran my fingers up and down over the length, enjoying the twitches that I got in response. He was turned on by that, too, it seemed. I chuckled to myself as I lowered my head onto his cock to suck on it. I didn't want to just throw myself onto him without first letting him warm up. He needed to be nice and ready, and the harder that he was, the better.

As I sucked on his cock, I heard him groan in pleasure, thrusting his cock closer to me as he did. He pushed up toward me, and I chuckled on his cock, letting my tongue linger as I let go of it. "Someone's ready for a good fuck," I purred as I looked up at him from his cock, my lips still touching it right around the frenulum as I spoke. His hips thrust forward as I did. "Aren't you going to say anything at all?" I asked him as I licked at his frenulum some more.

"You are fucking hot as hell," he managed to get out between heavy breaths. "I've wanted to get you over my desk ever since I hired you."

I laughed, rubbing over his cock. "Well, who's got whom now?" I asked as I took off my shirt, revealing my toned stomach and perky, D-cup breasts. I lowered them around his cock, letting him rub it between the soft, warm skin as I held them together and kneaded at my nipples for even more pleasure than before. I loved every moment of what I was doing, and from the look on Mr. Roberts' face, he did too.

I felt his dick getting harder as I rubbed him down with my breasts. "Oh, Mr. Roberts," I moaned, looking up at him, "Don't cum already. I've got so much more in store for you than this." Just saying that as I rubbed my tits over him got him cumming, and he squirted all over my tits and my face.

He seemed almost embarrassed that he had cum already, but he didn't say a word.

"Uh, oh, someone made a mess," I purred, using my finger to clean up every last drop of cum from my skin and licking it up, enjoying the taste in my mouth. I leaned forward to suck the last of it from his cock, too. There was no use in wasting the good stuff when I was right there and more than willing to suck it up if there was nowhere else to put it. I licked it up and looked at him with a smirk. He was watching me in awe, as if he had never seen someone do that before. His cock stayed mostly hard, even after he had spilled so much. As it started to soften, I sucked on it and licked at it, trying to keep the blood flow there. I rubbed myself on it, getting back onto his lap and straddling him. I removed my panties and left the skirt on, letting myself rub up on him over and over to bring him back to life. I put my tits in his face for him, letting them bounce with every motion that I made to try to wake his softening dick up again for more.

He leaned over and took control then. He sucked on my left tit first, licking desperately at it and then finally pulling the whole thing into his mouth, his tongue spinning all around it as he did. He was rough, but not hurtful as he tugged at my nipples. He licked and sucked on them carefully, and the more that I rubbed on him, the closer to finishing that I got. I couldn't hold out for much longer, I realized. I needed to fuck him soon, or I wouldn't be satisfied, but his cock was still woefully unready for that.

Instead, I chose to let myself grind on him longer, waiting for that refractory period to end. I lost myself in the moment, rubbing the tip of his cock against my clit and letting his shaft rub up against the lips. Up and down, up and down I went, and I used my other hand to play with my other nipple as well. I lost myself in my mind again, imagining what would happen if I were to undo his ties right that moment. Would he bend me over? Would he fuck me raw? What would he do for me? I wanted to know.

I imagined him taking me from behind, his cock reaching the deepest part of me while his balls slapped at my clit with every thrust, fucking me to the best climax that I had ever felt. I imagined him flipping me over and fucking me silly on my back, his hands on my breasts and mouth on mine as he fucked harder and harder. His cock was large enough to make that happen; I had to admit that much. It looked like it would be exactly what I needed to finish myself off that night. All I needed to do was get it back to hard again.

I rubbed harder against it, desperation in my aching pussy apparent as I did it more and more. I felt him finally starting to respond, and as his dick swelled against me, I came atop him. My whole body betrayed me, with me rubbing harder and harder against him as my hips gyrated atop his own as I did.

He chuckled at me as he continued to suck on my tit. "Someone's enjoying themselves," he murmured, the sensation of his lips moving making me realize that even after a spectacular orgasm, I wanted *more*. I wanted to be selfish.

"You're going to fuck me," I told him, getting off of his lap and clipping the zip ties off of him so that he could get up. He rubbed his wrists as he regarded me with lust shining in his eyes and dick, pointing at the ready to keep going.

"I can do that," he replied, his hands suddenly on my hips as he turned me around and bent me onto his desk, sending items clattering to the ground. Neither of us paid any attention to it as we did, and I felt his hand on the back of my head, pushing it down and then shifting to my hips to line himself up just right. "I'll fuck you so hard that you won't be able to walk those pretty little legs out of here," he growled in my ear before he thrust into me.

He wasn't kidding. And I was all the happier for it. I wanted a good, hard fuck, and if he was willing to give it to me, I was happy. After all, all I had wanted was a hard cock inside of me one way or another.

I felt him thrust so deeply into me that I let out a guttural moan of pleasure, my back arching on its own accord as he did. He let his cock linger there inside of me, letting me finally enjoy what I had wanted more than anything. He let me clench against it tightly as he lingered there, and I was happy to do so. I clenched all around it over and over again, letting myself enjoy it.

Slowly, he pulled his rock hard cock out of me, and I tightened up again as if I could prevent it from leaving if I tightened up enough.

It slipped out, leaving just the tip keeping my lips apart so that he would be able to thrust in again when he was ready. He let it rub against me, moving his hips in a circle to tease those sensitive, swollen, needy lips of mine, and it was driving me *crazy*. I wanted that cock back inside of me so bad.

I wanted it so bad that I shoved my ass toward him, plunging his cock right back into me without him being able to protest. I rode it harder on my own this time. I fucked it standing up, pushing myself onto him over and over again. His cock felt so good to ride as it glided in and out of my wet pussy, and I needed it so bad.

I pulled away and turned around to face him, pushing him to the floor. He obliged, laying across the thin carpet as I had requested, and I straddled him, preparing to ride him as hard and long as I wanted to. I pushed myself around him, letting his cock deepen, pushing my whole weight down to sit on him as I moaned in pleasure.

He reached around to play with my ass, placing his hands on either cheek before he started to guide my movements. He pushed up and pulled me back down to his own rhythm, and I was more than willing to oblige as we did. I felt myself getting hotter and tighter around him. His mound of fur around his cock was glistening with my juices and the smell of sex, hot and heady, filled the room as we fucked harder and with reckless abandon. I rode him gleefully, head tilted back as I did. I bounced harder on his cock, letting it get deeper and deeper into me as I did. I put his hands on my boobs to hold them in place as I looked into his eyes. He was watching me with an impressed, turned on expression as he rode me harder and harder. He wanted to fuck me just as much as I needed him, it seemed.

He let me have my fun before flipping me over, pulling my hair as he thrust deeper into me. He had one hair in my hair and another clawing at my chest, clenching down on my breasts tightly. His nails dug into my skin, just hard enough to avoid breaking the skin. He left his hands there, smashing his palm into my nipple and teasing me harder.

"It's my turn to do the fucking and the leading," he whispered in my ear. "And I want you to be a good girl and cum when I tell you to. Do you understand me?" His voice was breathy in my ear as he spoke, slamming into me as hard as he could.

I could barely speak as the pleasure began to build up again, and I nodded my head to him.

"Good girl. Now I'm going to ride your little ass hard until you cum when I tell you to." He wasn't joking, either. He fucked me so hard that all of the fantasies that I had been having, all of the visualization that I had been doing, was gone. He fucked me so hard that all I could focus on was the feeling of his cock inside of me, ramming me harder and harder.

He stopped suddenly, and I gasped at the sudden lack of sensation, suddenly flipping me over.

"I thought you were going to ride me?" I asked between heavy breaths with a smart ass smirk on my face.

"Oh, I will. But we're going to do something else first. He laid down on the floor and pushed my head toward his cock, soaked with my moisture. "Lick it."

I obliged, tasting the sex on his skin with a long moan of pleasure. It was so hot to taste our fluids combining. He pulled me closer and positioned me just above his face, and suddenly, I felt his tongue on me as well. He was tonguing me as I blew him, and I moaned on his cock again. I kept my grip on him tight. I could see that his balls were starting to tighten up, and I could feel the tension in his cock the more that I sucked him off, and I knew that if I kept it up, I'd be able to get him to cum.

But more importantly, he was licking me so much that I wasn't sure that I'd be able to hold out. His tongue skated across the tip of my clit as he slammed a finger into my pussy, reaching for the g-spot as he tongued me, and the feeling was so intense that I almost came right then and there. I was getting desperate as my poor, aching, soaking pussy craved to be filled up, and I stood up suddenly as I felt myself approaching the point of no return. I slipped past the grip he tried to use to hold me in place, and I got on his cock as quickly as I could, letting the pleasure build up even more until I could no longer take it. With a cry out that would make anyone blush, if they heard it, I came on that hard cock just as I felt him thrust up into me. We both moaned in pleasure, enjoying the ecstasy of each other's bodies as we came, our bodies spasming to each other in almost perfect harmony as we both finally got the big moment.

It felt like it went on for ages as my body, desperate for that release, clenched against him again and again until finally, spent and exhausted, I collapsed against his chest, sweaty, breathing heavily, and hearing his heart thundering against my ear. We weren't going to cuddle, but I took the moment to enjoy myself before getting up and straightening myself out. I cleaned myself up, taking a moment to glance in the mirror to see that I was looking quite disheveled.

Wordlessly, I put my clothes on and tried to make my appearance as appropriate to going out into the real world as I could. When I was satisfied, I turned to look at Mr. Roberts for a moment. He was reclining back in his chair, arms behind his head and looking fully satisfied himself as if it were not just his cock that had been stroked, but his ego as well. "I'll see you Monday, Krissy," he said with a smirk and a knowing look that said that this would probably become a regular thing.

I smirked right back at him as well. "See you on Monday," I replied cheerfully with a wave as I left, fully aware that my walking was not quite right. It seemed he had kept that promise after all.

www.ingramcontent.com/pod-product-compliance
Lightning Source LLC
Chambersburg PA
CBHW071956290426
44109CB00018B/2036